IN QUEST OF THE HERO

I ODed last night, so not great. You?

I'm a mess, but hanging in there. ODed how badly? Were you hospitalized at any point?

Nah, fuck hospitals. It's really hard to kill yourself on the stuff I have anyway and I didn't drink enough to make it toxic. Sorry to hear you're a mess. Is there anything I can do?

Taking care of yourself, honestly, is the #1 thing you could do for me. The

 iMessage

IN QUEST OF THE HERO

THE MYTH OF THE BIRTH OF THE HERO

THE HERO:
A STUDY IN TRADITION,
MYTH, AND DRAMA,
PART II

THE HERO PATTERN AND THE
LIFE OF JESUS

PRINCETON UNIVERSITY PRESS

PRINCETON, NEW JERSEY

CONTENTS

INTRODUCTION: IN QUEST OF THE HERO

by Robert A. Segal

T HE STUDY of hero myths goes back at least to 1871, when the English anthropologist Edward Tylor[1] argued that many of them follow a uniform plot, or pattern: the hero is exposed at birth, is saved by other humans or animals, and grows up to become a national hero. Tylor sought only to establish a common pattern, not to analyze the origin, function, or meaning of it. He appeals to the uniformity of the pattern to make the standard comparativist claim that whatever the origin, function, or meaning of hero myths, it must be the same in all myths to account for the resulting similarities:

> The treatment of similar myths from different regions, by arranging them in large compared groups, makes it possible to trace in mythology the operation of imaginative processes recurring with the evident regularity of mental law; and thus stories of which a single instance would have been a mere isolated curiosity, take their place among well-marked and consistent structures of the human mind.[2]

While some theorists are more attentive to the differences among hero myths than others, by definition all seek similarities and so are necessarily comparativists.

In 1876 the Austrian scholar Johann Georg von Hahn[3] used fourteen cases to argue that all "Aryan" hero tales follow a more comprehensive "exposure and return" formula. In each case the hero is born illegitimately, out of the fear of the prophecy of his future greatness is abandoned by his father, is saved by animals and raised by a lowly couple, fights wars, returns home triumphant, defeats his persecutors, frees his mother, becomes king, founds a city, and dies young. Though himself a solar mythologist, von Hahn, too, tried only to establish, not to analyze, the pattern.[4]

Similarly, in 1928 the Russian folklorist Vladimir Propp[5] sought to demonstrate that Russian fairy tales follow a common biographical plot, in which the hero goes off on a successful adventure and upon his return marries and gains the throne. Propp's pattern skirts both the birth and the death of the hero. Like von Hahn and Tylor, Propp attempted only to establish, not to analyze, his scheme.

Of the scholars who have analyzed the hero patterns they have delineated, by far the most influential have been the Viennese psychoanalyst Otto Rank (1884–1939), the American mythographer Joseph Campbell (1904–1987), and the English folklorist Lord Raglan (1885–1964). Rank wrote *The Myth of the Birth of the Hero* (1909)[6] as an outright disciple of Sigmund Freud; Campbell wrote *The Hero with a Thousand Faces* (1949)[7] as a kindred soul of Carl Jung; and Raglan wrote *The Hero* (1936)[8] as a theoretical ally of James Frazer.

Otto Rank

Only in passing does Freud himself analyze myth. Because he always compares myths with dreams, it is most fitting as well as most notable that his brief interpretation of the story of Oedipus occurs in *The Interpretation of Dreams*.[9] In *Dreams in Folklore*, written with D. E. Oppenheim, Freud interprets dreams in folklore, but none of the pieces of folklore is a myth.[10]

Along with Rank's *Myth of the Birth of the Hero*, the other classic Freudian analysis of myth is Karl Abraham's *Dreams and Myths*, also originally published in 1909.[11] Abraham and Rank alike follow the master in comparing myths with dreams and in deeming both the disguised, symbolic fulfillment of repressed, overwhelmingly Oedipal wishes lingering in the adult mythmaker or reader. But Rank's work is by far the richer and sprightlier of the two. He considers more myths, analyzes them in more detail, and above all establishes a common plot for them—a manifest pattern, which he then translates into latent, Freudian terms. Most importantly, he focuses on hero myths. Rank later broke irrevocably with Freud, but at the time he wrote *The Myth of the Birth of the Hero* he was an apostle and indeed soon emerged as Freud's heir apparent. In fact, Freud himself wrote the section of the essay on the "family romance."[12]

The title of Rank's monograph is at once misleading and prescient. It is misleading because Rank's Freudian emphasis is not on the hero's birth but on his later, Oedipal relationship to his parents. The birth is decisive not because of the hero's separation from his mother but because of the parents' attempt to fend off at birth the prophesied parricidal consequences. The title is prescient because Rank, like Sandor

Ferenczi, Géza Róheim, and Melanie Klein, came to reject the ortho-dox Freudian priority of the Oedipal stage over any other. Rank came to view birth, not the Oedipus Complex, as the key trauma and the key source of neurosis.[13] While Freud, at least as early as 1909, was prepared to grant that "the act of birth is the first experience of anxi-ety, and thus the source and prototype of the affect of anxiety,"[14] he was never prepared to make birth the prime, let alone sole, source of anxiety and neurosis.[15] Freud never subordinated the Oedipus Com-plex, and so relations with the father, to the trauma of birth, which necessarily centers on the mother. It is revealing that in Freud's writ-ings on religion even the nurturing and protective god, not just the threatening one, is male, not female.

The Myth of the Birth of the Hero evinces not only early Rank's but also early Freud's views. Psychoanalytic theory has evolved consider-ably since 1909. Contemporary Freudians, spurred by the development of ego psychology, regard myth far more positively than early Rank and Freud did. Myths solve problems rather than perpetuate them, are progressive rather than regressive, and abet adjustment to the world rather than flight from it. Myths serve not, or not just, to vent bottled-up drives but also to sublimate them. They are as different from dreams as akin to them. Finally, they serve everyone, not just neurotics.[16] Still, Rank's essay remains the classic Freudian analysis of hero myths and offers a striking foil to Campbell's largely Jungian analysis.

Joseph Campbell

Despite the commonly applied epithet, Joseph Campbell was never a straightforward Jungian. He did edit both The Portable Jung and the six-volume selection from the Eranos-Jahrbücher, which, while not uniformly Jungian, is Jungian in "spirit." Campbell himself twice gave lectures published in the Jahrbücher. Several volumes of his works ap-pear in the Bollingen Series, which is likewise broadly Jungian. Two of Campbell's works even constitute the inaugural and final entries in the series. He also edited other Bollingen volumes. He was both a fel-low and a trustee of the Bollingen Foundation.

Still, Campbell was not a Jungian analyst and underwent no analy-sis. Not only did he never call himself a Jungian, but he even denied that he was: "You know, for some people, 'Jungian' is a nasty word, and it has been flung at me by certain reviewers as though to say,

'Don't bother with Joe Campbell: he's a Jungian.' I'm not a Jungian!"[17] Of all rival theorists of myth, Campbell does praise Jung most: "As far as interpreting myths, Jung gives me the best clues I've got."[18] But Campbell refuses to defer to Jung: "he [Jung]'s not the final word—I don't think there is a final word."[19]

Campbell differs most with Jung over the origin and function of myth. Where for Jung the archetypal contents of myth arise out of the unconscious, only in some works of Campbell's do they do so. Even then, sometimes the unconscious for Campbell is, as for Freud, acquired rather than, as for Jung, inherited. Other times the contents of myth—contents that Campbell calls "archetypal" simply because they are similar worldwide—emerge from the imprint of either recurrent or traumatic experiences. In all of these cases, as for Jung, each society creates its own myths—whatever the source of the material it uses. Other times, however, myths for Campbell, in contrast to Jung, originate in one society and spread elsewhere.

Where for Jung myth functions at once to reveal the existence of the archetypes of the unconscious, to enable humans to encounter those archetypes, and to guide humans in encountering them, for Campbell myth serves additional functions as well. Campbell comes to declare repeatedly that myth serves four distinct functions: to instill and maintain a sense of awe and mystery before the world; to provide a symbolic image for the world such as that of the Great Chain of Being; to maintain the social order by giving divine justification to social practices like the Indian caste system; and above all to harmonize human beings with the cosmos, society, and themselves. Jung, ever seeking a balance between the internal and the external worlds, would doubtless applaud many of these functions for keeping humans anchored to the outer, everyday, conscious world, but he himself is more concerned with reconnecting humans to the inner, unconscious world, with which they have ordinarily lost contact. Since only the fourth of Campbell's litany of functions deals with the relationship of humans to themselves, and since even it deals with more than the unconscious, Jung would likely consider Campbell's quaternity of functions askew to his own.

For all Jung's praise of myth, he does not regard it as indispensable. Religion, art, dreams, and what he calls the "active imagination" can work as well, even if at times Jung uses the term "myth" so loosely as to encompass these alternatives to it. For Campbell, by contrast, myth is irreplaceable. Campbell attributes to myth so many disparate functions that it is hard to envision any possible substitute. Moreover, he defines myth so broadly that religion, art, and dreams become instances of myth rather than substitutes for it.

Jung considers myth neither necessary nor sufficient for human fulfillment. Campbell considers it both. Where for Jung therapy supplements myth, for Campbell myth precludes therapy, which is only for those bereft of myth. For Jung, one should reflect on a myth rather than heed it blindly. For Campbell, one should follow a myth—any myth—faithfully. Where for Jung a myth can lead one astray, for Campbell it never can.[20]

Despite these conspicuous differences, Campbell stands close to Jung and stands closest in *The Hero with a Thousand Faces*, which is still the classic Jungian analysis of hero myths. Campbell himself, to be sure, states that he became ever more of a Jungian *after* writing *Hero*: "When I wrote *The Hero with a Thousand Faces* they [Freud and Jung] were equal in my thinking: Freud served in one context, Jung in another. But then, in the years following, Jung became more and more eloquent to me. I think the longer you live, the more Jung can say to you."[21] But Campbell is likely basing this characterization of *Hero* on his reliance on the Freudian Géza Róheim, who, however, strayed from Freudian orthodoxy in a manner that Campbell adopts and carries still further to Jung.

Lord Raglan

Neither Rank nor Campbell is especially interested in the relationship between myth and ritual. Campbell would doubtless assume that every ritual has an accompanying myth, but neither he nor Rank assumes that every myth has a ritualistic counterpart. Only Lord Raglan does. He alone therefore qualifies as a "myth-ritualist."

The specific connection between myth and ritual varies from myth-ritualist to myth-ritualist. For Biblicist William Robertson Smith, the pioneering myth-ritualist, myth is inferior to ritual. It arises as an explanation of ritual only once a ritual is no longer considered magically potent and so is no longer understood. For classicist and anthropologist James Frazer, myth is the equal of ritual and arises with it to serve doing? <3

Very sad, but dealing w it. <3

Did _____ come in last night and chat with you for a bit?

Yeah, I couldn't tho.

Fair enough. I hope you're okay, or at least somewhere where 'okay' is at least visible in the distance

Wed 22 Jul 1:20 pm

How are you holding up?

Wed 22 Jul 3:07 pm

iMessage

as its script: myth explains what ritual enacts. Myth operates *while* ritual retains its magical power. The classicist Jane Harrison and the Biblicist S. H. Hooke follow Frazer's version of myth-ritualism but bestow magical efficacy on myth itself, not just on ritual. The Semiticist Theodor Gaster and the anthropologist Adolf Jensen propose versions of myth-ritualism that make myth superior to ritual. The structural anthropologist Claude Lévi-Strauss argues that whenever myth and ritual work in tandem, they work as dialectical opposites. Not only myths and rituals but also texts and practices of other kinds have been traced back to one version or another of myth-ritualism.[22]

Raglan's brand of myth-ritualism derives ultimately from Frazer: myth for Raglan arises alongside ritual to provide the script and is of equal importance. Yet Frazer himself is a less than uniform myth-ritualist.[23] On the one hand the heart of especially the second and third editions of *The Golden Bough* is exactly the ritualistic enactment of the myths of dying and rising gods of vegetation. On the other hand Frazer's theoretical statements increasingly sever myth from ritual. Indeed, in his introduction to his translation of the Library of Apollodorus, an introduction published only six years after the appearance of the twelfth and final volume of the third edition of *The Golden Bough* in 1915, Frazer attacks, though not by name, the very group of Cambridge classicists who deemed him their mentor.[24] The fact that S. H. Hooke and his Near Eastern counterparts to these classicist myth-ritualists single out Frazer as their anti-ritualist nemesis underscores Frazer's inconsistent stands.[25]

Frazer's ambivalence toward myth-ritualism manifests itself in Raglan, who at once applies Frazer's form of myth-ritualism yet takes it considerably from Frazer's antagonist Hooke. Having cited Frazer for support of myth-ritualism, Raglan quietly notes that "Sir James elsewhere expresses views difficult to reconcile with this."[26]

Rank's Freudian Hero

For Rank, following Freud, heroism deals with what Jungians call the first half of life. The first half—birth, childhood, adolescence, and young adulthood—involves the establishment of oneself as an independent person in the external world. The attainment of independence expresses itself concretely in the securing of a job and a mate. The securing of either requires both separation from one's parents and mastery of one's instincts. Independence of one's parents means not the rejection of them but self-sufficiency. Likewise independence of one's instincts means not the rejection of them but control over them: it means not the denial of instincts but the rerouting of them into socially acceptable outlets. When Freud says that the test of happiness is the capacity to work and love, he is clearly referring to the goals of the first half of life, which for him apply to all of life.

Freudian problems involve a lingering attachment to either parents or instincts. Either to depend on one's parents for the satisfaction of instincts or to satisfy instincts in antisocial ways is to be stuck, or fixated, at childhood.

Rank's pattern, which he applies fully to fifteen hero myths, is limited to the first half of life. Roughly paralleling von Hahn's pattern, of which he was unaware, Rank's goes from the hero's birth to his attainment of a "career":

> The hero is the child of most distinguished parents, usually the son of a king. His origin is preceded by difficulties, such as continence, or prolonged barrenness, or secret intercourse of the parents due to external prohibition or obstacles. During or before the pregnancy, there is a prophecy, in the form of a dream or oracle, cautioning against his birth, and usually threatening danger to the father (or his representative). As a rule, he is surrendered to the water, in a box. He is then saved by animals, or by lowly people (shepherds), and is suckled by a female animal or by an humble woman. After he has grown up, he finds his distinguished parents, in a highly versatile fashion. He takes his revenge on his father, on the one hand, and is acknowledged, on the other. Finally he achieves rank and honors.[27]

Literally, or consciously, the hero, who is always male, is a historical or legendary figure like Oedipus. The hero is heroic because he rises from obscurity to the throne. Literally, he is an innocent victim of either his parents or, ultimately, fate. While his parents have yearned for a child and abandon him only to save the father, they nevertheless do abandon him. The hero's revenge, if the parricide is even committed knowingly, is, then, understandable: who would not consider killing one's would-be killer?

Symbolically, or unconsciously, the hero is heroic not because he dares to win a throne but because he dares to kill his father. The killing is definitely intentional, and the cause is not revenge but frustration. The father has refused to surrender his wife—the real object of the son's efforts: "the deepest, generally unconscious root of the dislike of the son for the father, or of two brothers for each other, is related to be competition for the tender devotion and love of the mother."[28]

Too horrendous to face, the true meaning of the hero myth gets covered up by the concocted story. Rather than the culprit, the hero becomes an innocent victim or at worst a justified avenger: "The fictitious romance is the excuse, as it were, for the hostile feelings which the child harbors against his father, and which in this fiction are projected against the father."[29] What the hero seeks gets masked as power, not incest. Most of all, who the hero is becomes some third party, a historical or legendary figure, rather than either the creator of the myth or anyone stirred by it. Identifying himself with the literal hero, the mythmaker or reader vicariously revels in the hero's triumph, which in fact is his own. He is the real hero of the myth.

Why the literal hero is usually the son of royalty Rank never explains. Perhaps the filial clash thereby becomes even more titanic: it is over power as well as revenge. Indeed, when, as in Oedipus's case, the hero kills his father unknowingly, the conscious motive can hardly be revenge, so that ambition or something else non-Freudian provides an overt motive.

Literally, the myth culminates in the hero's attainment of a throne. Symbolically, the hero gains a mate as well. One might, then, conclude that the myth fittingly expresses the Freudian goal of the first half of life.

In actuality, it expresses the opposite. The wish it fulfills is not for detachment from one's parents and from one's antisocial instincts but, on the contrary, for the most intense possible relationship to one's parents and the most antisocial of urges: parricide and incest, even rape. Taking one's father's job and one's mother's hand does not quite spell independence of them.

The mythmaker or reader is an adult, but the wish vented by the myth is that of a child of three to five: "Myths are, therefore, created by adults, by means of retrograde childhood fantasies, the hero being credited with the mythmaker's personal infantile history."[30] The fantasy is the fulfillment of the Oedipal wish to kill one's father in order to gain access to one's mother. The myth fulfills a wish never outgrown by the adult who either invents or uses it.[31] That adult is psychologically an eternal child. Having never developed an ego strong enough to master his instincts, he is neurotic: "There is a certain class of persons, the so-called psychoneurotics, shown by the teachings of Freud to have remained children, in a sense, although otherwise appearing grown-up."[32] Since no mere child can overpower his father, the mythmaker imagines being old enough to do so. In short, the myth expresses not the Freudian goal of the first half of life but the fixated childhood goal that keeps one from accomplishing it.

To be sure, the Oedipal wish is fulfilled in only a limited fashion. The fullfillment is symbolic rather than literal, disguised rather than overt, unconscious rather than conscious, vicarious rather than direct, and mental rather than physical. By identifying himself with the hero, the creator or reader of the myth acts out in his mind deeds that he would dare not act out in the proverbial real world. Still, the myth does provide fulfillment of a kind and, in light of the conflict between the neurotic's impulses and the neurotic's morals, provides the best possible fulfillment.

As brilliant as it is, Rank's theory can be criticized on multiple grounds. One can grant the pattern while denying the Freudian meaning, which, after all, *reverses* the manifest one. Or one can deny the pattern itself. Certainly the pattern fits only those hero myths, or the portions of them, that cover heroes in the first half of life. Excluded, for example, would be the bulk of the myths of Odysseus and Aeneas, who are largely adult heroes. Rank's own examples come from Europe, the Near East, and India and may not fit heroes from elsewhere.

Indeed, Rank's pattern does not even fit all of his own examples. Moses, for example, is hardly the son of Pharaoh, does not kill or seek to kill Pharaoh, and does not succeed Pharaoh. Moses is the son of lowly rather than noble parents, is exposed by his parents to save rather than to kill him, and is saved by the daughter of Pharaoh.

Far from oblivious to these departures from his scheme, Rank, in defense, appeals both to non-Biblical versions of the Moses saga that come closer to his pattern and, still more, to aspects of the Biblical account that hint at the pattern: above all Pharaoh's fear of the coming generation of Israelite males and his consequent attempt to have them killed at birth. The mighty Pharaoh's terror before mere newborns parallels that of the hero's father before his infant son.

Still, why is there any disparity between the Moses story itself and the pattern it purportedly typifies? Rank would say that it is for the same reason that there is a disparity between that pattern and the

Freudian meaning it purportedly harbors: even the pattern, not just the meaning of it, bears too ugly a truth for the creator or user of the myth to confront. The disparity keeps this truth sequestered. Rank assumes that the Moses story is nevertheless close enough to the pattern to be said to fit it. A skeptic might contend that in Moses's case and that of others the divide is so wide that no hero pattern lurks beneath.

Even the case of Oedipus, which should surely be paradigmatic, does not fit fully. Oedipus is not abandoned to the water,[33] is raised by a royal rather than lowly couple, and does not consciously seek revenge on his father. Had he known Laius to be his father, he would have shuddered at the idea of killing him.[34]

Campbell's Jungian Hero

Where for Freud and Rank heroism is limited to the first half of life, for Carl Jung it involves the second half even more. For Freud and Rank, heroism involves relations with parents and instincts. For Jung, heroism in even the first half involves, in addition, relations with the unconscious. Heroism here means separation not only from parents and anti-social instincts but also from the unconscious: every child's managing to forge consciousness of the external world is for Jung heroic.

For Freud, the unconscious is the product of the repression of instincts. For Jung, it is inherited rather than created and includes more than repressed instincts. Independence of the Jungian unconscious therefore means more than independence of instincts. It means the formation of consciousness, the initial object of which is the external world.

The goal of the uniquely Jungian second half of life is likewise consciousness, but now consciousness of the Jungian unconscious rather than of the external world. One must return to the unconscious, from which one has invariably become severed. But the aim is not thereby to sever one's ties to the external world. On the contrary, the aim is to return in turn to the external world. The ideal is a balance between consciousness of the external world and consciousness of the unconscious. The aim of the second half of life is to supplement, not abandon, the achievements of the first half.

Just as classic Freudian problems involve the failure to establish oneself externally, so distinctively Jungian problems involve the failure to reestablish oneself internally. Freudian problems stem from excessive attachment to the world of childhood; Jungian ones, from excessive attachment to the world one enters upon breaking free of the childhood world: the external world. To be severed from the internal world is to feel empty and lost.

Jung himself allows for heroism in both halves of life,[35] but Campbell does not. Just as Rank confines heroism to the first half of life, so Campbell restricts it to the second half. Rank's scheme begins with the hero's birth; Campbell's with his adventure. Where Rank's scheme ends, Campbell's begins: with the adult hero ensconced at home. Rank's hero must be young enough for his father and in some cases even his grandfather still to be reigning. Campbell does not specify the age of his hero, but he must be no younger than the age at which Rank's hero myth therefore ends: young adulthood. He must, again, be in the second half of life. Campbell does acknowledge heroism in the first half of life and even cites Rank's monograph, but he demotes this youthful heroism to mere preparation for adult heroism: he calls it the "childhood of the human hero." Birth itself he dismisses as unheroic because it is not done consciously.[36]

Rank's hero must be the son of royal or at least distinguished parents. Campbell's need not be, though often he is. Campbell later allows for female heroes,[37] but in *Hero* he, like Rank, limits himself to male ones. More accurately, his scheme presupposes male heroes even though some of his examples are female! Likewise some of his heroes are young, even though his scheme presupposes adult heroes!

Where Rank's hero returns to his birthplace, Campbell's marches forth to a strange, new world, which he has never visited or even known existed:

> destiny has summoned the hero and transferred his spiritual center of gravity from within the pale of his society to a zone unknown. This fateful region of both treasure and danger may be variously represented: as a distant land, a forest, a kingdom underground, beneath the waves, or above the sky, a secret island, lofty mountaintop, or profound dream state.[38]

In this exotic, supernatural world the hero encounters above all a supreme female god and a supreme male god. The maternal goddess is loving and caring: "She is the paragon of all paragons of beauty, the reply to all desire, the bliss-bestowing goal of every hero's earthly and unearthly quest."[39] By contrast, the male god is tyrannical and merciless—an "ogre."[40] The hero has sex with the goddess and marries her. He then kills and eats the god. Yet with both, not just the goddess, he becomes mystically one.[41]

Where Rank's hero *returns* home to encounter his father and mother, Campbell's hero *leaves* home to encounter a male and a female god, who are neither his parents nor mates. Yet the two heroes' encounters are remarkably akin: just as Rank's hero kills his father and, if usually only latently, marries his mother, so Campbell's hero, in reverse order, first marries the goddess and then kills the god.

The differences, however, are even more significant. Because the goddess is not the hero's mother, sex with her does not constitute incest. Moreover, the two not only marry but become mystically one.

Despite appearances, the hero's relationship to the male god is for Campbell no less positive. Seemingly, the relationship is blatantly Oedipal. Campbell even cites Géza Róheim's Freudian analysis of aboriginal myths and rituals of initiation, which evince the son's fear of castration by his father and the father's prior fear of death at the hands of his son:

> The native Australian mythologies teach that the first initiation rites were carried out in such a way that all the young men were killed. The ritual is thus . . . a dramatized expression of the Oedipal [counter-] aggression [on the part] of the elder generation; and the circumcision, a mitigated castration. But the rites provide also for the cannibal, patricidal impulse of the younger, rising group of males.[42]

Róheim, however, departs from a strictly Freudian interpretation.[43] The sons seek not sex with their mothers but *reunion* with them. They seek to fulfill not their Oedipal desires but their even earlier, infantile ones—a booming echo of the later Rank. Their fathers oppose those desires not because they want to keep their wives for themselves but because they want to break their sons of the sons' prenatal ties to their mothers. If the fathers try to sever those ties by threatening their sons with castration, they also try to sever the ties by offering themselves as substitutes for their wives. The fathers selflessly nourish their sons with their own blood, occasionally dying in the process.

Campbell adopts Róheim's more harmonious, non-Freudian interpretation of the clash between sons and fathers and carries it even further. Since Campbell's hero is in the second half of life, he is not, like Róheim's initiates, seeking separation from his mother—for Róheim, as for the renegade Rank, the central experience of life. He is seeking reintegration with her. Furthermore, he is seeking reintegration with his father as well. Indeed, he is not really fighting with his father over his mother. For again, the two gods are neither his parents nor a couple. The hero is seeking from the god the same love that he has just won from the goddess. To secure it he need not give up the goddess but only trust in the god, who is symbolized by the father: "One must have a faith that the father is merciful, and then a reliance on that mercy."[44] The father sacrifices himself to his son.

When Campbell says that initiation rituals and myths "reveal the benign self-giving aspect of the *archetypal* father,"[45] he is using the term in its Jungian sense. For Freudians, gods symbolize parents. For Jungians, parents symbolize gods, and gods symbolize father and mother archetypes, components of the hero's personality. The hero's relationship to these gods thus symbolizes not, as for Freud, Rank, and Róheim, a son's relationship to other persons—his parents—but the relationship of one side of a male's personality—his ego—to another side—his unconscious. The father and the mother are but two of the archetypes of which the Jungian, or collective, unconscious is composed. Archetypes are unconscious not because they have been repressed but only because they have not yet been made conscious. For Jung and Campbell, myth originates and functions not, as for Freud and Rank, to satisfy neurotic urges that cannot be manifested openly but to express normal sides of the personality that have just not had a chance at realization.

By identifying himself with the hero of a myth, Rank's mythmaker or reader vicariously lives out in his mind an adventure that, if ever directly fulfilled, would be acted out on his parents themselves. While also identifying himself with the hero of a myth, Campbell's mythmaker or reader vicariously lives out in his mind an adventure that even when directly fulfilled would still take place in his mind. For parts of his mind are what he is really encountering.

Campbell's Hero versus Jung's

Having managed to break free of the secure, everyday world and go off to a dangerous new one, Campbell's hero, to complete his journey, must in turn break free of the new world, in which he has by now

become ensconced, and return to the everyday one. So enticing is the
new world that leaving *it* proves harder than leaving home. Circe, Ca-
lypso, the Sirens, and the Lotus Eaters thus tempt Odysseus with not
just a comfortable, long life but a carefree, immortal one.

Though often misconstrued, Jung no less than Freud opposes a state
of sheer unconsciousness. Both strive to make the unconscious conscious. While they differ over the origin of the unconscious and over
its capacity to become conscious, the ideal for both remains consciousness. Jung opposes the rejection of ordinary, or ego, consciousness for
unconsciousness as vigorously as he opposes the rejection of unconsciousness for ego consciousness. He seeks a balance between ego consciousness and the unconscious, between consciousness of the external
world and consciousness of the unconscious. For Jung, the hero's failure to return to the everyday world would spell his failure to resist the
allure of the unconscious.

Where Jung seeks a balance between ego consciousness and the
unconscious, Campbell seeks pure unconsciousness. Campbell's hero
never returns to the everyday world: he surrenders to the unconscious.
Yet Campbell himself demands the hero's return to the everyday
world. How, then, can his hero really be spurning it? The answer is
that the world to which Campbell's hero returns is not really the
everyday world. It is the strange, new world, which turns out to per-
vade the everyday one. No separate everyday world exists. It and the
new world are really one:

> The two worlds, the divine [i.e., new] and the human [i.e. everyday],
> can be pictured only as distinct from each other—different as life and
> death, as day and night. . . . Nevertheless . . . the two kingdoms are
> actually one. . . . The values and distinctions that in normal life seem
> important disappear with the terrifying assimilation of [what is now] the
> self into what formerly was [to the ego] only otherness.[46]

The hero need never have left home after all: "Hence separateness,
withdrawal, is no longer necessary. Wherever the hero may wander,
whatever he may do, he is ever in the presence of his own essence—for
he has the perfected eye to see. There is no separateness."[47]

To say that the everyday world and the new world are one is to say
that no distinctive everyday world exists. Campbell thus dismisses as
illusory the "values and distinctions" of the everyday world. If no
everyday world exists, then the hero's apparent return to it is a sham.

If no everyday world exists, then the ego, which provides conscious-ness of it, is itself a sham as well.

By contrast to Campbell, Jung never denies the existence of the everyday world and so of the ego. He rejects the everyday world, the object of ego consciousness, as the *sole* reality, not as *a* reality. While he seeks to integrate the everyday world with the new one, ego con-sciousness with the unconscious, he denies that it is possible to fuse them, at least without thereby dissolving both the everyday world and the ego itself.

Campbell's hero returns or, better, remains home not only because he finds the new world back home but also because he wants selflessly to save others:

> The full round, the norm of the monomyth, requires that the hero shall now begin the labor of bringing the runes of wisdom, the Golden Fleece, or his sleeping princess, back into the kingdom of humanity, where the boon may redound to the renewing of the community, the nation, the planet, or the ten thousand worlds.[48]

If the hero's return is selfless, then the everyday world to which he is returning is worthless. Indeed, he is returning only to apprise others of the fact: whatever the literal "boon," the symbolic one is knowl-edge, knowledge of the status of the everyday world. To be sure, the everyday world here *is* distinct from the new one, but for exactly that reason it is no less worthless now than when the two worlds are one. Campbell's chief heroes consequently include the selfless Buddha, Moses, Aeneas, and Jesus.

Campbell's characterization of the hero's return as triumphant re-veals another fundamental departure from Jung: Campbell's hero iron-ically remains bound to the *first* half of life. Even though Campbell's hero has undeniably already accomplished the goals of the first half of life, truly re-encounters the unconscious, must even guard against suc-cumbing to it, and returns home transformed, he also returns *trium-phant*. He thinks he has *tamed* the unconscious and can do the same for others.

Jung would say that Campbell's hero has in fact missed the power and depth of the unconscious. A Jungian hero would return home humbled rather than elevated, wary rather than brash, the saved rather than the savior. A Jungian hero would seek only a *modus vivendi* with the unconscious, not control over it. Campbell's hero is, in

Bus on Heller St just drove right past me :-O

Next one's in half an hour, so I'm walking. See you in a bit

That sucks! But see you soon-ish.

Hey I'm here!

Sat 18 Jul 4:17 am

Hey Andy, I'm sorry. Are you okay?

Sat 18 Jul 10:32 am

I'm okay. How are you doing? <3

 iMessage

Jungian lingo, merely an "inflated" ego. Only Jung's is a full-fledged "self." If on the one hand Campbell ventures well beyond Jung in seeing heroism as the transcendence of the ego in mystical oneness with the unconscious, on the other hand he stops far short of Jung in simultaneously seeing heroism as the ego's mastery over the unconscious. Only because Campbell assumes that the ego stays in control can he, without trepidation, espouse the fusion of the ego with the unconscious. Jung would deny that in a deeper encounter with the unconscious the ego either could or should remain in control. To underscore the difference between Campbell's and Jung's notions of heroism, Jungian analyst Joseph Henderson goes so far as to restrict heroism per se to Campbell's variety and to relabel the Jungian ideal "initiation."[49]

Like Rank's theory, Campbell's can be faulted on various grounds. As with Rank's theory, one might grant the pattern but deny the meaning. Or one might question the pattern itself. Since it obviously applies only to myths about heroes in the second half of life, it excludes all of Rank's hero myths, or at least all Rank's portions of them. Whether it even fits Campbell's own examples is not easy to tell, for Campbell, unlike either Rank or Raglan, provides no set of hero myths to accompany his pattern. While he continually cites scores of hero myths to illustrate individual *parts* of his pattern, he does not apply his full pattern to even one myth. Campbell himself acknowledges this point, but then he declares confidently that "should he [the reader] wish to prove whether all [the myths cited merely in part] might have been cited for every section of the monomyth, he need only turn to some of the source volumes enumerated in the footnotes and ramble through a few of the multitude of tales."[50]

Yet one might question even so seemingly transparent a confirmation of Campbell's pattern as the myth of Aeneas, which Campbell names as an example of his pattern.[51] Aeneas's descent to Hades and return does fit Campbell's scheme snugly, but Aeneas's larger itinerary does not. Rather than returning home to Troy upon completion of his journey, he proceeds to Italy to found a new civilization. Similarly, Odysseus's descent to the underworld fits Campbell's pattern, but his larger journey, which Campbell cites,[52] does not. Odysseus, unlike Aeneas, does return home, but also unlike Aeneas he arrives with no boon in hand. His return is an entirely personal triumph. Since Campbell distinguishes a myth from a fairy tale on exactly the grounds that the triumph of a mythic hero is more than personal,[53] Odysseus's story would logically be disqualified as a myth.[54]

Raglan's Frazerian Hero

Rank's hero triumphs at the expense of everyone else; Lord Raglan's, like Campbell's, saves everyone else. Campbell's saving hero need not die; Raglan's must. Campbell's hero undertakes a dangerous journey to aid his community; Raglan's hero in the myth is driven *from* his community and, in the accompanying ritual, is sacrificed *by* the community. Campbell's hero can be any adult male; Raglan's must be a king, though he can be divine.

Raglan is indebted to myth-ritualists James Frazer and S. H. Hooke not merely for their link of myth to ritual but also for their identification of the specific ritual involved: the killing of the king by the community in order to ensure its welfare.[55] For Hooke, following Frazer, the ritual in which the king is killed enacts the myth of the life of the god of vegetation: his death, rebirth, victory, marriage, and inauguration. The enactment by the king of the death and rebirth of the god functions magically to yield the rebirth of crops. The enactment works by the first of Frazer's two laws of magic: that the imitation of what one wants to happen effects it. The king, himself merely human, is thus not the god of vegetation but only his representative.[56] He imitates, not incarnates, that god. His action automatically causes the god and in turn vegetation to do the same: while the god is dead, the land is infertile; when he is revived, so is the land. The ritual is performed annually at the end of winter.

For Hooke, the king is only symbolically, not literally, killed. Strictly speaking, the king himself is not even symbolically killed. It is the god whose part he plays[57] who dies, and dies literally—not through the effect of magic but at the hands of his enemy.[58] It is the literal rebirth of the god that is magically produced.

In Raglan's version,[59] which he attributes to Hooke but which really derives from Frazer,[60] the king does not merely play the part of the god but *is* the god.[61] Consequently, the king's death, which initially is literal but later merely symbolic, does not magically cause the death of the god but *is* the death of that god and therefore of vegetation.[62] Similarly, the installation of a successor does not magically induce but *is* the rebirth of the god and therefore of vegetation. For Raglan, as for Frazer and Hooke, the myth describes the life of the god and the ritual enacts it. The function of the ritual, which is performed either at the end of a fixed term or upon the weakening of the incumbent, is, as for Frazer and Hooke, to aid the community. Besides the fertility of the earth, that aid can take the form of success in war, good health, and human fertility.

Venturing beyond both Frazer and Hooke, Raglan equates the king with the hero. For Frazer and Hooke, the king may in effect be a hero to his community, but only Raglan labels him one. In addition, Raglan introduces his own detailed hero pattern, which he applies to twenty-one hero myths.[63] That pattern extends all the way from the hero's conception to his death. In contrast to Rank's and Campbell's patterns, it therefore covers both halves of life:

(1) The hero's mother is a royal virgin;

(2) His father is a king, and

(3) Often a near relative of his mother, but

(4) The circumstances of his conception are unusual, and

(5) He is also reputed to be the son of a god.

(6) At birth an attempt is made, usually by his father or his maternal grandfather, to kill him, but

(7) He is spirited away, and

(8) Reared by foster-parents in a far country.

(9) We are told nothing of his childhood, but

(10) On reaching manhood he returns or goes to his future kingdom.

(11) After a victory over the king and/or a giant, dragon, or wild beast,

(12) He marries a princess, often the daughter of his predecessor, and

(13) Becomes king.

(14) For a time he reigns uneventfully, and

(15) Prescribes laws, but

(16) Later he loses favour with the gods and/or his subjects, and

(17) Is driven from the throne and city, after which

(18) He meets with a mysterious death,

(19) Often at the top of a hill.

(20) His children, if any, do not succeed him.

(21) His body is not buried, but nevertheless

(22) He has one or more holy sepulchres.[64]

Clearly, parts one to thirteen correspond roughly to Rank's entire scheme, though Raglan himself never read Rank.[65] Six of Raglan's cases duplicate Rank's, and the anti-Freudian Raglan nevertheless also takes the case of Oedipus as his standard.[66] The victory that gives the hero the throne is not, however, Oedipal, for the vanquished is not necessarily his father, even if, as for Rank, the father is usually the one who had sought his son's death at birth. Parts fourteen to twenty-two do not correspond at all to Campbell's scheme. The hero's exile is loosely akin to the hero's journey, but for Raglan there is no return. The hero's sepulchres do serve as a kind of boon, but not for his native community. For Rank, the heart of the hero pattern is gaining kingship. For Raglan, the heart is losing it. Wherever Campbell's heroes are kings, the heart is their accomplishments *as* kings.

For all Raglan's touting of the symbiosis of myth and ritual, his hero myth and ritual seem incongruously out of sync. In the myth the protagonist is usually human. In the ritual the protagonist is always divine. The myth runs from the birth of the protagonist to his mysterious death. The ritual enacts only the portion of the myth that corresponds to the replacement of the king: the exile of the incumbent.

Raglan nevertheless equates the hero of the myth with the god of the ritual: "The conclusion that suggests itself is that the god is the hero as he appears in ritual, and the hero is the god as he appears in myth; in other words, the hero and the god are two different aspects of the same superhuman being."[67]

But how can a god lose power, let alone die? Raglan's answer is that it is the hero, not the god, who loses power and then dies—even though the hero and the god are identical!

Still, how can the myth that purportedly provides the script for the ritual be so at odds with it? Raglan's rejoinder is that the myth and the ritual are not so far apart. In both, the central figure is the king. Moreover, many of the events in the life of the hero are supernatural, so that the hero must in fact be a god himself. Above all, what Raglan considers the core of the myth—the toppling of the king—corresponds to the undeniable core of the ritual—the killing of the king when he either weakens or finishes his term.

For Rank, heroes are heroic because they dare to serve themselves. For both Campbell and Raglan, heroes are heroic because they willingly or unwillingly serve their communities. For Raglan, heroes in myth serve their communities by their victories over those who threaten their peoples' physical welfare. Hence Oedipus defeats the Sphinx, who is starving Thebes. Heroes in ritual serve their communities by their sacrificial deaths. In both myths and rituals heroes are really ideal kings. For Campbell, heroes in myth serve their communities by their return home with a boon, typically secured only by defeating or at least taming supernatural entities. Where the boon bestowed by Raglan's hero is entirely material, that bestowed by Campbell's is immaterial: it is not food but, again, wisdom. Without Raglan's hero the community would die; without Campbell's it would remain benighted.

Like Rank's and Campbell's theories, Raglan's can be questioned on various counts. One might grant the mythic pattern but deny a connection to ritual. One might grant some connection but deny that, in the light of the disparity between the myth and the ritual, it takes Raglan's form. Or one might deny the pattern itself—denying either that it applies worldwide[68] or that it even applies substantially to Raglan's own cases. By Raglan's own tally none of his examples scores all twenty-two points, and one scores only nine. Rank can at least assert, albeit nonfalsifiably, that hero myths which stray from his own scheme are distortions created to keep the true pattern hidden. Raglan can use no comparable ploy: there is nothing in his pattern to be kept a secret. Why, then, one might ask, do not all of his hero myths, if not all hero myths, attain perfect scores?[69]

The Three Theories Compared

The theories of Rank, Campbell, and Raglan typify the array of analyses of hero myths. For Rank, the true subject of hero myths is the family. For Campbell, it is the mind. For Raglan, it is the physical world and, even more, the gods who control that world.

Both Rank and Campbell read myth symbolically. Because the real subject of hero myths for Rank is the family, the figures in a hero myth symbolize the mythmaker or reader and his parents. It is, then, confusing for Rank to identify the hero with the ego[70]—as if the hero's parents represent other parts of the mind. Because the real subject of hero myths for Campbell *is* the mind, figures in a hero myth symbolize parts of the mythmaker's or reader's mind: the ego and the archetypes of the collective unconscious.

By contrast to both Rank and Campbell, Raglan reads myth literally. Stories about heroes are really about heroes. While Raglan relentlessly impugns the historicity of heroes, he takes for granted that stories about them are *meant* literally.[71] While Raglan *equates* heroes with gods, heroes for him do not *symbolize* gods. They *are* gods.

For Rank, hero myths originate and function to fulfill a blocked need: the need to fulfill socially and personally unacceptable impulses. The fulfillment that myth provides is compensatory: it is a disguised, unconscious, and merely fantasized venting of impulses that cannot be vented directly. The meaning of myth is therefore unconscious. One cannot face it openly.

For Campbell, hero myths originate and function to fulfill not a blocked need but simply a yet unrealized one: the need to discover and nurture a latent side of one's personality. There is nothing socially or personally objectionable about that side, in which, indeed, one revels. Rather than a merely compensatory fulfillment, myth provides a direct and full one—in fact, the best possible one. Where the meaning of myth is unconscious, that meaning has not been kept hidden. It has merely gone unrecognized. For Rank, deciphering the meaning is like breaking a code. For Campbell, it is equivalent to figuring out the Rosetta stone. Campbell, however, goes beyond even Jung, not merely Rank, when he insists both that, except for literalist moderns, the meaning of myth is always conscious and that myth works only *when* the meaning is conscious.

For Raglan, hero myths originate and function to fulfill neither a blocked need nor a potential one but an ever-beckoning one: the need for food and other necessities. Myth serves the same function as applied science: controlling the physical world in order to survive. For those without science, myth is not just a compensatory way or even the best way of serving its function but the sole way. Raglan himself, to be sure, does not assume that believers in myth would die without it, only that they think they would. They take for granted that myth alone enables them to control the gods who control vegetation.

For Rank and Campbell, hero myths work. For Rank, they provide a partial satisfaction of Oedipal wishes. For Campbell, they reveal an otherwise unknown side of the personality. For Raglan, however, hero myths do nothing: they are an illusory means of delivering the goods. Science provides the only true means. For both Rank and Campbell, hero myths work as long as adherents believe in heroes. For Raglan, hero myths would work only if the mythicized figures in whom persons believed were real.

Rank allows for modern as well as primitive hero myths. As long as there are neurotics, there will be hero myths. Because hero myths for Rank can be secular as well as religious, there is no automatic conflict between myth and science and so between myth and modernity. Campbell does not merely allow for modern as well as primitive hero myths but proclaims their existence. All humans for him spontaneously spin myths. Relentlessly pitting religion against science, Campbell not only distinguishes religious hero myths from the rest of religion but also maintains that religious heroes are gradually being superseded by secular ones—most recently by heroes whose adventures take them to outer space. If myth fell within the realm of religion, then myth and science, hence myth and modernity, would stand opposed, but myth does not.

By contrast to both Rank and Campbell, Raglan denies the existence of modern hero myths. While he doubtless grants the existence of modern heroes, his equation of heroes in myths with gods of nature commits adherents to hero myths to the belief in one or more gods who are incarnate in humans and who directly will the course of nature. For Raglan, this belief conflicts with modern science, so that to have science is not to have myth. Adherence to hero myths also commits one to kingship, for gods deign to reside only in royalty, never in commoners. Myth for Raglan, following Frazer, is an exclusively prescientific phenomenon. Where for Rank hero myths will disappear only if neurosis ever does, and where for Campbell hero myths will never disappear, for Raglan hero myths *have* disappeared.

Alan Dundes on Jesus as Hero

Alan Dundes, the Berkeley folklorist, begins his essay "The Hero Pattern and the Life of Jesus"[72] by asking why hero patterns have not been applied more fully to the case of Jesus. While Rank does use Jesus as one of his fifteen heroes, Raglan does not—despite the conspicuous fit. Because Campbell cites all heroes, including Jesus, only in passing, he does not count here. Dundes suggests that the paucity of folkloristic analyses of the life of Jesus stems from the fear that folklore means falsehood: viewed folkloristically, Jesus would seemingly become an imaginary rather than a historical figure.

Of the three theorists of hero myths, Campbell never denies that mythical heroes can also be historical ones. But his symbolic interpretation of the meaning of heroism trivializes any historical meaning: to say that the life of Jesus symbolizes the development of the myth-maker's or reader's ego out of the unconscious and the eventual return of the ego to unconsciousness is surely to make at best coincidental the historicity of the symbol used. While Rank does not broach the issue of the historicity of heroes, no doubt the same holds for him: to say that the life of Jesus symbolizes the fulfillment of the mythmaker's or reader's extant Oedipal yearnings is likewise to make at most incidental the historicity of Jesus. Indeed, Rank's theory renders the historicity of Jesus even less credible than Campbell's since the manifest level, the level of both the Gospels themselves and the pattern, is for Rank a distortion invented to keep the real, symbolic meaning from surfacing.

Despite Raglan's literal reading of myth, he rails against the historicity of heroes more fervently than either Rank or Campbell. While granting that heroes may be *based* on historical figures, he denies that any aspects of their *heroism* are.[73] Those aspects would include the "high points" of Jesus's life: his lineage, birth, teaching, and death.

Raglan offers various arguments against the historicity of heroes. He notes that many of the twenty-two aspects of the lives of his mythical heroes scarcely correspond to what is ordinarily recorded of real persons; that the lives of his mythical heroes involve supernatural events; that his heroes' lives parallel those of gods; and that the similarities in the lives of so many heroes are much too coincidental for historical comfort.[74]

Striving to disentangle folkloristic concerns from historical ones, Dundes points to folklorist Francis Lee Utley's "somewhat tongue-in-cheek" application of Raglan's pattern to the case of Abraham Lincoln—an incontestably historical figure who nevertheless garners a full twenty-two points.[75] Concludes Dundes:

> The fact that a hero's biography conforms to the Indo-European hero pattern does not necessarily mean that the hero never existed. It suggests rather that the folk repeatedly insist upon making their versions of the lives of heroes follow the lines of a specific series of incidents. Accordingly, if the life of Jesus conforms in any way with the standard hero pattern, this proves nothing one way or the other with respect to the historicity of Jesus.[76]

Of course, the historical Jesus for most Christians *includes* much of Raglan's pattern.

As a folklorist rather than a historian, Dundes turns from the compatibility of folklore with history to folklore itself. On the one hand he shows how early theologians and religious historians themselves appealed to folkloristic patterns in reconstructing the historical Jesus. On the other hand he laments the failure of modern scholars to utilize the hero patterns of Raglan and others in analyzing the life of Jesus as *either* folklore or history.[77] He most helpfully charts the history of hero patterns, which, he notes, fall properly under the folkloristic rubrics of legend or tale *rather than* myth.[78]

Without attempting to reconcile the differences among different hero patterns, Dundes shows how three of them—von Hahn's, Rank's, and Raglan's—illuminate aspects of the folkloristic, whether or not historical, life of Jesus. For example, Dundes observes that the paucity of attention accorded Jesus's childhood, at least in the canonical Gospels, fits Raglan's scheme. To the extent that Raglan's pattern holds generally, one would, then, *expect* scant interest in Jesus the boy and adolescent: "Bible scholars have bemoaned the lack of information about the youth of and growing up of Jesus. . . . The point is that this is precisely the case with nearly all heroes of tradition. That is why Raglan included his trait 9 'We are told nothing of his childhood.' "[79]

Dundes stresses that a pattern is as illuminating when it does not fit as when it does. Rather than insisting that a pattern either fit or fail, he permits variations, which reflect the differences between one culture and another. Von Hahn, Rank, and Raglan would doubtless also attribute variations to the particularities of each culture, but they are more concerned with the patterns themselves. Moreover, as proponents of those patterns, they would surely prefer to relegate variations to details not covered by their patterns rather than to violations of those patterns: the more violations, the less credible the pattern itself.

Contrary to Raglan's pattern, Jesus does not quite marry a princess. Dundes uses this issue as a take-off point for his own provocative speculations about family relations in Mediterranean society. Though his speculations are triggered by an exception to *Raglan's* pattern, Dundes explains the anomaly in Freudian, not ritualist, terms. Furthermore, Dundes's Freudian approach is of a classical rather than contemporary variety. He analyzes heroism in unblinkingly Oedipal terms.[80] He even chides the early Rank for diverting attention from the Oedipal trauma to the infantile one.

Dundes suggests that the case of Jesus typifies the forced options of Mediterranean males. Jesus's celibacy symbolizes submission to his father, who opposes his son's budding sexuality. The crucifixion symbolizes the enactment of the father's threatened punishment: castration—here carried out preemptively. Yet Jesus actually triumphs over his tyrannical father. That triumph is symbolized by not only his resurrection but also his ties to Mary Magdalene, who stands for the real Mary of his affections, and his ascent to heaven, where he joins his father as a reigning equal:

> So Jesus has it both ways: he is the dutiful son obeying a distant, powerful father, but he becomes one with that father—just as boys growing up in circum-Mediterranean households have to learn to progress from a close and prolonged association with protective mothers to a world of men dominated by elders to a time finally when they themselves become distant fathers to their own children as they seek virgin wives and attempt not to become cuckolded (like Joseph).[81]

For Mediterranean sons, torn between a desire for their smothering mothers and a fear of their overpowering fathers, even the fantasy of a straightforward Oedipal victory in the form of Rank's pattern would be impossible. One does not have to concur wholly in Dundes's interpretation of the folkloristic life of Jesus[82] to admire this imaginative use of the hero pattern.[83]

Notes

1. See Edward B. Tylor, *Primitive Culture*, 5th ed. (New York: Harper Torchbooks, 1958 [1871]), vol. 1 (retitled *The Origins of Culture*), 281–82. In an earlier essay Tylor amasses stories of children raised by beasts, but only in passing does he connect them to myths of future heroes: see "Wild Men and Beast-Children," *Anthropological Review* 1 (May 1863): 21–32.

2. Tylor, *Primitive Culture*, 1:282.

3. See Johann Georg von Hahn, *Sagwissenschaftliche Studien* (Jena: Mauke, 1876), 340. Trans. Henry Wilson in John C. Dunlop, *History of Prose Fiction*, rev. Wilson (London: Bell, 1888), in an unnumbered attachment to the last page of volume 1.

4. For an application of von Hahn's otherwise neglected pattern, see Alfred Nutt, "The Aryan Expulsion-and-Return-Formula in the Folk and Hero Tales of the Celts," *Folk-lore Record* 4 (1881): 1–44.

5. See Vladimir Propp, *Morphology of the Folktale*, trans. Laurence Scott, 2d ed., rev. and ed. Louis A. Wagner, Publications of the American Folklore

persistent fantasy. Even now, when I'm anxious or depressed, I'll often find myself trying to mentally "load a savegame." It's a tic that doesn't involve any outward expression, but I just try to *click* on where I think the menu might be hidden in my mind. The hope is that one of these times, the menu will simply unfurl, and I'll realize it's been autosaving for me this whole time, and I'll finally be able to load up July of 2015 and get to work.

In *Life is Strange*, the fantasy of saving is turned into the game's core mechanic. While the thematic point of the game ends up being that this kind of perfection is unattainable—that some losses are unavoidable—the experience of playing it tells you the opposite. Every time you fuck something up, you can hop back in time and reverse it. Every time you're curious how someone would react to a different rhetorical strategy, you can zip back and test it out. The whole thing is about re-experiencing situations, folding a single life over itself again and again in the pursuit of better outcomes.

Until the roof. Then you're on your own, stripped of your powers through a convenient plot contrivance. Then you're watching your friend teeter closer to killing herself, with only one chance to avoid saying the wrong thing. In that situation, you're a pianist whose hands have fallen off. Every sinking platitude you say is like the *klumpf* of your handless arms smashing against the keys. To be fair, this is realistic. This is what it feels like to try to convince someone not to kill themselves. An atonal jumble of helpless notes that never quite makes the chord.

These are the last text messages Kat and I sent to each other:

Society Bibliographical and Special Series, vol. 9; Indiana University Research Center in Anthropology, Folklore, and Linguistics Publication 10 (Austin: University of Texas Press, 1968 [1928]). For Propp's later, more historical work, see his *Theory and History of Folklore*, ed. Anatoly Liberman, trans. Ariadna Y. Martin and Richard P. Martin, Theory and History of Literature, vol. 5 (Minneapolis: University of Minnesota Press, 1984), esp. chap. 5; and "Oedipus in the Light of Folklore," trans. Polly Coote, in *Oedipus: A Folklore Casebook*, ed. Lowell Edmunds and Alan Dundes, Garland Folklore Casebooks, no. 4 (New York: Garland, 1983), 76–121. On Propp, see Alan Dundes's introduction to *Morphology of the Folktale*; Anatoly Liberman's introduction to *Theory and History of Literature*; Archer Taylor, "The Biographical Pattern in Traditional Narrative," *Journal of the Folklore Institute* 1 (1964): 121–29; and Isidor Levin, "Vladimir Propp: An Evaluation on His Seventieth Birthday," *Journal of the Folklore Institute* 4 (June 1967): 32–49.

6. Otto Rank, *The Myth of the Birth of the Hero*, trans. F. Robbins and Smith Ely Jelliffe, Nervous and Mental Disease Monograph Series, no. 18 (New York: Journal of Nervous and Mental Disease Publishing, 1914 [1909]); reprinted (New York: Brunner, 1952); reprinted, *The Myth of the Birth of the Hero and Other Writings*, ed. Philip Freund (New York: Vintage Books, 1959), 3–96. The second, enlarged 1922 edition of the work has never been translated into English. Citations are to the reprint in *In Quest of the Hero*.

7. Joseph Campbell, *The Hero with a Thousand Faces* (New York: Pantheon Books, 1949); 2d ed. (Princeton, N.J.: Princeton University Press, 1972). Citations are from the second edition. While not excerpted in *In Quest of the Hero*, the book is now part of the same Mythos Series.

8. Lord Raglan, *The Hero* (London: Methuen, 1936); reprinted (New York: Vintage Books, 1956). Chapters 16–17 were originally published as "The Hero of Tradition," *Folk-Lore* 45 (September 1934): 212–31. The excerpt in *In Quest of the Hero* represents the second of the three parts of the book—the part on myth. Citations are to the reprint in *In Quest of the Hero*.

9. See Sigmund Freud, *The Interpretation of Dreams*, trans. James Strachey (New York: Avon Books, 1965 [1900]), 294–98.

10. Sigmund Freud and D. E. Oppenheim, *Dreams in Folklore*, trans. A. M. O. Richards (New York: International Universities Press, 1958).

11. Karl Abraham, *Dreams and Myths*, trans. William A. White, Nervous and Mental Disease Monograph Series, no. 15 (New York: Journal of Nervous and Mental Disease Publishing, 1913 [1909]); rev. trans.: "Dreams and Myths," in Abraham, *Clinical Papers and Essays on Psycho-Analysis*, ed.

Hilda C. Abraham, trans. Hilda C. Abraham and D. R. Ellison (London: Hogarth, 1955), 151–209. Other early Freudian works on myth and kindred literature include Rank's own *Der Künstler*, 1st ed. (Vienna and Leipzig: Heller, 1907); Rank, *Das Inzest-Motif in Dichtung und Sage*, 1st ed. (Leipzig and Vienna: Deuticke, 1912); Rank, *The Double*, ed. and trans. Harry Tucker, Jr. (Chapel Hill: University of North Carolina Press, 1971 [1914]); Rank, *Psychoanalytische Beiträge zur Mythenforschung*, Internationale Psychoanalytische Bibliothek, no. 4, 1st ed. (Leipzig and Vienna: Internationaler Psychoanalytischer Verlag, 1919), esp. chs. 1, 7; Rank, *The Don Juan Legend*, ed. and trans. David G. Winter (Princeton, N.J.: Princeton University Press, 1975 [1922, 1924]); Rank, "Dreams and Myths"—an appendix to chap. 6 of the 4th through the 7th and penultimate edition of *The Interpretation of Dreams*; Rank and Hanns Sachs, *The Significance of Psychoanalysis for the Mental Sciences*, trans. Charles R. Payne, Nervous and Mental Disease Monograph Series, no. 23 (New York: Nervous and Mental Publishing, 1916 [1913]), chap. 2; Franz Ricklin, *Wishfulfillment and Symbolism in Fairy Tales*, trans. William A. White, Nervous and Mental Disease Monograph Series, no. 21 (New York: Nervous and Mental Publishing, 1915 [1908]); Herbert Silberer, "Phantasie und Mythos," *Jahrbuch für Psychoanalytische und Psychopathologische Forschungen* 2 (1910): 541–622; Ernest Jones, *Hamlet and Oedipus* (New York: Norton, 1949 [1910]), chap. 7; Karl Johan Karlson, "Psychoanalysis and Mythology," *Journal of Religious Psychology* 7 (November 1914), esp. 182–206; and Clarence O. Cheney, "The Psychology of Mythology," *Psychiatric Quarterly* 1 (April 1927): 198–209. See also Justin Glenn, "Psychoanalytic Writings on Classical Mythology and Religion: 1909–1960," *Classical World* 70 (December 1976–January 1977): 225–47; Richard S. Caldwell, "Selected Bibliography on Psychoanalysis and Classical Studies," *Arethusa* 7 (Summer 1974): 115–34; and Lowell Edmunds and Richard Ingber, "Psychoanalytical Writings on the Oedipus Legend: A Bibliography," *American Imago* 34 (Winter 1977): 374–86.

12. See Ernest Jones, *Sigmund Freud*, II (London: Hogarth, 1955), 273, 332.

13. See Otto Rank, *The Trauma of Birth*, trans. not given (London: Kegan Paul; New York: Harcourt, Brace, 1929 [1924]).

14. Freud, *The Interpretation of Dreams*, 436 n. 2.

15. For Freud's view of the significance of birth in the wake of the break with Rank, see his *The Problem of Anxiety*, trans. Henry Alden Bunker (New York: Psychoanalytic Press and Norton, 1936 [1926]), chaps. 8–10; and *New Introductory Lectures on Psychoanalysis*, trans. James Strachey (New York: Nor-

ton, 1965 [1933]), 87–88, 143–44. At the same time Freud employs Rank's analysis of hero myths as late as his *Moses and Monotheism* (trans. Katherine James [New York: Vintage Books, 1965 (1939)], pt. 1).

16. For contemporary Freudian approaches to myth, see Jacob A. Arlow, "Ego Psychology and the Study of Mythology," *Journal of the American Psychoanalytic Association* 9 (July 1961): 371–93; Sidney Tarachow and others, "Mythology and Ego Psychology," in *The Psychoanalytic Study of Society*, ed. Warner Muensterberger and Sidney Axelrad, III (New York: International Universities Press, 1964), 9–97; and Martin S. Bergman, "The Impact of Ego Psychology on the Study of the Myth," *American Imago* 23 (Fall 1966): 257–64. Ironically, contemporary Freudian Bruno Bettelheim says roughly the same as Arlow and others of fairy tales *rather than* myths, where he is more like early Rank: see his *The Uses of Enchantment* (New York: Vintage Books, 1970), 35–41, 194–99.

17. Joseph Campbell, *An Open Life*, with Michael Toms, ed. John M. Maher and Dennie Briggs (Burdett, N.Y.: Larson, 1988), 123.

18. Ibid.

19. Ibid., 121.

20. On the differences between Campbell and Jung, see, more fully, my *Joseph Campbell: An Introduction*, rev. ed. (New York: New American Library, 1990), chap. 12.

21. Campbell, *An Open Life*, 121.

22. Other leading myth-ritualists include anthropologists A. M. Hocart and Clyde Kluckhohn; historian of religion E. O. James; classicists Gilbert Murray, F. M. Cornford, and A. B. Cook; Biblicists Ivan Engnell, Aubrey Johnson, and Sigmund Mowinckel; literary critics Jessie Weston, E. M. Butler, Francis Fergusson, C. L. Barber, and most fervently Stanley Edgar Hyman, while at times Herbert Weisinger. On myth-ritualism, see John J. Gross, "After Frazer: The Ritualistic Approach to Myth," *Western Humanities Review* 5 (Autumn 1951): 379-91; Stanley Edgar Hyman, "The Ritual View of Myth and the Mythic," *Journal of American Folklore* 68 (October–December 1955): 462–72; Stith Thompson, "Myths and Folktales," *Journal of American Folklore* 68 (October–December 1955): 482–88; Herbert Weisinger, "Notes and Queries," *Journal of American Folklore* 69 (October–December 1956): 387–90; Joseph Fontenrose, *The Ritual Theory of Myth*, Folklore Studies, no. 18 (Berkeley: University of California Press, 1966); William Bascom, "The Myth-Ritual Theory," *Journal of American Folklore* 70 (April–June 1957): 103–14; Hans H. Penner, "Myth and Ritual: A Wasteland or a Forest of Symbols?" *History and Theory*, Beiheft 9 (1968): 46–57; G. S. Kirk, *Myth*, Sather Classi-

cal Lectures 1969 (Berkeley: University of California Press, 1970), 12–31; Kirk, *The Nature of Greek Myths* (Harmondsworth, Middlesex, U.K.: Penguin, 1974), chap. 10; my "The Myth-Ritualist Theory of Religion," *Journal for the Scientific Study of Religion*, 19 (June 1980): 173–85; H. S. Versnel, "What's Sauce for the Goose Is Sauce for the Gander: Myth and Ritual, Old and New," in *Approaches to Greek Myth*, ed. Lowell Edmunds (Baltimore: Johns Hopkins University Press, 1990), chap. 1; Henri Frankfort, *Kingship and the Gods* (Chicago: University of Chicago Press, 1948); Frankfort, *The Problem of Similarity in Ancient Near Eastern Religions*, Frazer Lecture 1950 (Oxford: Clarendon Press, 1951); S.G.F. Brandon, "The Myth and Ritual Position Critically Examined," in *Myth, Ritual, and Kingship*, ed. S. H. Hooke (Oxford: Clarendon Press, 1958), chap. 9; "The Mythical-Ritual Pattern in Civilization," *Proceedings of the 7th Congress for the History of Religions*, Amsterdam, 4–9 September 1950, ed. C. J. Bleeker, G.W.J. Drewes, and K.A.H. Hidding (Amsterdam: North-Holland Publishing, 1951); *The Sacral Kingship: Contributions to the Central Theme of the VIIIth International Congress for the History of Religions*, Rome, April 1955, Supplements to *Numen*, no. 4 (Leiden: Brill, 1959); and A. N. Marlow, "Myth and Ritual in Early Greece," *Bulletin of the John Rylands Library* 43 (March 1961): 373–402.

23. See Robert Ackerman, "Frazer on Myth and Ritual," *Journal of the History of Ideas* 36 (January–March 1975): 115–34; and J. G. *Frazer* (Cambridge: Cambridge University Press, 1987), 231–35, 253–55, and 282–83.

24. See James George Frazer, introduction to Apollodorus, *The Library*, trans. Frazer, Loeb Classical Library (London: Heinemann; New York: Putnam's, 1921), 1:xxviii n. 1.

25. See S. H. Hooke, "The Myth and Ritual Pattern of the Ancient East," in *Myth and Ritual*, ed. Hooke (London: Oxford University Press, 1933), 1. Even more confusingly, Hooke's critics castigate him for employing Frazer's myth–ritualism: see Frankfort, *The Problem of Similarity*, 6–7; and Brandon, "The Myth and Ritual Position," 263. See, in reply, Hooke, "Myth and Ritual: Past and Present," in *Myth, Ritual, and Kingship*, 4–5.

26. Raglan, *The Hero*, 98 n. 19.

27. Rank, *The Myth of the Birth of the Hero*, 57.

28. Ibid., 66.

29. Ibid., 63.

30. Ibid., 71.

31. Still following Freud, Rank introduces a second, non-Oedipal, nonsexual wish that likewise arises in childhood and continues in adult neurotics: a wish for perfect parents. "The entire endeavor to replace the real father by

a more distinguished one is merely the expression of the child's longing for the vanished happy time, when his father still appeared to be the strongest and greatest man, and the mother seemed the dearest and most beautiful woman" (ibid., 62). The child invents the "family romance" and the adult the full-fledged myth to satisfy both wishes. Rank never tries to reconcile these seemingly incompatible wishes. On the contrary, he, like Freud, thinks that the two wishes work in tandem: both get rid of the father. But the Oedipal aim is to get rid of the real, noble father; the non-Oedipal one, to get rid of the adopted, lowly father—and of the mother as well.

32. Ibid., 58.

33. Contrary to Rank (ibid., 17), Cithaeron is a mountain rather than a river. After all, why pierce Oedipus's ankles if he is to be shipped out to sea?

34. On Rank's Freudian theory of heroism, see, in addition to Alan Dundes's comments in "The Hero Pattern and the Life of Jesus," his *Interpreting Folklore* (Bloomington: Indiana University Press, 1980), 51–52; Bascom, "The Myth-Ritual Theory," 109–12; Clyde Kluckhohn, "Recurrent Themes in Myths and Mythmaking," in *Myth and Mythmaking*, ed. Henry A. Murray (New York: Braziller, 1960), 53–58; Melville J. and Frances S. Herskovits, *Dahomean Narrative*, Northwestern University African Studies, no. 1 (Evanston, Ill.: Northwestern University Press, 1958), 85–95; and Taylor, "The Biographical Pattern in Traditional Narrative," 117, 128–29. On Rank's whole psychology, both before and long after his split with Freud, see Jessie Taft, *Otto Rank* (New York: Julian Press, 1958); Fay B. Karpf, *The Psychology and Psychotherapy of Otto Rank* (New York: Philosophical Library, 1953); Esther Menaker, *Otto Rank* (New York: Columbia University Press, 1982); E. James Lieberman, *Acts of Will* (New York: Free Press, 1985); Ruth L. Munroe, *Schools of Psychoanalytic Thought* (New York: Holt, Rinehart, 1955), ch. 14; Samuel Eisenstein, "Otto Rank: The Myth of the Birth of the Hero," in *Psychoanalytic Pioneers*, ed. Franz Alexander, Eisenstein, and Martin Grotjahn (New York: Basic Books, 1966), 36–50; Jack Jones, "Otto Rank: A Forgotten Heresy," *Commentary* 30 (September 1960): 219–29; Jones, "Rank, Otto," *International Encyclopedia of the Social Sciences* 13 (1968): 314–19; Ira Progoff, *The Death and Rebirth of Psychology* (New York: Julian Press, 1956), chap. 7; Dennis B. Klein, *Jewish Origins of the Psychoanalytic Movement* (New York: Praeger, 1981), ch. 4; Ernest Jones, *Sigmund Freud*, III (London: Hogarth, 1957), chap. 2; Paul Roazen, *Freud and His Followers* (New York: Knopf, 1975), chap. 8; and Peter Gay, *Freud* (New York: Norton, 1988), 470–89.

35. For Jung's interpretation of heroism in both halves of life, see C. G. Jung, "The Psychology of the Child Archetype," in his *The Archetypes and the Collective Unconscious*, Collected Works, ed. Sir Herbert Read and others,

trans. R.F.C. Hull and others, vol. 9, pt. 1, 1st ed. (New York: Pantheon Books, 1959), 151–81; *Symbols of Transformation,* Collected Works, vol. 5, 1st ed. (New York: Pantheon Books, 1956), 171–444; *Psychology and Alchemy,* Collected Works, vol. 12, 1st ed. (New York: Pantheon Books, 1953), 333–39; and *Analytical Psychology* (New York: Vintage Books, 1970), 117–23. On Jungian heroism, see Joseph L. Henderson, "Ancient Myths and Modern Man," in Jung and others, *Man and His Symbols* (New York: Dell Laurel Editions, 1968), 103–25; Marie-Louise von Franz, *An Introduction to the Psychology of Fairy Tales* (New York: Spring, 1970), 41–46; M. Esther Harding, *Psychic Energy,* 2d ed. (Princeton, N.J.: Princeton University Press, 1963), chap. 9; Jolande Jacobi, *The Way of Individuation,* trans. R.F.C. Hull (New York: Harcourt, Brace, 1967), 60–79; and John Weir Perry, "The Messianic Hero," *Journal of Analytical Psychology* 17 (July 1972): 184–98.

36. See Campbell, *The Hero with a Thousand Faces,* 318–34; and *The Power of Myth,* with Bill Moyers, ed. Betty Sue Flowers (New York: Doubleday, 1988), 124–25. On Rank's view of heroism, see also Campbell, *The Masks of God: Occidental Mythology* (New York: Viking, 1964), 73–74, 77.

37. See Campbell, *The Power of Myth,* 125. On female Jungian heroes, see Coline Covington, "In Search of the Heroine," *Journal of Analytical Psychology* 34 (July 1989): 243–54.

38. Campbell, *The Hero with a Thousand Faces,* 58.

39. Ibid., 110–11.

40. Ibid., 126.

41. To be sure, Campbell, in his second, longer summary of his pattern (ibid., 246) makes these specific relationships to gods optional.

42. Ibid., 139.

43. See my *Joseph Campbell,* 222–29.

44. Campbell, *The Hero with a Thousand Faces,* 130.

45. Ibid., 139–40.

46. Ibid., 217.

47. Ibid., 386.

48. Ibid., 193.

49. See Joseph L. Henderson, *Thresholds of Initiation* (Middletown, Conn: Wesleyan University Press, 1967), esp. 101–2, 134–35, 151–52, 159, and 178–80; "Ancient Myths and Modern Man," esp. 101–25; and introduction to Henderson and Maud Oakes, *The Wisdom of the Serpent,* Patterns of Myth Series (New York: Braziller, 1963), esp. chap. 5. See also John Beebe, introduction to *Aspects of the Masculine,* ed. Beebe (Princeton, N.J.: Princeton University Press, 1989), esp. xi–xiii.

50. Campbell, *The Hero with a Thousand Faces,* 58 n. 10.

51. Ibid., 30.

52. Ibid., 58.

53. Ibid., 37–38.

54. As I discovered in writing my book on Campbell, surprisingly little has been written about him. Prior to the 1988 Bill Moyers interviews, from which comes *The Power of Myth*, there were barely any articles on him. There were really only book reviews and interviews, though there were many applications of his hero pattern, especially to literary works. Since the Moyers series there have appeared posthumous paeans to the man—for example, the hagiographical *Hero's Journey*, ed. Phil Cousineau (San Francisco: Harper, 1990)—but scholarly appraisals are still scant. Mine remains the sole scholarly book on Campbell, though forthcoming is a collection of essays, *Paths to the Power of Myth*, ed. Daniel C. Noel (New York: Crossroad, 1990). Kenneth L. Golden is editing another collection for Garland. On Campbell's theory of heroism, see, in addition to Dundes's brief but pointed remarks in "The Hero Pattern and the Life of Jesus," Dundes's headnotes to my "Joseph Campbell's Theory of Myth," in *Sacred Narrative*, ed. Dundes (Berkeley: University of California Press, 1984), 256–57; my *Joseph Campbell*, chaps. 2–3; Taylor, "The Biographical Pattern in Traditional Narrative," 119–21, 128–29; and Jean Dalby Clift and Wallace B. Clift, *The Hero's Journey in Dreams* (New York: Crossroad, 1988), chaps. 2–3. On Campbell's theory of myth as a whole, see, in addition to my *Joseph Campbell*, Stanley Edgar Hyman, "Myth, Ritual, and Nonsense," *Kenyon Review* 11 (Summer 1949): 455–56, 470–75; Richard Chase, *The Democratic Vista* (Garden City, N.Y.: Doubleday Anchor Books, 1958), 74–86; Florence Sandler and Darrell Reeck, "The Masks of Joseph Campbell," *Religion* 11 (January 1981): 1–20; M. C. D'Arcy, "God and Mythology," *Heythrop Journal* 1 (April 1960): 95–104; Richard M. Dorson, "Current Folklore Theories," *Current Anthropology* 4 (February 1963): 107–8; Dorson, "Mythology and Folklore," *Annual Review of Anthropology* 2 (1973): 108–9; William Kerrigan, "The Raw, The Cooked and the Half-Baked," *Virginia Quarterly Review* 51 (Autumn 1975): 646–56; and Alfred Sundel, "Joseph Campbell's Quest for the Holy Grail," *Sewanee Review* 78 (January–March 1970): 211–16.

55. See James George Frazer, *The Golden Bough*, 3rd ed., 12 vols. (London: Macmillan, 1911–1915); Frazer, *The Golden Bough*, 1-vol. abridgment (London: Macmillan, 1922)—the edition cited unless otherwise noted; S. H. Hooke, "The Myth and Ritual Pattern of the Ancient East" and "Traces of the Myth and Ritual Pattern in Canaan," in *Myth and Ritual*, chaps. 1, 4; Hooke, introduction and "The Myth and Ritual Pattern in Jewish and Chris-

tian Apocalyptic," in *The Labyrinth*, ed. Hooke (London: SPCK, 1935), v–x, chap. 6; Hooke, *The Origins of Early Semitic Ritual*, Schweich Lectures 1935 (London: Oxford University Press, 1938); Hooke, *The Siege Perilous* (London: SCM Press, 1956), chaps. 3, 12; and Hooke, "Myth and Ritual: Past and Present," chap. 1.

56. More precisely, Frazer supplies this scenario for the god of vegetation (chap. 29), and Hooke adds the role of the king. When Frazer considers kingship, the king is the incarnation, not merely the representative, of the god of vegetation (chaps. 24–26).

57. Sometimes Hooke says, inconsistently, that the king *is* god—a possibility that would render Hooke's version of the ritual absurd: see Hooke, introduction to *The Labyrinth*, v.

58. For Frazer, in contrast to Hooke, the death of the god can be voluntary, as in Adonis's descent to Hades.

59. See Raglan, *The Hero*, 89–136; *Death and Rebirth* (London: Watts, 1945), passim; and *The Origins of Religion* (London: Watts, 1949), esp. chaps. 9–10.

60. See Frazer, *The Golden Bough*, chaps. 24–26.

61. Going beyond both Frazer and Hooke, Raglan speculates that in the earliest form of the ritual the victim was not the king and that in the next stage of the ritual the king was not the god: see *The Origins of Religion*, chaps. 9–10. By contrast, in "Myth and Ritual," *Journal of American Folklore* 68 (October–December 1955): 459, Raglan places divine kingship in the *first* stage of the ritual.

62. Strictly speaking, the chief god for Raglan is of the sky rather than, as for Frazer and Hooke, of vegetation.

63. Raglan, *The Hero*, 137–56. Raglan claims to be following Hooke but actually devises his own pattern.

64. Ibid., 138.

65. Raglan, "Notes and Queries," *Journal of American Folklore* 70 (October–December 1957): 359. Elsewhere Raglan ironically scorns what he assumes to be "the Freudian explanation" as "to say the least inadequate, since it only takes into account two incidents out of at least [Raglan's] twenty-two and we find that the rest of the story is the same whether the hero marries his mother, his sister or his first cousin" ("The Hero of Tradition," 230—not included in *The Hero*). Raglan disdains psychological analyses of all stripes: in response to the Jungian H. G. Baynes, "On the Psychological Origins of Divine Kingship," *Folk-Lore* 47 (March 1936): 74–104, see his "Psychology and the Divine Kingship," *Folk-Lore* 47 (September 1936): 340–44.

66. For Raglan's own ritualist analysis of the Oedipus myth, see his *Jocasta's Crime* (London: Methuen, 1933), esp. chap. 26.

67. Raglan, *The Hero*, 162.

68. See Victor Cook, "Lord Raglan's Hero—A Cross Cultural Critique," *Florida Anthropologist* 18 (September 1965): 147–54.

69. On Raglan's theory of heroism and of myth as a whole, see, in addition to Cook's "Lord Raglan's Hero" and to Dundes's observations in "The Hero Pattern and the Life of Jesus," Fontenrose, *The Ritual Theory of Myth*, chap. 1; Bascom, "The Myth-Ritual Theory," 103–14; Bascom, "Notes and Queries," *Journal of American Folklore* 71 (January–March 1958): 79–80; Stanley Edgar Hyman, "Notes and Queries," *Journal of American Folklore* 71 (April–June 1958): 152–55; Bascom, "Notes and Queries," *Journal of American Folklore* 71 (April–June 1958): 155–56; Kluckhohn, "Recurrent Themes in Myths and Mythmaking," 53–58; Herskovitses, *Dahomean Narrative*, 104–5, 111–16; Taylor, "The Biographical Pattern in Traditional Narrative," 118–19, 128–29; F. A. de Caro, "The Chadwicks and Lord Raglan: A Retrospective Analysis," *Folklore Forum* 6 (April 1973): 75–86; and Edmund Leach, "Testament of an English Eccentric," *New York Review of Books* 5 (September 16, 1965): 16–17. See Raglan's response to Bascom, "Notes and Queries," *Journal of American Folklore* 70 (October–December 1957): 359–60. For an application of Raglan's pattern, see Alwyn D. Rees, "The Divine Hero in Celtic Hagiology," *Folk-Lore* 47 (March 1936): 30–41.

70. See Rank, *The Myth of the Birth of the Hero*, 62, 70–71.

71. On the distinction between a literal and a historical interpretation, see my *Joseph Campbell*, 198–201.

72. Alan Dundes, *The Hero Pattern and the Life of Jesus*, Protocol of the Twenty-fifth Colloquy, The Center for Hermeneutical Studies in Hellenistic and Modern Culture, 12 December 1976 (Berkeley, Calif.: The Center for Hermeneutical Studies in Hellenistic and Modern Culture, 1977). Contains sixteen responses and discussion. Reprinted, minus responses and discussion, in Dundes, *Interpreting Folklore*, 223–61. Citations are to the reprint in *In Quest of the Hero*.

73. See Raglan, *The Hero*, 158, 165–75.

74. Ibid., 148–75; "The Hero of Tradition," 229.

75. See Francis Lee Utley, "Lincoln Wasn't There, or Lord Raglan's Hero," Supplement to *CEA Critic* 22 (June 1965), CEA Chap Book (Washington, D.C.: College English Association, 1965).

76. Dundes, "The Hero Pattern and the Life of Jesus," 190.

77. Dundes mentions (ibid., 179, 203) Frazer's attention to the case of

Jesus, but he accords it insufficient due: see *The Golden Bough*, 3rd ed., esp. vol. 5, bk. 1, chap. 10; bk. 2, chap. 6; and vol. 9, 412–23.

78. See William Bascom, "The Forms of Folklore: Prose Narratives," *Journal of American Folklore* 78 (January–March 1965): 3–20; Dundes, *Analytic Essays in Folklore*, Studies in Folklore, no. 2 (The Hague: Mouton, 1975), 164–65.

79. Dundes, "The Hero Pattern and the Life of Jesus," 191.

80. Dundes boldly dismisses ego psychology as "not all that relevant" because "folklore represents primary-process or id products" (*Parsing through Customs* [Madison: University of Wisconsin Press, 1987], 33).

81. Dundes, "The Hero Pattern and the Life of Jesus," 216.

82. For Freud's own interpretation of Jesus as a son who, similarly, is at once a submissive sacrifice to the father and his father's successor, see *Totem and Taboo*, trans. James Strachey (New York: Norton, 1950 [1913]), 153–55; and *Moses and Monotheism*, 109–14.

83. For other books by Dundes, see esp. *The Morphology of North American Indian Folktales*, FF Communications, no. 195, vol. 81 (Helsinki: Suomalainen Tiedeakatemia, Academia Scientiarum Fennica, 1964); *Analytic Essays in Folklore*, esp. sec. 3; *Essays in Folkloristics*, Kirpa Dai Series in Folklore and Anthropology, vol. 1 (Meerut, India: Folklore Institute, 1978); the overlapping *Interpreting Folklore*; *Parsing through Customs*, esp. chap. 1; *Folklore Matters* (Knoxville: University of Tennessee Press, 1989), esp. 57–82; *Life is Like a Chicken Coop Ladder* (New York: Columbia University Press, 1984); *Sacred Narrative*; and *The Flood Myth*, ed. Dundes (Berkeley: University of California Press, 1988).

Imagine an abscess in your brain. Every day, your neurons direct electricity through habitualized routes, doing jobs they're used to doing. The more regularly those electrical impulses travel to particular places, the quicker and more efficient their journey becomes. The tubes get oiled, the lanes get expanded, and they get settled into their route. But when someone you love dies —when a central component of your mental map is suddenly gone—your neurons don't stop directing electricity down those well-worn paths. After all, the infrastructure is already built. They go down that way every day. How would they know to stop?

And so your neurons steer you off a cliff. Every day. This is what losing a loved one means: the daily careening of mental electricity into the gaping chasm of their absence. The daily plunge and crash of a whole highway's worth of cognitive impulses, plummeting into the smoldering wreckage of yesterday's.

The abscess never goes away. Gradually, over months and years, your neurons learn to direct traffic around it. The topography of your brain is always marred, but you just learn to live with it. You work around the abscess. This is the best way I can describe grief.

—◆•✦•◆—

Most video games are power fantasies. But the most significant power-fantasy afforded by video games isn't the ability to kill monsters with fireballs from your hands, or direct the rise and fall of civilizations, or assassinate your way to world peace. It's not saving a princess, or saving the world, or saving the universe. It's just *saving*. The most important power fantasy afforded by most video games is the ability to save and load your game.

It's a colossal power, when you think about it. Saving and loading gives you the power to make a mistake, and then go back in time and do it better. It empowers you to be imperfect, but also, where it matters, perfect. It lets you live every possible iteration of yourself, while still being yourself, both inside and comfortably outside of the pull of time. It allows you to experience death while remaining immortal.

When I was a kid, having savegames in real life was my most

PART I

THE MYTH OF THE BIRTH OF THE HERO

by Otto Rank

Introduction

THE prominent civilized nations—the Babylonians and Egyptians, the Hebrews and Hindus, the Persians, the Greeks and the Romans, as well as the Teutons and others—all began at an early stage to glorify their national heroes—mythical princes and kings, founders of religions, dynasties, empires, or cities—in a number of poetic tales and legends. The history of the birth and of the early life of these personalities came to be especially invested with fantastic features, which in different nations—even though widely separated by space and entirely independent of each other—present a baffling similarity or, in part, a literal correspondence. Many investigators have long been impressed with this fact, and one of the chief problems of mythological research still consists in the elucidation of the reason for the extensive analogies in the fundamental outlines of mythical tales, which are rendered still more puzzling by the unanimity in certain details and their reappearance in the most of the mythical groupings.[1]

The mythological theories, aiming at the explanation of these remarkable phenomena, are, in a general way, as follows:[2]

1. The "Idea of the People," propounded by Adolf Bastian.[3] This theory assumes the existence of *elemental ideas*, so that the unanimity of the myths is a necessary sequence of the uniform disposition of the human mind and the manner of its manifestation, which within certain limits is identical at all times and in all places. This interpretation was urgently advocated by Adolf Bauer as accounting for the wide distribution of the hero myths.[4]

2. The explanation by *original community*, first applied by Theodor Benfey to the widely distributed parallel forms of folklore and fairy tales.[5] Originating in a favorable locality (India), these tales were first accepted by the primarily related (Indo-Germanic) peoples, then continued to grow while retaining the common primary traits, and ultimately radiated over the entire earth. This mode of explanation was first adapted to the wide distribution of the hero myths by Rudolf Schubert.[6]

3. The modern theory of *migration*, or *borrowing*, according to which individual myths originate from definite peoples (especially the Babylo-

nians) and are accepted by other peoples through oral tradition (commerce and traffic) or through literary influences.[7]

The modern theory of migration and borrowing can be readily shown to be merely a modification of Benfey's theory, necessitated by newly discovered and irreconcilable material. This profound and extensive research of modern investigations has shown that India, rather than Babylonia, may be regarded as the first home of the myths. Moreover, the tales presumably did not radiate from a single point, but traveled over and across the entire inhabited globe. This brings into prominence the idea of the interdependence of mythological structures, an idea which was generalized by Braun as the basic law of the nature of the human mind: Nothing new is ever discovered as long as it is possible to copy.[8] The theory of elemental ideas, so strenuously advocated by Bauer over a quarter of a century ago, is unconditionally declined by the most recent investigators (Winckler,[9] Stucken), who maintain the migration theory.

There is really no such sharp contrast between the various theories or their advocates, for the concept of elemental ideas does not interfere with the claims of primary common possession or of migration. Furthermore, the ultimate problem is not whence and how the material reached a certain people; the question is: Where did it come from to begin with? All these theories would explain only the variability and distribution of the myths, but not their origin. Even Schubert, the most inveterate opponent of Bauer's view, acknowledges this truth, by stating that all these manifold sagas date back to a single very ancient prototype. But he is unable to tell us anything of the origin of this prototype. Bauer likewise inclines to this mediating view; he points out repeatedly that in spite of the multiple origin of independent tales, it is necessary to concede a most extensive and ramified borrowing, as well as an original community of the concepts in related peoples.[10] The same conciliatory attitude is maintained by Lessmann in a recent publication (1908), in which he rejects the assumption of elemental ideas, but admits that primary relationship and borrowing do not exclude each other.[11] As pointed out by Wundt, however, it must be kept in mind that the appropriation of mythological contents always represents at the same time an independent mythological construction; because only that can be retained permanently which corresponds to the borrower's stage of mythological ideation. The faint recollections of preceding narratives would hardly suffice for the re-figuration of the same material, without the persistent presence of the underlying motifs; but precisely for this reason, such motifs may pro-duce new contents that agree in their fundamental themes, even in the absence of similar associations.[12]

Leaving aside for the present the inquiry as to the mode of distri-bution of these myths, the origin of the hero myth in general is now to be investigated, fully anticipating that migration (or borrowing) will prove to be directly and fairly positively demonstrable in a num-ber of cases. When this is not feasible, other viewpoints will have to be conceded, at least for the present, rather than bar the way to further progress by the somewhat unscientific attitude of Hugo Winckler, who says: When human beings and products, exactly corresponding to each other, are found at remote parts of the earth, we must conclude that they have wandered thither; whether we have knowledge of the how or when makes no difference in the assumption of the fact itself.[13] Even granting the migration of all myths, the origin of the first myth would still have to be explained.[14]

Investigations along these lines will necessarily help to provide a deeper insight into the contents of the tales. Nearly all authors who have hitherto been engaged in the interpretation of the birth myths of heroes find in them a personification of the processes of nature, fol-lowing the dominant mode of natural mythological interpretation.[15] The newborn hero is the young sun rising from the waters, first con-fronted by lowering clouds, but finally triumphing over all obstacles.[16] The taking into consideration of all natural (chiefly atmospheric) phe-nomena—as was done by the first representatives of this method of myth interpretation[17]—and the regarding of the legends, in a more restricted sense, as astral myths (Stucken, Winckler, and others) are approaches not so essentially distinct as the followers of each individ-ual direction believe to be the case. Nor does it seem a basic improve-ment when the purely solar interpretation, as advocated especially by Frobenius,[18] was no longer accepted and the view was advanced that all myths were orginally lunar. Hüsing holds this theory in his discus-sion of the myth of Cyrus the Great; Siecke also claims this view as the only legitimate, obvious interpretation of the birth myths of the he-roes; and it is a concept that is beginning to gain popularity.[19]

The interpretation of the myths themselves will be taken up in de-tail later on, and we shall refrain here from all detailed critical comments on the above mode of explanation. Although significant, and undoubtedly in part correct, the astral theory is not altogether satisfactory and fails to afford an insight into the motives of myth formation. The objection may be raised that the tracing to astronomical processes does not fully represent the content of these myths, and that much clearer and simpler relations might be established through another mode of interpretation. The much abused theory of elemental ideas indicates a practically neglected aspect of mythological research. At the beginning, as well as at the end of his contribution, Bauer points out how much more natural and probable it would be to seek the reason for the general unanimity of these myths in the very general traits of the human psyche, rather than in primary community or migration. This assumption appears to be more justifiable, since such general movements of the human mind are also expressed in still other forms and in other domains, where they can be demonstrated as universal.[20]

Concerning the character of these general movements of the human mind, the psychological study of the essence of these myths might help to reveal the source from which has flowed uniformly, at all times and in all places, an identical mythological content. Such a derivation of an essential constituent, from a common human source, has already been successfully attempted with one of these legendary motifs. Freud, in his *Interpretation of Dreams*, reveals the connection of the Oedipus fable—where Oedipus is told by the oracle that he will kill his father and marry his mother, as he unwittingly does later—with two typical dreams experienced by many now living: the dream of the father's death, and the dream of sexual intercourse with the mother. Of King Oedipus he says:[21]

> His fate moves us only because it might have been our own, because the oracle laid upon us before our birth the very curse which rested upon him. It may be that we were all destined to direct our first sexual impulses toward our mothers, and our first impulses of hatred and resistance toward our fathers; our dreams convince us that we were. King Oedipus, who slew his father Laius and wedded his mother Jocasta, is nothing more or less than a wish-fulfillment—the fulfillment of the wish of our childhood.[22]

The manifestation of the intimate relationship between dream and myth—not only in regard to the content but also as to the form and motor forces of this and many other, more particularly pathological, psyche structures—entirely justifies the interpretation of the myth as a dream of the masses of the people, which I have recently shown elsewhere.[23] At the same time, the transference of the method, and in part also of the results, of Freud's technique of dream interpretation to the myths would seem to be justifiable, as was defended by Abraham, and illustrated in an example, in his paper on "Dreams and Myths."[24] In the circle of myths that follow, the intimate relations between dream and myth find further confirmation, with frequent opportunity for reasoning from analogy.

The hostile attitude of the most modern mythological tendency (chiefly represented by the Society for Comparative Mythological Research) against all attempts at establishing a relation between dream and myth is for the most part the outcome of the restriction of the parallelization to the so-called nightmares (*Alpträume*), as attempted in Laistner's notable book, and also of ignorance of the relevant teachings of Freud.[25] The latter not only help us to understand the dreams themselves but also show their symbolism and close relationship with all psychic phenomena in general, especially with daydreams or fantasies, with artistic creativeness, and with certain disturbances of the normal psychic function. A common share in all these productions belongs to a single psychic function: the human imagination. It is to this imaginative faculty—of humanity at large rather than of the individual—that the modern myth theory is obliged to concede a high rank, perhaps the first, as the ultimate source of all myths. The interpretation of the myths in the astral sense—or more accurately speaking, as "almanac tales"—gives rise to the query: In view of a creative imagination in humanity, should we seek (with Lessmann) for the first germ of the origin of such tales precisely in the processes of the heavens, or on the contrary, should we conclude that readymade tales of an entirely different (but presumably psychic) origin were only subsequently transferred to the heavenly bodies?[26] Ehrenreich makes a more positive admission: The mythologic evolution certainly begins on terrestrial soil, in so far as experiences must first be gathered in the immediate surroundings before they can be projected into the heavenly universe.[27] And Wundt tells us that the theory of the evolution of mythology according to which it first originates in the heavens, whence at a later date it descends to earth, is contradictory both to the history of the myth (which is unaware of such a migration) and to the psychology of myth formation (which must repudiate such a translocation as internally impossible).[28] We are also convinced that the myths,[29] originally at least, are structures of the human faculty of imagination, which were at some time projected for certain reasons upon the heavens, and may be secondarily transferred to the heavenly bodies, with their baffling phenomena. The significance of the unmistakable traces—the fixed figures, and so forth—that have been imprinted upon the myth by this transference must by no means be underrated, although the origin of these figures was possibly psychic in character; they were subsequently made the basis of the almanac and firmament calculations precisely on account of this significance.

In a general way, it would seem as if the investigators who apply an exclusively "natural" scheme of interpretation have been unable, in any sense—in their endeavor to discover the original sense of the myths—to get away entirely from a psychological process such as must be assumed similarly for the creators of the myths.[30] The motive is identical, and led to the same course for myth-creators and for myth-interpreters. It is most naïvely uttered by one of the founders and champions of comparative myth investigation and of the natural mythological mode of interpretation; Max Müller points out in his *Essays* that this procedure not only invests meaningless legends with a significance and beauty of their own but also helps to remove some of the most revolting features of classical mythology, as well as to elucidate their true meaning.[31] This readily understandable revulsion naturally prevents the mythologist from assuming that such motifs—incest with mother, sister, or daughter; murder of father, grandfather, or brother—could be based on universal fantasies, which according to Freud's teachings have their source in the infantile psyche, with its peculiar interpretation of the external world and its denizens. This revulsion is, therefore, only the reaction of the dimly sensed painful recognition of the actuality of these relations; and this reaction impels the myth interpreters, for their own subconscious rehabilitation, and that of all mankind, to credit these motifs with an entirely different meaning from their original significance. The same internal repudiation prevents the myth-creating people from believing in the possibility of such revolting thoughts, and this defense probably was the first reason for projecting these relations onto the firmament. The psychological pacifying through such a rehabilitation, by projection upon external and remote objects, can still be realized—to a certain degree, at least—by a glance at one of these interpretations, for instance that of the objectionable Oedipus fable, as given by Goldhizer, a representative of the natural school of myth interpreters: Oedipus (who kills his father, marries his mother, and dies old and blind) is the solar hero who murders his procreator, the darkness; he shares his couch with his mother, the gloaming, from whose lap, the dawn, he has been born; he dies, blinded, as the setting sun.[32]

It is understandable that some such interpretation is more soothing to the mind than the revelation of the fact that incest and murder impulses against their nearest relatives are found in the fantasies of most people, as remnants of infantile ideation. But this is not a scientific argument, and revulsion of this kind—although it may not always be equally conscious—is altogether out of place in view of existing facts. One must either become reconciled to these indecencies, provided they are felt to be such, or one must abandon the study of psychological phenomena. It is evident that human beings, even in the earliest times, and with a most naïve imagination, never saw incest and parricide in the firmament on high,[33] but it is far more probable that these ideas are derived from another source, presumably human. In what way they came to reach the sky, and what modifications or additions they received in the process, are questions of a secondary character that cannot be settled until the psychic origin of the myths in general has been established.

At any rate, besides the astral conception, the claims of the part played by the psychic life must be credited with the same rights for myth formation, and this argument will be amply vindicated by the results of our method of interpretation. With this object in view, we shall first take up in the following pages the legendary material on which such a psychological interpretation is to be attempted on a large scale for the first time.

Notes

1. *Editor's note*: There are, indeed, widespread correspondences in the myths of early and primitive peoples—very often the same stories, with only slight variations, are told by the Eskimos and the aborigines of South Africa, by the Carib Indians and the natives of Polynesia, and around the globe. Among the stories are those describing the creation of the world and its first inhabitants—or, at least, the ancestors of the tribe—and later a great deluge,

was the republishing of two out-of-print chapbooks. Staying true to our do-it-yourself roots, we did all of the copyediting, design, printing, and binding ourselves—just like in the nineteenth century, when publishers and printers were the same people. As our commercial printing workload became heavier, that dream was put on the back burner. In early 2017, the unthinkable happened: Donald Trump became the president of the United States.

Following the election, we quickly realized how imminent things felt, how dangerous and uncharted the territory that lay before us was. Trump's bigotry and xenophobia hung in the air like a poisonous fog, and many people felt that his being in power would enable a whole host of others who would seek to do irreparable harm to the fabric of our society. Every day that passed, every executive order signed, every crumbling piece of the social safety net that had been fought for and won over previous decades, all of it demanded action. It didn't take long for our role in all of this to come into focus. We knew then that we had to begin publishing.

To us, publishing isn't synonymous with the big New York publishing houses. It's not about the elite, corporate structure or the fancy offices. As designers and printers, we see publishing as the beautiful moment when thoughts, hopes, and dreams come together. We see it as the freedom for people to tell their own stories without asking for permission from industry gatekeepers. In a world where the odds are stacked against so many, we have dedicated our publishing to lifting up the voices of emerging artists and writers, especially those who have historically been rejected and discouraged by the mainstream publishing industry.

We put out an open call for submissions in May 2017, asking writers and visual artists to share how they would interpret loss and grief. That open call received almost a thousand submissions. For some, this was the most difficult writing they've ever done. With great effort and care, we whittled it all down to thirty-three contributors from around the world. These writers and artists generously share their heartbreak and breakthroughs as they face some of the most difficult moments of their lives. Within these pages you'll find stories about gentrification, the loss of loved ones, the loss of home, even stories that take a glimpse presents you with a choice between two Bible verses, and you can feel yourself dissociating. You have to say the right words or she'll kill herself. There's a throbbing in your head. You pause the game, and find yourself staring at biblegateway.com, trying to figure out what these verses will mean in this context. It's hard to remember how sentences hang together. Matthew 11:28 goes like this:

Come to me, all you who are weary and burdened, and I will give you rest.

This seems like a dangerous thing to say to an extremely religious person on the brink of suicide. You don't want her to come to Jesus for rest; you want her to step down from the ledge. The other verse, Proverbs 21:15, is angrier:

When justice is done, it brings joy to the righteous but terror to evildoers.

Kate's not the fire-and-brimstone type, but she did seem heartened when you told her that you were looking for evidence to nail Nathan Prescott, the preppy sociopath who drugged her. Her soft heart is clearly stung by the injustice of what happened, so maybe a little Old Testament retribution could help the situation.

You choose the Proverbs verse. It's the wrong one.

Kate steps off the roof of the building. She falls in slow motion, her body bending in the slipstream of the air. You bring your hands to your face, making a horrified mask over your mouth and nose. Kate is dead. You emit a strangled noise, and slump back in your chair. You're staring at the computer screen. You glance across your room, towards the secret compartment where you keep the stash of sleeping pills your friend gave you the last time you saw her. You don't leave the house for a week.

My friend who killed herself was named Kat.

a vast and destructive conflagration, and the coming of the tribe's culture hero. It is to the stories of this typical culture hero that Rank addresses himself in his present essay. The legends he compiles and discusses, however, are those that have already become more refined and sophisticated.

2. A short and fairly complete review of the general theories of mythology, and of the principal advocates of each, is to be found in Wilhelm Wundt: *Völkerpsychologie* (Leipzig, 1905–9), Vol. II, Part I, p. 527.

3. *Das Beständige in den Menschenrassen und die Spielweise ihrer Veränderlichkeit* (Berlin, 1868).

4. *"Die Kyros Sage und Verwandtes,"* Sitzungsberichte der Wiener Akademie, No. 100 (1882), p. 495.

5. *Pantschatantra* (1859).

6. *Herodots Darstellung der Cyrussage* (Breslau, 1890).

7. Compare E. Stucken: *Astral Mythen* (Leipzig, 1896–1907), especially Part V, "Moses"; and H. Lessmann: *"Die Kyrossage in Europe,"* Wissen. beit. z. Jahresbericht d. städt. Realschule zu Charlottenburg (1906).

8. *Naturgeschichte der Sage*, 2 vols. (Munich, 1864–5), tracing all religious ideas, legends, and systems back to their common family tree and primary root.

9. Some of the important writings by Winckler will be mentioned in the course of this article.

10. *Zeitschrift für der Oesterr. Gymnasium* (1891), pp. 161 ff. Schubert's reply is also found here, pp. 594 ff.

11. "Object and Aim of Mythological Research," *Mytholog. Bibliot.* (Leipzig), Vol. I, No. 4.

12. Wundt, op. cit., Part III.

13. *"Die babylonische Geisteskultur in ihren Beziehungen zur Kulturentwicklung der Menschheit,"* Wissenschaft und Bildung, Vol. XV (1907), p. 47.

14. Of course no time will be wasted here on the futile question as to what the first legend may have been; in all probability this never existed, any more than "the first human couple."

15. *Editor's note:* At the time Rank wrote this essay, there was a well-established school of German and American mythologists and anthropologists, among whom Leo Frobenius was particularly prominent, who held that all myths had an original allegorical reference to the sun: its rising, setting, and supernatural influence. The figures who appeared as actors in the myths could be interpreted as disguises o the sun in its various aspects. A rival school soon claimed that all myths were lunar—referring allegorically to the moon, instead. Thus the culture hero would really be a representation of the sun, or of

the moon. The two schools, and others with a similar trend of thought, lumped together, are referred to by Rank in the course of this essay as the "astral school." Because of its popularity and the authority of many of its proponents, he was constrained to speak of it with some respect. But this "naturalistic" approach to mythology has since sharply declined, and in his later writings Rank pays it scant attention.

16. Brodbeck: *Zoroaster* (Leipzig, 1893), p. 138.

17. As an especially discouraging example of this mode of procedure may be mentioned a contribution by the well-known natural mythologist Schwartz, which touches on this circle of myths, and is entitled: *Der Ursprung der Stamm und Gründungssage Roms unter dem Reflex indogermanischer Mythen* (Jena, 1898).

18. Leo Frobenius: *Das Zeitalter des Sonnengotten* (Berlin, 1904).

19. G. Hüsing: *Contributions to the Kyros Myth* (Berlin, 1906). Siecke, "Hermes als Mondgott," *Mytholog. Bibliot.*, Vol. II, No. 1 (1908), p. 48. Compare, for example, Paul Koch: *Sagen der Bibel und ihre Übereinstimmung mit der Mythologie der Indogermanen* (Berlin, 1907). Compare also the partly lunar, partly solar, but at any rate entirely one-sided conception of the hero myth in Gustav Friedrich: *Grundlage, Entstehung und genaue Einzeldeutung der bekanntesten germanischen Märchen, Mythen and Sagen* (Leipzig, 1909), p. 118.

20. *Editor's note*: The problem of "elemental ideas" (and their continuing influence in modern life) is one which has much concerned Carl Jung and his disciples; it has led to their famous if controversial theories of the "archetype" and the "collective unconscious." It has been pointed out that it is not fully appreciated how close Rank came to Jung's theory of the "archetype," though of course Rank's emphasis is rather different. If anything, it is less mystical.

21. *Editor's note*: First published in 1900. The translation used here is that of Dr. A. A. Brill in his Modern Library edition: *The Basic Writings of Sigmund Freud* (New York, 1938), p. 308.

22. The fable of Shakespeare's Hamlet also permits of a similar interpretation, according to Freud. It will be seen later on how mythological investigators bring the Hamlet legend from entirely different viewpoints into the correlation of the circle of myths.

23. *Editor's note*: The reference here is to *Der Künstler* ("The Artist"), Rank's first published work (1907).

24. *Editor's note*, Karl Abraham's contribution was published in German in the same year as this essay (1909). English translation by W. A. White in Nervous and Mental Diseases Monograph Series, No. 15 (New York, 1913).

25. Laistner: *The Riddle of the Sphinx* (1889). Compare Lessmann, "Object

and Aim . . . ," loc. cit. Ehrenreich alone (*General Psychology*, p. 149) admits the extraordinary significance of dream-life for the myth-fiction of all times. Wundt does so likewise, for individual mythological motifs.

26. Stucken (op. cit., p. 432) says in this sense: The myth transmitted by the ancestors was transferred to natural processes and interpreted in a naturalistic way, not vice versa. "Interpretation of nature is a motive in itself" (p. 636n.). In a very similar way, Eduard Meyer (*Geschichte des Altertums*, 1884–1902, Vol. V. p. 48) has written: "In many cases, the natural symbolism, sought in the myths, is only apparently present or has been secondarily introduced, as often in the Vedas and in the Egyptian myths; it is a primary attempt at interpretation, like the myth-interpretations that arose among the Greeks as early as the fifth century."

27. Op. cit., p. 104.

28. Op. cit., p. 282.

29. For fairy tales, in this as well as in other essential features, Thimme advocates the same point of view as is here claimed for the myths. Compare Adolf Thimme: *Das Märchen*, Vol. II of *Handbücher zur Volkskunde* (Leipzig, 1909).

30. Of this myth interpretation, Wundt (op. cit., p. 352) has well said that it really should have accompanied the original myth formation.

31. Vol. II, p. 143, in the German translation (Leipzig, 1869).

32. See Ignaz Goldhizer: *Der Mythus bei den Hebräern und seine geschichtliche Entwickelung* (Leipzig, 1876), p. 125. According to the writings of Siecke (loc. cit., p. 39), the incest myths lose all unusual features through being referred to the moon and its relation to the sun. His explanation is quite simple: the daughter (the new moon) is the repetition of the mother (the old moon); with her the father (the sun) (also the brother, the son) becomes reunited.

33. Is it to be believed? In an article entitled *"Urreligion der Indogermanen"* (Berlin, 1897), where Siecke points out that the incest myths are descriptive narrations of the seen but inconceivable process of nature, he objects to the assumption by Oldenburg (*Religion der Veda*, p. 5) of a primeval tendency of myths to the incest motif, with the remark that in the days of yore the theme was thrust upon the narrator, without an inclination of his own, through the forcefulness of the witnessed facts.

THE CIRCLE OF MYTHS

FROM the mass of chiefly biographic hero myths, we have selected those that are best known and some that are especially
characteristic.[1] These myths will be given in abbreviated form, as
far as relevant for this investigation, with statements concerning the
sources. Attention will be called to the most important and constantly
recurring motifs by the use of italic type.

Sargon

Probably the oldest transmitted hero myth in our possession is derived
from the period of the foundation of Babylonia (about 2800 B.C.)[2] and
concerns the birth history of its founder, Sargon the First.[3] The literal translation of the report—according to the mode of rendering, it
appears to be an original inscription by King Sargon himself—is as
follows:

> Sargon, the mighty king, King of Agade, am I. *My mother was a vestal,
> my father I knew not*, while my father's brother dwelt in the mountains.
> In my city Azuripani, which is situated on the bank of the Euphrates,
> my mother, the vestal, bore me. *In a hidden place she brought me forth. She
> laid me in a vessel made of reeds*, closed my door with pitch, *and dropped
> me down into the river*, which did not drown me. The river carried me to
> Akki, the water carrier. Akki the water carrier lifted me up in the kind-
> ness of his heart, Akki the water carrier raised me as his own son, Akki
> the water carrier made of me his gardener. In my work as a gardener I
> was beloved by Ishtar, I became the king, and for forty-five years I held
> kingly sway.[4]

Moses

The biblical birth history of Moses, which is told in the second chapter of Exodus, presents the greatest similarity to the Sargon legend,

even an almost literal correspondence of individual traits.[5] Already the first chapter (22) relates that Pharaoh commanded his people to throw into the river all sons that were born to Hebrews, while the daughters were permitted to live; the reason for this order is given as fear of the overfertility of the Israelites. The second chapter continues as follows:

And there went a man of the house of Levi, and took to wife a daughter of Levi.[6] And the woman conceived, and bare a son: and when she saw him that he was a goodly child, she hid him three months. And when she could not longer hide him, she took for him an ark of bulrushes, and daubed it with slime and with pitch, and put the child therein; and she laid it in the flags by the river's brink. And his sister stood afar off, to wit what would be done to him. And the daughter of Pharaoh came down to wash herself at the river; and her maidens walked along by the river's side; and when she saw the ark among the flags, she sent her maid to fetch it. And when she had opened it, she saw the child and, behold, the babe wept. And she had compassion on him and said, this is one of the Hebrews' children. Then said his sister to Pharaoh's daughter, Shall I go and call to thee a nurse of the Hebrew women, that she may nurse the child for thee? And Pharaoh's daughter said to her, Go. And the maid went and called the child's mother. And Pharaoh's daughter said unto her, Take this child away, and nurse it for me, and I will give thee thy wages. And the woman took the child, and nursed it. And the child grew, and she brought him unto Pharaoh's daughter, and he became her son. And she called his name Moses:[7] and she said, Because I drew him out of the water.

This account is ornamented by rabbinical mythology with an account of the events preceding Moses' birth. In the sixtieth year after Joseph's death, the reigning Pharaoh saw in a dream an old man who held a pair of scales; all the inhabitants of Egypt lay on one side, with only a suckling lamb on the other, but nevertheless this outweighed all the Egyptians. The startled king at once consulted the wise men and astrologers, who declared the dream to mean that a son would be born to the Israelites who would destroy all Egypt. The king was frightened, and at once ordered the death of all newborn children of the Israelites in the entire country. On account of this tyrannical order, the Levite Amram, who lived in Goshen, decided to separate from his wife Jochebed, so as not to foredoom to certain death the children conceived through him. But this resolution was opposed later on by his daughter Miriam, who foretold with prophetic assurance that precisely the child suggested in the king's dream would come forth from her mother's womb, and would become the liberator of his people.[8]

Amram therefore rejoined his wife, from whom he had been separated for three years. At the end of three months, she conceived, and later on bore a boy at whose birth the entire house was illuminated by an extraordinary luminous radiance, suggesting the truth of the prophecy.[9]

Similar accounts are given of the birth of the ancestor of the Hebrew nation, Abraham. He was a son of Terah—Nimrod's captain—and Amtelai. Prior to his birth, it was revealed to King Nimrod from the stars that the coming child would overthrow the thrones of powerful princes and take possession of their lands. King Nimrod planned to have the child killed immediately after its birth. But when the boy was requested from Terah, he said, "Truly a son was born to me, but he has died." He then delivered a strange child, concealing his own son in a cave underneath the ground, where God permitted him to suck milk from a finger of the right hand. In this cave, Abraham is said to have remained until the third (according to others the tenth) year of his life.[10]

In the next generation, in the story of Isaac, the same mythological motifs appear. Prior to his birth, King Abimelech is warned by a *dream* not to touch Sarah, as this would cause woe to betide him. After a long period of barrenness, she finally bears her son, who (in later life, in this report) after having been destined to be *sacrificed by his own father*, Abraham, is ultimately rescued by God. But Abraham casts out his elder son Ishmael, with Hagar, the boy's mother.[11]

Karna

A close relationship with the Sargon legend is also shown in certain features of the ancient Hindu epic Mahabharata, in its account of the birth of the hero Karna.[12] The contents of the legend are briefly rendered by Lassen.[13]

The princess Pritha, also known as Kunti, bore as a virgin the boy Karna, whose father was the sun-god Surya. The young Karna was born with the golden ear ornaments of his father and with an unbreakable coat of mail. The mother in her distress concealed and exposed the boy. In the adaptation of the myth by A. Holtzmann, verse 1458 reads: "Then my nurse and I made a large basket of rushes, placed a lid thereon, and lined it with wax; into this basket I laid the boy and carried him down to the river Acva." Floating on the waves, the basket reaches the river Ganges and travels as far as the city of Campa. "There was passing along the bank of the river, the charioteer, the noble friend of Dhritarashtra, and with him was Radha, his beautiful and pious spouse. She was wrapt in deep sorrow, because no son had been given to her. On the river she saw the basket, which the waves carried close to her on the shore; she showed it to Azirath, who went and drew it forth from the waves." The two take care of the boy and raise him as their own child.

Kunti later on marries King Pandu, who is forced to refrain from conjugal intercourse by the curse that he is to die in the arms of his spouse. But Kunti bears three sons, again through divine conception, one of the children being born in the cave of a wolf. One day Pandu dies in the embrace of his second wife. The sons grow up, and at a tournament which they arrange, Karna appears to measure his strength against the best fighter, Arjuna, the son of Kunti. Arjuna scoffingly refuses to fight the charioteer's son. In order to make him a worthy opponent, one of those present anoints him as king. Meanwhile Kunti has recognized Karna as her son, by the divine mark, and prays him to desist from the contest with his brother, revealing to him the secret of his birth. But he considers her revelation as a fantastic tale, and insists implacably upon satisfaction. He falls in the combat, struck by Arjuna's arrow.[14]

A striking resemblance to the entire structure of the Karna legend is presented by the birth history of Ion, the ancestor of the Ionians. The following account is based on a relatively late tradition.[15]

Apollo, in the grotto of the rock of the Athenian Acropolis, procreated a son with Creusa, the daughter of Erechtheus. In the grotto the boy was also born, and exposed; the mother leaves the child behind in a woven basket, in the hope that Apollo will not leave his son to perish. At Apollo's request, Hermes carries the child the same night to Delphi, where the priestess finds him on the threshold of the temple in the morning. She brings the boy up, and when he has grown into a youth makes him a servant of the temple. Erechtheus later gave his daughter Creusa in marriage to Xuthus. As the marriage long remained childless, they addressed the Delphian oracle, praying to be blessed with progeny. The god reveals to Xuthus that the first to meet him on leaving the sanctuary is his son. He hastens outside and meets the youth, whom he joyfully greets as his own son, giving him the name Ion, which means "walker." Creusa refuses to accept the youth as her son; her attempt to poison him fails, and the infuriated people turn against her. Ion is about to attack her, but Apollo, who does not wish the son to kill his own mother, enlightens the mind of the priestess so that she understands the connection. By means of the basket in which the newborn child had lain, Creusa recognizes him as her son, and reveals to him the secret of his birth.

Oedipus

The parents of Oedipus, King Laius and his queen, Jocasta, lived for a long time in childless wedlock. Laius, who longs for an heir, asks the Delphic Apollo for advice. The oracle answers that he may have a son if he so desires; but fate has ordained that his own son will kill him. Fearing the fulfillment of the oracle, Laius refrains from conjugal relations, but being intoxicated one day he nevertheless procreates a son, whom he causes to be exposed in the river Cithaeron, barely three days after his birth. In order to be quite sure that the child will perish, Laius orders his ankles to be pierced. According to the account of Sophocles, which is not the oldest, however, the shepherd who has been intrusted with the exposure, surrenders the boy to a shepherd of King Polybus, of Corinth, at whose court he is brought up, according to the universal statement. Others say that the boy was exposed in a box on the sea, and was taken from the water by Periböa, the wife of King Polybus, as she was rinsing her clothes by the shore.[16] Polybus brought him up as his own son.

Oedipus, on hearing accidentally that he is a foundling, asks the Delphian oracle about his true parents, but receives only the prophecy that he will kill his father and marry his mother. In the belief that this prophecy refers to his foster parents, he flees from Corinth to Thebes, but on the way unwittingly kills his father Laius. By solving a riddle, he frees the city from the plague of the Sphinx, a man-devouring monster, and in reward is given the hand of Jocasta, his mother, as well as the throne of his father. The revelation of these horrors and the subsequent misfortune of Oedipus were a favorite subject for spectacular display among the Greek tragedians.

An entire series of Christian legends have been elaborated on the pattern of the Oedipus myth, and the summarized contents of the Judas legend may serve as a paradigm of this group.[17] Before his birth, his mother, Cyboread, is warned by a dream that she will bear a wicked son, to the ruin of all his people. The parents expose the boy in a box on the sea. The waves cast the child ashore on the Isle of Scariot, where the childless queen finds him, and brings him up as her son. Later on, the royal couple have a son of their own, and the foundling, who feels himself slighted, kills his foster brother. As a fugitive from the country, he takes service at the court of Pilate, who makes a confidant of him and places him above his entire household. In a fight, Judas kills a neighbor, without knowing that he is his father. The widow of the murdered man—his own mother—then becomes his wife. After the revelation of these horrors, he repents and seeks the Saviour, who receives him among his apostles. His betrayal of Jesus is known from the Gospels.

The legend of St. Gregory on the Stone—the subject of the narrative of Hartmann von Aue—represents a more complicated type of this mythological cycle. Gregory, the child of the incestuous union of royal lovers, is exposed by his mother in a box on the sea, saved and raised by fishermen, and is then educated in a convent for the church. But he prefers the life of a knight, is victorious in combats, and in reward is given the hand of the princess, his mother. After the discovery of the incest, Gregory does penance for seventeen years on a rock in the midst of the sea, and he is finally made the Pope, at the command of God.[18]

A very similar legend is the Persian epic of King Darab, told by the poet Firdausi.[19] The last Kiranian Behmen nominated as his successor his daughter and simultaneous wife Humâi; his son Sâsân was grieved and withdrew into solitude. A short time after the death of her husband, Humâi gave birth to a son, whom she resolved to expose. He was placed in a box, which was put into the Euphrates and drifted downstream, until it was stopped by a stone that had been placed in the water by a tanner. The box with the child was found by him, and he carried the boy to his wife, who had recently lost her own child. The couple agreed to raise the foundling. As the boy grew up, he soon became so strong that the other children were unable to resist him. He did not care for the work of his foster father, but learned to be a warrior. His foster mother was forced by him to reveal the secret of his origin, and he joined the army that Humâi was then sending out to fight the king of Rûm. Her attention being called to him by his bravery, Humâi readily recognized him as her son, and named him her successor.

Paris

The famed Greek legend of the birth of Paris relates that King Priam of Troy had with his wife Hecuba a son, named Hector. When Hecuba was about to bear another child, *she dreamed* that she brought forth a burning log of wood, which set fire to the entire city. Priam asked the advice of Aisakos, who was his son with his first wife, Arisbe, and an expert in the interpretation of dreams. Aisakos declared that the child would bring trouble upon the city, and advised that it be exposed. Priam gave the little boy to a slave, Agelaos, who carried him to the top of Mount Ida. *The child was nursed during five days by a she-bear.* When Agelaos found that he was still alive, he picked him up, and carried him home to raise him. He named the boy Paris; but after the child had grown into a strong and handsome youth, he was called Alexander, because he fought the robbers and protected the flocks. Before long he discovered his parents. How this came about is told by Hyginus, according to whose report the infant is *found by shepherds.* One day messengers, sent by Priam, come to these herders to fetch a bull which is to serve as the prize for the victor in some commemorative games. They selected a bull that Paris valued so highly that he followed the men who led the beast away, assisted in the combats, and won the prize. This aroused the anger of his brother Deiphobus, who threatened him with his sword, but his sister Cassandra recognized him as her brother, and Priam joyfully received him as his son. The misfortune which Paris later brought to his family and his native city, through the abduction of Helen, is well known from Homer's *Iliad*, as well as from countless earlier and later poems.

A certain resemblance with the story of the birth of Paris is presented by the poem of Zal, in Firdausi's Persian hero myths.[20] The first son is born to Sam, king of Sistan, by one of his consorts. Because he and assaulted by a group of rich assholes at a party. She is virtually disowned by her hyper-conservative mother because of it. The game gives you a number of small opportunities to help Kate, like rubbing something mean off the slate outside her door, or stepping in when she's getting bullied by the school's head of security. You try to support her, but you always get the sense that you could be doing more. Then, all of a sudden, towards the end of the game's second chapter, Kate is standing on the edge of the roof of the school.

Everything slows down at this point. Grey rain hisses all around you. Kate blurs from place to place like the misaligned frames of an old photograph. You manage to pause time long enough to stagger up to the roof, but by the time you're up there, your powers are totally conked out. You can't control time anymore. A crowd has gathered down below, phone cameras pointed up, but you're on your own. Something inside your chest feels like it's trying to punch its way out.

"What are you doing here, Max?" Kate turns around to glare at you, her face flush with tears. The small crucifix around her neck seems neon against her soaked cotton blouse. This is the first time you've seen her angry. "Max, seriously, don't come near me! *I will jump!*"

Kate's voice is loud and strained, but her mouth doesn't quite match the sounds she's making. Tears mingle with the rain on her face, but her hair is dry. You try not to think about how wrong her mouth looks. Something you did once mattered, and she mentions it. Another thing you did was disappointing; she mentions that, too. One by one, your past actions are totted up in a list. How did you support her? How did you make her feel? Suddenly, two options appear in the sky:

[left click] *Things will get better.* [right click] *You matter, not just to me.*

The first option feels phony, so you choose the right click. Every choice afterward is like this. Kate continues to cry, insisting on her hopelessness, and you have to choose the least-worst of the binary choices that hover in the sky. You can't take too long to choose, though. That's its own choice.

The clicks of the mouse start to seem heavy and far away. The game had white hair, *his mother concealed the birth.*[21] But the nurse reveals the birth of his son to the king. Sam is disappointed, and commands that the child be exposed. The servants carry it to the top of Mount Elburz, where it is raised by the Seemurgh, a powerful bird. The full-grown youth is seen by a traveling caravan, whose members speak of him as "whose nurse a bird is sufficient." King Sam once *sees his son in a dream*, and sallies forth to seek the exposed child. He is unable to reach the summit of the elevated rock where he finally espies the youth. But the Seemurgh bears his son down to him; he receives him joyfully and nominates him as his successor.

Telephus

Aleos, King of Tegea, was informed by the *oracle* that his sons would perish through a descendant of his daughter. He therefore made his daughter Auge a priestess of the goddess Athena, and threatened her with death should she mate with a man. But when Hercules dwelt as a guest in the sanctuary of Athena, on his expedition against Augeas, he saw the maiden, and while intoxicated, he raped her. When Aleos became aware of her pregnancy, he delivered her to Nauplius, a rough sailor, with the command to throw her into the sea. But on the way she gave birth to Telephus on Mount Parthenios, and Nauplius, unmindful of the orders he had received, carried both her and the child to Mysia, where he delivered them to King Teuthras.

According to another version, Auge secretly brought forth as a priestess, but kept the child hidden in the temple. When Aleos discovered the sacrilege, he cause the child to be exposed in the Parthenian mountains. Nauplius was instructed to sell the mother in foreign lands, or to kill her. She was delivered by him into the hands of Teuthras.[22]

According to the current tradition, *Auge exposes the newborn child* and escapes to Mysia, where the childless King Teuthras adopts her as his daughter. The boy, however, is nursed by a doe, and is found by shepherds who take him to King Corythos. The king brings him up as his son. When Telephus has grown into a youth, he betakes himself to Mysia, on the advice of the oracle, to seek his mother. He frees Teuthras, who is in danger from his enemies, and in reward receives the hand of the supposed daughter of the king, namely his own mother

Auge. But she refuses to submit to Telephus, and when he in his ire is about to pierce the disobedient one with his sword, she calls on her lover Hercules in her distress, and Telephus thus recognizes his mother. After the death of Teuthras he becomes King of Mysia.

Perseus

Acrisius, the king of Argos, had already reached an advanced age without having male progeny. As he desired a son, he consulted the Delphian oracle, but this warned him against male descendants, and informed him that his daughter Danaë would bear a son through whose hand he would perish. In order to prevent this, he had his daughter locked up in an iron tower, which he caused to be carefully guarded. But Zeus penetrated through the roof, in the guise of a golden shower, and Danaë became the mother of a boy.[23] One day Acrisius heard the voice of young Perseus in his daughter's room, and in this way learned that she had given birth to a child. *He killed the nurse*, but carried his daughter with her son to the domestic altar of Zeus, to have an oath taken on the true father's name. But he refuses to believe his daughter's statement that Zeus is the father, and *he encloses her with the child in a box, which is cast into the sea.*[24] The box is carried by the waves to the coast of Seriphos, where *Dictys, a fisherman*, usually called a brother of King Polydectes, *saves mother and child by drawing them out of the sea with his nets.* Dictys leads the two into his house and keeps them as his relations. Polydectes, however, becomes enamored of the beautiful mother, and *as Perseus was in his way, he tried to remove him* by sending him forth to fetch the head of the Gorgon Medusa. But against the king's anticipations Perseus accomplishes this difficult task, and a number of heroic deeds besides. Later, in throwing the discs during a contest, he accidentally kills his grandfather, as foretold by the oracle. He becomes the king of Argos, then of Tiryns, and the builder of Mycenae.[25]

Gilgamesh

Aelian, who lived about 200 A.D., relates in his "Animal Stories" the history of *a boy who was saved by an eagle:*

Animals have a characteristic fondness for man. An eagle is known
to have nourished a child. I shall tell the entire story, in proof of my
assertion. When Senechoros reigned over the Babylonians, the Chal-
dean fortunetellers foretold that the son of the king's daughter would
take the kingdom from his grandfather; this verdict was a prophecy of
the Chaldeans. The king was afraid of this prophecy, and humorously
speaking, he became a second Acrisius for his daughter, over whom he
watched with the greatest severity. But his daughter, fate being wiser
than the Babylonian, conceived secretly from an inconspicuous man.
For fear of the king, the guardians threw the child down from the acropolis, where the royal daughter was imprisoned. The eagle, with his keen
eyes, saw the boy's fall, and before the child struck the earth, he caught
it on his back, bore it into a garden, and set it down with great care.
When the overseer of the place saw the beautiful boy, he was pleased
with him and raised him. The boy received the name Gilgamesh, and
became the king of Babylonia. If anyone regards this as a fable, I have
nothing to say, although I have investigated the matter to the best of my
ability. Also of Achaemenes, the Persian, from whom the nobility of the
Persians is derived, I learn that he was the pupil of an eagle.[26]

Cyrus

The myth of Cyrus the Great, which the majority of investigators
place in the center of this entire mythical circle—without entirely sufficient grounds, it would appear—has been transmitted to us in several
versions. According to the report of Herodotus (about 450 B.C.), who
states that among four renderings known to him, he selected the least
"glorifying" version,[27] the story of the birth and youth of Cyrus is as
follows:

Royal sway over the Medes was held, after Cyaxares, by his son
Astyages, who had a daughter named Mandane. Once he saw, in a
dream, so much water passing from her as to fill an entire city and inundate all Asia. He related his dream to the dream interpreters among the
magicians, and was in great fear after they had explained it all to him.
When Mandane had grown up, he gave her in marriage, not to a Mede,
his equal in birth, but to a Persian, by name of Cambyses. This man
came of a good family and led a quiet life. The king considered him of

lower rank than a middle-class Mede. After Mandane had become the wife of Cambyses, Astyages saw another dream-vision in the first year. He dreamed that a vine grew from his daughter's lap, and this vine over-shadowed all Asia. After he had again related this vision to the dream interpreters, he sent for his daughter, who was with child, and after her arrival from Persia, he watched her, because he meant to kill her off-spring. For the dream interpreters among the magicians had prophesied to him that his daughter's son would become king in his place. In order to avert this fate, he waited until Cyrus was born, and then sent for Harpagos, who was his relative and his greatest confidant among the Medes, and whom he had placed over all his affairs. Him he addressed as follows: "My dear Harpagos, I shall charge thee with an errand which thou must conscientiously perform. But do not deceive me, and let no other man attend to it, for all might not go well with thee. Take this boy, whom Mandane has brought forth, carry him home, and kill him. Afterwards thou canst bury him, how and in whatsoever manner thou desirest." But Harpagos made answer: "Great King, never hast thou found thy servant disobedient, and also in future I shall beware not to sin before thee. If such is thy will, it behooves me to carry it out faith-fully." When Harpagos had thus spoken, and the little boy with all his ornaments had been delivered into his hands, for death, he went home weeping. On his arrival he told his wife all that Astyages had said to him. But she inquired, "What art thou about to do?" He made reply: "I shall not obey Astyages, even if he raved and stormed ten times worse than he is doing. I shall not do as he wills, and consent to such a murder. I have a number of reasons: in the first place, the boy is my blood rela-tive; then, Astyages is old, and he has no male heir. Should he die, and the kingdom go to his daughter, whose son he bids me kill at present would I not run the greatest danger? But the boy must die, for the sake of my safety. However, one of Astyages' men is to be his murderer, not one of mine."

Having thus spoken, he at once despatched a messenger to one of the king's cattle herders, by name Mithradates, who, as he happened to know, was keeping his herd in a very suitable mountain pasturage, full of wild animals. The herder's wife was also a slave of Astyages', by name Cyno in Greek, or Spako ("a bitch") in the Median language. When the herder hurriedly arrived, on the command of Harpagos, the latter said to him: "Astyages bids thee take this boy and expose him in the wildest mountains, that he may perish as promptly as may be, and the

King has ordered me to say to thee: If thou doest not kill the boy, but let him live, in whatever way, thou art to die a most disgraceful death. And I am charged to see to it that the boy is really exposed." When the herder had listened to this, he took the boy, went home, and arrived in his cottage. His wife was with child, and was in labor the entire day, and it happened that she was just bringing forth, when the herder had gone to the city. They were greatly worried about each other. But when he had returned and the woman saw him again so unexpectedly, she asked in the first place why Harpagos had sent for him so hurriedly. But he said: "My dear wife, would that I had never seen what I have seen and heard in the city, and what has happened to our masters. The house of Harpagos was full of cries and laments. This startled me, but I entered, and soon after I had entered, I saw a small boy lying before me, who struggled and cried and was dressed in fine garments and gold. When Harpagos saw me, he bid me quickly take the boy, and expose him in the wildest spot of the mountains. He said Astyages had ordered this, and added awful threats if I failed to do so. I took the child and went away with it, thinking that it belonged to one of the servants, for it did not occur to me whence it had come. But on the way, I learned the entire story from the servant who led me from the city, and placed the boy in my hands. He is the son of Mandane, daughter of Astyages, and Cambyses, the son of Cyrus; and Astyages has ordered his death. Behold, here is the boy."

Having thus spoken, the herder uncovered the child and showed it to her, and when the women saw that he was a fine strong child, she wept, and fell at her husband's feet, and implored him not to expose it. But he said he could not do otherwise, for Harpagos would send servants to see if this had been done; he would have to die a disgraceful death unless he did so. Then she said again: "If I have failed to move thee, do as follows, so that they may see an exposed child: I have brought forth a dead child; take it and expose it, but the son of the daughter of Astyages we will raise as our own child. In this way, thou wilt not be found a disobedient servant, nor will we fare ill ourselves. Our stillborn child will be given a kingly burial, and the living child's life will be preserved." The herder did as his wife had begged and advised him to do. He placed his own dead boy in a basket, dressed him in all the finery of the other, and exposed him on the most desert mountain. Three days later he announced to Harpagos that he was now enabled to show the boy's cadaver. Harpagos sent his most faithful body guardians, and ordered the burial of the cattle herder's son. The other boy, however, who was known later on as Cyrus, was brought up by the herder's wife. They did not call him Cyrus, but gave him another name.

When the boy was twelve years old the truth was revealed, through the following accident. He was playing on the road, with other boys of his own age, in the village where the cattle were kept. The boys played "King," and elected the supposed son of the cattle herder.[28] But he commanded some to build houses, others to carry lances; one he made the king's watchman, the other was charged with the bearing of messages; briefly, each received his appointed task. One of the boy's playmates, however, was the son of Artembares, a respected man among the Medes, and when he did not do as Cyrus ordained, the latter made the other boys seize him. The boys obeyed, and Cyrus chastised him with severe blows. After they let him go, he became furiously angry, as if he had been treated improperly. He ran into the city and complained to his father of what Cyrus had done to him. He did not mention the name of Cyrus for he was not yet called so, but said the cattle herder's son. Artembares went wrathfully with his son to Astyages, complained of the disgraceful treatment, and spoke thus: "Great king, we suffer such outrageous treatment from thy servant, the herder's son," and he showed him his own son's shoulders. When Astyages heard and saw this, he wished to vindicate the boy for the sake of Artembares, and he sent for the cattle herder with his son. When both were present, Astyages looked at Cyrus and said: "Thou, a lowly man's son, hast had the effrontery to treat so disgracefully the son of a man whom I greatly honor!" But he made answer: "Lord, he has only received his due. For the boys in the village, he being among them, were at play, and made me their king, believing me to be the best adapted thereto. And the other boys did as they were told, but he was disobedient, and did not mind me at all. For this he has received his reward. If I have deserved punishment, here I am at your service."

When the boy spoke in this way, Astyages knew him at once. For the features of the face appeared to him as his own, and the answer was that of a highborn youth; furthermore, it seemed to him that the time of the exposure agreed with the boy's age. This smote his heart, and he remained speechless for a while. Hardly had he regained control over himself, when he spoke to get rid of Artembares, so as to be able to question the cattle herder without witnesses. "My dear Artembares," he said, "I shall take care that neither thou nor thy son shall have cause for complaint." Thus he dismissed Artembares. Cyrus, however, was led into the palace by the servants, on the command of Astyages, and the cattle herder had to stay behind. When he was all alone with him, Astyages questioned him whence he had obtained the boy, and who had given the child into his hands. But the herder said that he was his own son, and that the woman who had borne him was living with him. Astyages remarked that he was very unwise, to look out for most cruel tortures, and he beckoned the sword-bearers to take hold of him. As he was being led to torture, the herder confessed the whole story, from beginning to end, the entire truth, finally beginning to beg and implore forgiveness and pardon. Meanwhile Astyages was not so incensed against the herder, who had revealed to him the truth, as against Harpagos; he ordered the sword-bearers to summon him, and when Harpagos stood before him, Astyages asked him as follows: "My dear Harpagos, in what fashion hast thou taken the life of my daughter's son, whom I once delivered over to thee?" Seeing the cattle herder standing near, Harpagos did not resort to untruthfulness, for fear that he would be refuted at once, and so he proceeded to tell the truth. Astyages concealed the anger which he had aroused in him, and first told him what he had learned from the herder; then he mentioned that the boy was still living, and that everything had turned out all right. He said that he had greatly regretted what he had done to the child, and that his daughter's reproaches had pierced his soul. "But as everything has ended so well, send thy son to greet the newcomer, and then come to eat with me, for I am ready to prepare a feast in honor of the Gods who have brought all this about."

When Harpagos heard this, he prostrated himself on the ground before the king, and praised himself for his error having turned out well, and for being invited to the king's table, in commemoration of a happy event. So he went home, and when he arrived there, he at once sent off his only son, a boy of about thirteen years, telling him to go to Astyages, and to do as he was bid. Then Harpagos joyfully told his wife what had befallen him. But Astyages butchered the son of Harpagos when he came, cut him to pieces, and roasted the flesh in part; another portion of the flesh was cooked, and when everything was prepared he kept it in readiness. When the hour of the meal had come, Harpagos and the other guests arrived. A table with sheep's meat was arranged in front of Astyages and the others, but Harpagos was served with his own son's flesh, without the head, and without the choppings of hands and feet, but with everything else. These parts were kept hidden in a basket. When Harpagos seemed to have taken his fill, Astyages asked him if the meat had tasted good to him, and when Harpagos answered that he had enjoyed it, the servants, who had been ordered to do so, brought in his own son's covered head, with the hands and feet, stepped up to Harpagos, and told him to uncover and take what he desired. Harpagos did so, uncovered the basket, and saw the remnants of his son. When he saw this, he did not give way to his horror, but controlled himself. Astyages then asked him if he knew of what game he had eaten; and he replied that he knew it very well, and that whatever the king did was well done. Thus he spoke, took the flesh that remained, and went home with it, where he probably meant to bury it together.

This was the revenge of Astyages upon Harpagos. Concerning Cyrus, he took counsel, and summoned the same magicians who had explained his dream, then he asked them how they had at one time interpreted his vision in a dream. But they said that the boy must become a king, if he remained alive, and did not die prematurely. Astyages made reply: "The boy is alive, and is here, and as he was staying in the country, the boys of the village elected him for their king. But he did everything like the real kings, for he ordained to himself as the master, sword-bearers, gate-keepers, messengers, and everything. How do you mean to interpret this?" The magicians made reply: "If the boy is alive, and has been made king without the help of anyone, thou canst be at ease so far as he is concerned, and be of good cheer, for he will not again be made a king. Already several prophecies of ours have applied to insignificant trifles, and what rests upon dreams is apt to be vain." Astyages made reply: "Ye sorcerers, I am entirely of your opinion that the dream has been fulfilled when the boy was king in name, and that I have nothing more to fear from him. Yet counsel me carefully as to what is safest for my house and for yourselves." Then the magicians said: "Send the boy away, that he may get out of thy sight, send him to the land of the Persians, to his parents." When Astyages had heard this, he was greatly pleased. He sent for Cyrus, and said to him: "My son, I have wronged thee greatly, misled by a deceitful dream, but thy good fortune has saved thee. Now go cheerfully to the land of the Persians: I shall give thee safe conduct. There wilt thou find a very different father, and a very different mother than the herders, Mithradates and his wife." Thus spake Astyages, and Cyrus was sent away. When he arrived in the house of Cambyses, his parents received him with great joy when they learned who he

was, for they believed him to have perished at that time, and they desired to know how he had been preserved. He told them that he had
believed himself to be the son of the cattle herder, but had learned
everything on the way from the companions whom Astyages had sent
with him. He related that the cattle herder's wife had saved him, and
praised her throughout. The "bitch" (Spako) played the principal part
in his conversation. The parents took hold of this name, so that the
preservation of the child might appear still more wonderful, and thus
was laid the foundation of the myth that the exposed Cyrus was nursed
by a bitch.

Later on, Cyrus, on the instigation of Harpagos, stirred up the
Persians against the Medes. War was declared, and Cyrus, at the head
of the Persians, conquered the Medes in battle. Astyages was taken
prisoner alive, but Cyrus did not harm him, and kept him with him
until his end. Herodotus' report concludes with the words: "But from
that time on the Persians and Cyrus reigned over Asia. Thus was
Cyrus born and raised, and made a king."

The report of Pompeius Trogus is preserved only in the extract by
Justin, according to whom Astyages had a daughter but no male heir.[29]
This version continues:

> In his dream he saw a vine grow forth from her lap, the sprouts of
> which overshadowed all Asia. The dream interpreters declared that the
> vision signified the magnitude of his grandson, whom his daughter was
> to bear; but also his own loss of his dominions. In order to banish this
> dread, Astyages gave his daughter in marriage neither to a prominent
> man nor to a Mede, so that his grandson's mind might not be uplifted
> by the paternal estate besides the maternal; but he married her to Cam-
> byses, a middle-class man from the then unknown people of the Per-
> sians. But this was not enough to banish the fears of Astyages, and he
> summoned his pregnant daughter, in order to have her infant destroyed
> before his eyes. When a boy had been born, he gave him to Harpagos,
> his friend and confidant, to kill him. For fear that the daughter of
> Astyages would take revenge upon him for the death of her boy, when
> she came to reign after her father's death, he delivered the boy to the
> king's herder for exposure. At the same time that Cyrus was born, a son
> happened to be born also to the herder. When his wife learned that the
> king's child had been exposed, she urgently prayed for it to be brought
> to her, that she might look at it. Moved by her entreaties, the herder

returned to the woods. There he found a bitch standing beside the child, giving it her teats, and keeping the beasts and birds away from it. At this aspect he was filled with the same compassion as the bitch; so that he picked up the boy and carried him home, the bitch following him in great distress. When his wife took the boy in her arms, he smiled at her as if he already knew her; and as he was very strong, and ingratiated himself with her by his pleasant smile, she voluntarily begged the herder to [expose her own child instead][30] permit her to raise the boy; be it that she was interested in his welfare, or that she placed her hopes on him.

Thus the two boys had to exchange fates; one was raised in place of the herder's child, while the other was exposed instead of the grandson of the king. The remainder of this apparently more primitive report agrees essentially with the account of Herodotus.

An altogether different version of the Cyrus myth is extant in the report of Ctesias, a contemporary of Herodotus. The original of his narrative, which comprised more than an entire book in his Persian history, has been lost; but a surviving fragment of Nicholas of Damascus summarizes the Ctesian account.[31] Astyages is said to have been the worthiest king of the Medes, after Abakes. Under his rule occurred the great transmutation through which the rulership passed from the Medes to the Persians, in the following manner:

The Medes had a law that a poor man who went to a rich man for his support, and surrendered himself to him, had to be fed and clothed and kept like a slave by the rich man, or in case the latter refused to do so, the poor man was at liberty to go elsewhere. In this way a boy by name of Cyrus, a Mard by birth, came to the king's servant who was at the head of the palace sweepers. Cyrus was the son of Atradates, whose poverty made him live as a robber, and whose wife, Argoste, Cyrus' mother, made her living by tending the goats. Cyrus surrendered himself for the sake of his daily bread, and helped to clean the palace. As he was diligent, the foreman gave him better clothing and advanced him from the outside sweepers to those who cleaned the interior of the king's palace, placing him under their superintendent. This man was severe, however, and often whipped Cyrus. The boy left him and went to the lamplighter, who liked Cyrus and moved him closer to the king, by placing him among the royal torch-bearers. As Cyrus distinguished himself also in his new position, he came to Artembares, who was at the head of the cupbearers and himself presented the cup to the king. Artembares gladly accepted Cyrus, and bade him

SAVEGAMES

Andy Connor

I'D BEEN WARNED ABOUT THIS PARTICULAR VIDEO GAME. "IT'S really good," a friend told me, "but there's some potentially triggering stuff about suicide in there." I go into these kinds of things with my eyes open.

The game is called *Life is Strange*. In it, you play an eighteen-year-old girl named Max from a small fishing town in Oregon. One day, in photography class, you discover that you can reverse time. When the game lets you, you have the option of holding down a button to move your consciousness back in the flow of time, re-experience a situation, and do things differently. The first tests are small: you hear an answer to a teacher's question in class, then go back and give it as though you'd always known it. Then things escalate. You save your friend Chloe from being shot dead in the girl's bathroom, and an elaborate mystery storyline unfurls from there. It's accompanied by eerie weather events that coincide with the advent of your powers. None of that has much to do with Kate Marsh.

A short, timid, Christian classmate of yours, Kate was drugged pour the wine for the guests at the king's table. Not long afterwards, Astyages noticed the dexterity and nimbleness of Cyrus' service, and his graceful presentation of the wine cup, so that he asked of Artembares whence this youth had come who was so skillful a cupbearer.

"O Lord," spake he, "this boy is thy slave, of Persian parentage, from the tribe of the Mards, who has surrendered himself to me to make a living." Artembares was old, and once on being attacked by a fever, he prayed the king to let him stay at home until he had recovered. "In my stead, the youth whom thou hast praised will pour the wine, and if he should please thee, the king, as a cupbearer, *I who am a eunuch, will adopt him as my son.*" Astyages consented, but the other confided in many ways in Cyrus *as in a son*. Cyrus thus stood at the king's side, and poured his wine by day and by night, showing great ability and cleverness. Astyages conferred upon him the income of Artembares, as if he had been his son, adding many presents, and Cyrus became a great man whose name was heard everywhere.

Astyages had a very noble and beautiful daugher,[32] whom he gave to the Mede Spitamas, adding all Media as her dowry. Then Cyrus sent for his father and mother, in the land of the Medes, and they rejoiced in the good fortune of their son, and *his mother told him the dream which she had at the time that she was bearing him*, while asleep in the sanctuary as she was tending the goats. *So much water passed away from her that it became as a large stream, inundating all Asia, and flowing as far as the sea.* When the father heard this, he ordered the dream to be placed before the Chaldeans in Babylon. Cyrus summoned the wisest among them, and communicated the dream to him. He declared that the dream foretold great good fortune to Cyrus, and *the highest dignity in Asia*; but Astyages must not learn of it, "for else he would disgracefully kill thee, as well as myself the interpreter," said the Babylonian. They swore to each other to tell no one of this great and incomparable vision. *Cyrus later on rose to still higher dignities, created his father a Satrap of Persia, and raised his mother to the highest rank and possessions among the Persian women.* But when the Babylonian was killed soon afterwards by Oebares, the confidant of Cyrus, his wife betrayed the fateful dream to the king, when she learned of Cyrus' expedition to Persia, which he had undertaken in preparation of the revolt. The king sent his horsemen after Cyrus, with the command to deliver him dead or alive. But Cyrus escaped them by a ruse. Finally a combat took place, terminating in the defeat of the Medes. Cyrus also conquered Egbatana, and here the daughter of

Astyages and her husband Spitamas, with their two sons, were taken prisoners. But Astyages himself could not be found, for Amytis and Spitamas had concealed him in the palace, under the rafters of the roof. Cyrus then ordered that Amytis, her husband, and the children should be tortured until they revealed the hiding place of Astyages, but he came out voluntarily, that his relatives might not be tortured on his account. *Cyrus commanded the execution of Spitamas*, because he had lied in affirming to be in ignorance of Astyages' hiding place; *but Amytis became the wife of Cyrus. He removed the fetters of Astyages*, with which Oebares had bound him, *honored him as a father*, and made him a Satrap of the Barkanians.

A great similarity to Herodotus' version of the Cyrus myth is found in the early history of the Persian royal hero, Kaikhosrav, as related by Firdausi in the *Shah Namah*. This myth is most extensively rendered by Spiegel.[33] During the warfare of King Kaikâus, of Bactria and Iran, against King Afrâsiâb, of Turan, *Kaikâus fell out with his son, Siâvaksh*, who applied to Afrâsiâb for protection and assistance. He was kindly received by Afrâsiâb, who gave him his daughter Feringis to wife, on the persuasion of his vizier, Pirân, *although he had received the prophecy that the son to be born of this union would bring great misfortune upon him*. Garsevaz, the king's brother, and a near relative of Siâvaksh, calumniates the son-in-law, and Afrâsiâb leads an army against him. *Before the birth of his son, Siâvaksh is warned by a dream, which foretold destruction and death to himself, but royalty to his offspring*. He therefore flies from Afrâsiâb, but is taken prisoner and killed, on the command of the Shah. His wife, who is pregnant, is saved by Pirân from the hands of the murders. On condition of announcing at once the delivery of Feringis to the king, Pirân is granted permission to keep her in his house. The shade of the murdered Siâvaksh once comes to him in a dream and tells him that an avenger has been born; Pirân actually finds in the room of Feringis a newborn boy, whom he names Kaikhosrav. Afrâsiâb no longer insisted upon the killing of the boy, but he ordered Pirân *to surrender the child with a nurse to the herders, who were to raise him in ignorance of his origin*. But his royal descent is promptly revealed in his courage and his demeanor; and as Pirân takes the boy back into his home, Afrâsiâb becomes distrustful, and orders the boy to be led before him. Instructed by Pirân, Kaikhosrav plays the fool,[34] and reassured as to his harmlessness, the Shah dismisses him to his mother, Feringis. Finally, Kaikhosrav is crowned as king by his grandfather, Kaikâus. After prolonged, complicated, and tedious combats, Afrâsiâb is at last taken prisoner, with divine assistance. Kaikhosrav strikes his head off, and also causes Garsevaz to be decapitated.

A certain resemblance to the preceding saga, although more remote is presented by the myth of Feridun, as told by Firdausi.[35] *Zohâk, the king of Iran, once sees in a dream three men of royal tribe.* Two of them are bent with age, but between them is a *younger man* who holds a club, with a bull's head, in his right hand; this man steps up to him, and *fells him with his club to the ground.* The dream interpreters declared to the king that the young hero who will dethrone him is Feridun, a scion of the tribe of Dschemschid. Zohâk at once sets out to look for the tracks of his dreaded enemy. Feridun is the son of Abtin, a grandson of Dschemschid. His father hides from the pursuit of the tyrant, but he is seized and killed. Feridun himself, a boy of tender age, *is save by his mother, Firânek, who escapes with him and entrusts him to the care of the guardian of a distant forest. Here he is suckled by a cow.* For three years he remains hidden in this place, but then his mother no longer believes him safe, and she carries him to a hermit on Mount Elburz. Soon afterwards Zohâk comes to the forest and kills the guardian as well as the cow.

When Feridun was sixteen years old, he came down from Mount Elburz, learned of his origin through his mother, and swore to avenge the death of his father and of his nurse. On the expedition against Zohâk he is accompanied by his two older brothers, Purmâje and Kayânuseh. He orders a club to be forged for his use, and ornaments it with the bull's head, in memory of his foster mother, the cow. With this club he smites Zohâk, as foretold by the dream.

Tristan

The theme of the Feridun story is pursued in the Tristan saga, as related in the epic poem by Gottfried von Strassburg. This is especially evident in the prologue of the Tristan saga, which is repeated later on in the adventures of the hero himself (duplication). Riwalin, king in the land of the Parmenians, in an expedition to the court of Mark, king of Cornwall and England, had become acquainted with the latter's beautiful sister, Blancheflure, and his heart was aflame with love for her. While assisting Mark in a campaign, Riwalin was mortally wounded and was carried to Tintajole. Blancheflure, *disguised as a beggar maid,* hastened to his sickbed, and her devoted love saved the king's life. She fled with her lover to his native land (obstacles) and was there proclaimed as his consort. But Morgan attacked Riwalin's country, for the sake of Blancheflure, whom the king entrusted to his *faithful retainer* Rual, because she was carrying a child. Rual placed the queen for safekeeping in the castle of Kaneel. Here *she gave birth to a son and died, while her husband fell in the battle against Morgan. In order to protect the king's offspring from Morgan's pursuits,* Rual spread the rumor that the infant had been born dead. The boy was named Tristan, because he had been conceived and born in sorrow. Under the care of his *foster parents,* Tristan grew up, equally straight in body and mind, until his fourteenth year, when he was kidnapped by Norwegian merchants, who then put him ashore in Cornwall because they feared the wrath of the gods. Here *the boy was found by the soldiers of King Mark,* who was so well pleased with the brave and handsome youth that he promptly made him his master of the chase (career), and held him in great affection. Meanwhile, faithful Rual had set forth to seek his abducted foster son, whom he found at last in Cornwall, where Rual had come begging his way. Rual *revealed Tristan's descent* to the king, who was delighted to see in him the son of his beloved sister, and raised him to the rank of knight. In order *to avenge his father,* Tristan proceeded with Rual to Parmenia, vanquished Morgan, the usurper, and gave the country to Rual as liege, while he himself returned to his uncle Mark.[36]

The actual Tristan saga goes on with a repetition of the principal themes. In the service of Mark, Tristan kills Morald, the bridegroom of Isolde, and being wounded unto death, he is saved by Isolde. He asks her hand in marriage on behalf of his uncle Mark. When he fulfills the condition of killing a dragon, she accompanies him reluctantly to Cornwall, to which they travel by ship. On the journey they partake unwittingly of the disastrous love potion which binds them together in frenzied passion; they betray King Mark. On the wedding night, Isolde's faithful maid, Brangäne, represents the queen, and sacrifices her virginity to the king. Next follows the banishment of Tristan, his several attempts to regain his beloved, although he had meanwhile married another Isolde—"Isolde the White Hand," of Brittany, who resembled his love, "Isolde the Fair." At last he is again wounded unto death, and Isolde arrives too late to save him.[37]

A plainer version of the Tristan saga—in the sense of the characteristic features of the myth of the birth of the hero—is found in the fairy tale "The True Bride," quoted by Riklin from Rittershaus.[38] A royal pair have no children. The king having threatened to kill his wife unless she bears a child by the time of his return from his sea voyage, she is brought to him during his journey, by his zealous maidservant, as the fairest of three promenading ladies, and he takes her into his tent without recognizing her.[39] She returns home without having been discovered, gives birth to a daughter, Isol, and dies. Isol later on finds, in a box by the seaside, a most beautiful little boy, whose name is Tristram, and she raises him to become engaged to him. The subsequent story, which contains the motif of the true bride, is noteworthy for present purposes only in so far as here again occurs the draught of oblivion, and two Isoldes. The king's second wife gives a potion to Tristram, which causes him to forget the fair Isol entirely, so that he wishes to marry the black Isota. Ultimately he discovers the deception, however, and becomes united with Isol.

Romulus

The original version of the story of Romulus and Remus—as told by the most ancient Roman annalist Quintus Fabius Pictor—is rendered as follows by Mommsen:[40]

> *The twins* borne by Ilia, the daughter of the preceding king Numitor, *from the embrace of the war-god Mars were condemned by King Amulius, the present ruler of Alba, to be cast into the river.* The king's servants took the children and carried them from Alba as far as the Tiber on the Palatine Hill; but when they tried to descend the hill to the river, to carry out the command, they found that the river had risen, and they were unable to reach its bed. The tub with the children was therefore thrust by them into the shallow water at the shore. *It floated* for a while; *but the water promptly receded*, and *knocking against a stone, the tub capsized*, and the screaming infants were upset into the river mud. *They were heard by a she-wolf who had just brought forth and had her udders full of milk; she came and gave her teats to the boys, to nurse them*, and as they were drinking she licked them clean with her tongue. Above them flew a woodpecker, which guarded the children, and also carried food to them. The father was providing for his sons: for the wolf and the woodpecker are animals

consecrated to father Mars. This was seen by one of the royal herdsmen, who was driving his pigs back to the pasture from which the water had receded. Startled by the spectacle, he summoned his mates, who found the she-wolf attending like a mother to the children, and the children treated her as their mother. The men made a loud noise to scare the animal away; but the wolf was not afraid; she left the children, but not from fear; slowly, without heeding the herdsmen, she disappeared into the wilderness of the forest, at the holy site of Faunus, where the water gushes from a gully of the mountain. Meanwhile the men picked up the boys and carried them to the chief swineherd of the king, Faustulus, for they believed that the gods did not wish the children to perish. *But the wife of Faustulus had just given birth to a dead child, and was full of sorrow. Her husband gave her the twins, and she nursed them; the couple raised the children, and named them Romulus and Remus.*

After Rome had been founded, later on, King Romulus built himself a house not far from the place where his tub had stood. The gully in which the she-wolf had disappeared has been known since that time as the Wolf's Gully, the Lupercal. The image in ore of the she-wolf with the twins was subsequently erected at this spot,[41] and the she-wolf herself, the Lupa, was worshipped by the Romans as a divinity.

The Romulus saga later on underwent manifold transmutations, mutilations, additions, and interpretations.[42] It is best known in the form transmitted by Livy (I, 3 ff.), where we learn something about the antecedents and subsequent fate of the twins:

King Proca bequeaths the royal dignity to his firstborn son, Numitor. But his *younger brother, Amulius, pushes him from the throne*, and becomes king himself. So that no scion from Numitor's family may arise, as the avenger, he kills the male descendants of his brother. *Rhea Silvia, the daughter, he elects as a vestal, and thus deprives her of the hope of progeny, through perpetual virginity* as enjoined upon her under the semblance of a most honorable distinction. But the vestal maiden was overcome by violence, and having *brought forth twins*, she named Mars as the *father of her illegitimate offspring*, be it from conviction, or because a god appeared more creditable to her as the perpetrator of the crime.

The narrative of the exposure in the Tiber goes on to relate that the floating tub, in which the boys had been exposed, was left on dry land by the receding waters, and that a thirsty wolf, attracted from the neighboring mountains by the children's cries, offered them her teats. The boys are said to have been found by the chief royal herder, supposedly named Faustulus, who took them to the homestead of his wife, Larentia, where they were raised. Some believe that Larentia was called Lupa ("she-wolf") by the herders because she offered her body, and that this was the origin of the wounderful saga.

Grown to manhood, the youths Romulus and Remus protect the herds against the attacks of wild animals and robbers. One day Remus is taken prisoner by the robbers, who accuse him of having stolen Numitor's flocks. But Numitor, to whom he is surrendered for punishment, was touched by his tender age, and when he learned of the twin brothers, he suspected that they might be his exposed grandsons. While he was anxiously pondering the resemblance with the features of his daughter, and the boy's age as corresponding to the time of the exposure, Faustulus arrived with Romulus, and a conspiracy was hatched when the descent of the boys had been learned from the herders. The youths armed themselves for vengeance, while Numitor took up weapons to defend his claim to the throne he had usurped. After *Amulius had been assassinated*, Numitor was reinstituted as the ruler, and the youths resolved to found a city in the region where they had been exposed and brought up. A furious dispute arose upon the question of which brother was to be the ruler of the newly erected city, for neither twin was favored by the right of primogeniture, and the outcome of the bird oracle was equally doubtful. The saga relates that Remus jumped over the new wall, to deride his twin, and *Romulus became so much enraged that he slew his brother*. Romulus then usurped the sole mastery, and the city was named Rome after him.

The Roman tale of Romulus and Remus has a close counterpart in the Greek myth of a city foundation by the twin brothers Amphion and Zethus, who were the first to found the site of Thebes of the Seven Gates. The enormous rocks which Zethus brought from the mountains were joined by the music drawn from Amphion's lyre strings to form the walls which became so famous later on. Amphion and Zethus passed as *the children of Zeus and Antiope*, daughter of King Nykteus. She escaped by flight from the punishment of her father, who died of grief; on his deathbed he implored *his brother and successor on the throne, Lycus*, to punish the wrongdoing of Antiope. Meantime she had married Epopeus, the king of Sicyon, who was killed by Lycus. Antiope was led away by him in fetters. She gave birth to twin sons in the Cithaeron, where she left them. A shepherd raised the boys and called them Amphion and Zethus. Later on, Antiope succeeded in escaping from the torments of Lycus and his wife, Dirce. She accidently sought shelter in the Cithaeron, with the twin brothers, now grown up. The shepherd reveals to the youths the fact that Antiope is their mother. Thereupon they cruelly kill Dirce, and deprive Lycus of the rulership.

The remaining twin sagas,[43] which are extremely numerous, cannot be discussed in detail in this connection. Possibly they represent a complication of the birth myth by another very ancient and widely distributed myth complex, that of the hostile brothers, the detailed discussion of which belongs elsewhere. The apparently late and secondary character of the twin type in the birth myths justifies the separation of this part of mythology from the present theme. As regards the Romulus saga, Mommsen considers it highly probable that it originally told only of Romulus, while the figure of Remus was added subsequently, and somewhat disjointedly, when it became desirable to invest the consulate with a solemnity founded on old tradition.[44]

Hercules[45]

After the loss of his numerous sons, Electryon betroths his daughter, Alcmene, to Amphitryon, the son of his brother, Alcaeus. However, Amphitryon, through an unfortunate accident, causes the death of Electryon, and escapes to Thebes with his affianced bride. He has not enjoyed her love, for she has solemnly pledged him not to touch her until he has avenged her brothers on the Thebans. An expedition is therefore started by him, from Thebes, and he conquers the king of the hostile people, Pterelaos, with all the islands. As he is returning to Thebes, Zeus in the form of Amphitryon betakes himself to Alcmene, to whom he presents a golden goblet as evidence of victory.[46] He rests with the beauteous maiden during three nights, according to the later poets, holding back the sun one day. In the same night, Amphitryon arrives, exultant in his victory and aflame with love. In the fullness of time, the fruit of the divine and the human embrace is brought forth, and Zeus announces to the gods his son, as the most powerful ruler of the future.[47] But his jealous spouse, Hera, knows how to obtain from him the pernicious oath that the first-born grandson of Perseus is to be

the ruler of all the other descendants of Perseus. Hera hurries to Mycenae, to deliver the wife of Perseus' third son, Sthenelos, of the seven-
months child, Eurystheus. At the same time she hinders and endangers
the confinement of Alcmene, through all sorts of wicked sorcery, precisely as at the birth of the god of light, Apollo. Alcmene finally gives
birth to Hercules and Iphicles, the latter in no way the former's equal
in courage or in strength, but destined to become the father of his
faithful friend, Iolaos.[48] In this way Eurystheus became the king in Mycenae, in the land of the Argolians, in conformity with the oath of
Zeus, and the later-born Hercules was his subject.

The old legend related the raising of Hercules on the strength-
giving waters of the Fountain of Dirce, the nourishment of all Theban
children. Later on, however, another version arose. Fearing the jealousy of Hera, Alcmene *exposed the child she had borne* in a place that for
a long time after was known as the Field of Hercules. About this time,
Athena arrived, in company with Hera. She marveled at the beautiful
form of the child, and persuaded Hera to put him to her breast. But the
boy took the breast with far greater strength than his age seemed to
warrant; Hera felt pains and angrily flung the child to the ground.
Athena, however, carried him to the neighboring city and *took him to
Queen Alcmene, whose maternity was unknown to her, as a poor foundling, whom she begged her to raise for the sake of charity.* This peculiar
accident is truly remarkable! The child's own mother allows him to
perish, disregarding the duty of maternal love, and the stepmother,
who is filled with natural hatred against the child, saves her enemy
without knowing it.[49] Hercules had drawn only a few drops from
Hera's breast, but the divine milk was sufficient to endow him with
immortality. An attempt on Hera's part to kill the boy, asleep in his
cradle, by means of two serpents, proved a failure, for the child awak-
ened and crushed the beasts with a single pressure of his hands. As a
boy, Hercules one day killed his tutor, Linos, being incensed over an
unjust chastisement. Amphitryon, fearing the wildness of the youth,
sent him to tend his ox-herds in the mountains, with the herders,
among whom he is said by some to have been raised entirely, like Amphion and Zethus, Cyrus, and Romulus. Here he lives from the hunt,
in the freedom of nature.[50]

The myth of Hercules suggests in certain features the Hindu saga of
the hero Krishna, who like many heroes escapes a general infanticide,
and is then brought up by a herder's wife, Iasodha. A wicked she-

demon appears, who has been sent by King Kansa to kill the boy. She takes the post of wet nurse in the home, but is recognized by Krishna, who bites her so severely in suckling—like Hera, when nursing Hercules, whom she also means to destroy—that she dies.

Jesus

The Gospel according to Luke (1:26–35) relates the prophecy of the birth of Jesus, as follows:

> And in the sixth month the angel Gabriel sent from God unto a city of Galilee, named Nazareth, *to a virgin espoused to a man whose name was Joseph,* of the house of David; and the virgin's name was Mary. And the angel came in unto her, and said, Hail! thou that art highly favored, the Lord is with thee: blessed art thou among women. And when she saw him, she was troubled at his saying, and cast in her mind what manner of salutation this should be. And the angel said unto her, Fear not, Mary: for thou hast found favour with God. And, behold, *thou shalt conceive in thy womb, and bring forth a son, and shalt call his name JESUS. He shall be great and shall be called the Son of the Highest:* and the Lord God shalt give unto him the throne of his father David. And he shall reign over the house of Jacob for ever; and of his kingdom there shall be no end. Then said Mary unto the angel, How shall this be, *seeing I know not a man?* And the angel answered and said unto her, The Holy Ghost shall come upon thee, and the power of the Highest shall overshadow thee: therefore also that holy thing which shall be born of thee *shall be called the Son of God.*

This report is supplemented by the Gospel according to Matthew (1:18–25), in the narrative of the birth and childhood of Jesus:[51]

> Now the birth of Jesus Christ was on this wise: when as his mother Mary was espoused to Joseph, before they came together, *she was found with child of the Holy Ghost.* Then Joseph, her husband, being a just man, and not willing to make her a publick example, was minded to put her away privily. But, while he thought on these things, behold, *the angel of the Lord appeared unto him in a dream,* saying, Joseph, thou son of David, fear not to take unto thee Mary thy wife: for that which is conceived in her is of the Holy Ghost. And she shall bring forth a son, and thou shall

call his name JESUS: for he shall save his people from their sins. Now all this was done that it might be fulfilled which was spoken of the Lord by the prophet, saying, Behold, a virgin shall be with child, and shall bring forth a son, and they shall call his name Emmanuel, which being interpreted is, God with us. Then Joseph being raised from sleep did as the angel of the Lord had bidden him and took unto him his wife: *And knew her not till she had brought forth her firstborn son:* and he called his name JESUS.

Here we interpolate the detailed account of the birth of Jesus, from Gospel of Luke (2:4–20):

And Joseph also went up from Galilee, out of the city of Nazareth, into Judaea, unto the city of David, which is called Bethlehem; (because he was of the house and lineage of David:) to be taxed with Mary his espoused wife, being great with child. And so it was, that, while they were there, the days were accomplished that she should be delivered. And *she brought forth her firstborn son, and wrapped him in swaddling clothes, and laid him in a manger;*[52] because there was no room for them in the inn. And there were in the same country shepherds abiding in the field, keeping watch over their flocks by night. And, lo, the angel of the Lord came upon them, and the glory of the Lord shone round about them, and they were sore afraid. And the angel said unto them, Fear not; for, behold, I bring you good tidings of great joy, which shall be to all people. For unto you is born this day in the city of David a Saviour, which is Christ the Lord. And this shall be a sign unto you; Ye shall find the babe wrapped in swaddling clothes, lying in a manger. And suddenly there was with the angel a multitude of heavenly host praising God, and saying, Glory to God in the Highest, and on earth peace, good will toward men. And it came to pass, as the angels were gone away from them into heaven, the shepherds said one to another, Let us now go even unto Bethlehem, and see this thing which has come to pass, which the Lord has made known unto us. And they came with haste, and found Mary, and Joseph, and the babe lying in a manger. And when they had seen it, they made known abroad the saying which was told them concerning this child. And all they that heard wondered at those things which were told them by the shepherds. But Mary kept all these things, and pondered them in her heart. And the shepherds returned, glorifying and praising God for all the things which they had heard and seen, as it was told unto them.

We now continue the account after Matthew, in the second chapter:

Now when Jesus was born in Bethlehem of Judaea in the days of Herod the king, behold, there came *wise men from the east* to Jerusalem, Saying, *Where is he that is born King of the Jews?* for we have seen his star in the east, and are come to worship him. When *Herod the king* had heard these things, he was troubled, and all Jerusalem with him. And when he had gathered all the chief priests and scribes of the people together, he demanded of them where Christ should be born. And they said unto him, In Bethlehem of Judaea: for thus it is written by the prophet, And thou Bethlehem, in the land of Juda, art not the least among the princes of Juda, for out of thee shall come a Governor, that shall rule my people Israel.

Then Herod, when he had privily called the wise men, enquired of them diligently what time the star appeared. And he sent them to Bethlehem, and said, Go and search diligently for the young child; and when ye have found him, bring me word again, that I may come and worship him also. When they had heard the king, they departed; and, lo, the star, which they saw in the east, went before them, till it came and stood over where the young child was. When they saw the star, they rejoiced with exceeding great joy.

And when they were come into the house, they saw the young child with Mary his mother, and fell down, and worshipped him: and when they had opened their treasures, they presented unto him gifts; gold, and frankincense, and myrrh. And being warned of God in a dream, that they should not return to Herod, they departed into their own country another way. And when they were departed, behold, *the angel of the Lord appeareth to Joseph in a dream, saying, Arise, and take the young child and his mother, and flee into Egypt,* and be thou there until I bring thee word: for Herod will seek the young child to destroy him. When he arose, he took the young child and his mother by night, and departed into Egypt: and was there until the death of Herod: that it might be fulfilled which was spoken of the Lord by the prophet saying, Out of Egypt have I called my son.

Then Herod, when he saw that he was mocked of the wise men, was exceeding wroth, and sent forth, and *slew all the children that were in Bethlehem, and in all the coasts thereof, from two years old and under,* according to the time which he had diligently enquired of the wise men. . . .

But when Herod was dead, behold, an angel of the Lord appeareth in a dream to Joseph in Egypt, Saying, Arise, and take the young child and his mother, and go into the land of Israel: *for they are dead which sought the young child's life.* And he arose, and took the young child and his mother, and came into the land of Israel. But when he heard Archelaus did reign in Judaea in the room of his father Herod, he was afraid to go thither: notwithstanding, being warned of God in a dream, he turned aside into the parts of Galilee: And he came and dwelt in a city called Nazareth: that it might be fulfilled which was spoken by the prophets, He shall be called a Nazarene.[53]

Similar birth legends to those of Jesus have also been transmitted of other founders of religions, such as Zoroaster, who is said to have lived about the year 1000 B.C.[54] His mother, Dughda, dreams, *in the sixth month of her pregnancy,* that the wicked and the good spirits are fighting for the embryonic Zoroaster; a monster tears the future Zoroaster from the mother's womb; but a light god fights the monster with his horn of light, re-encloses the embryo in the mother's womb, blows upon Dughda, and she becomes pregnant again. On awakening, she hurries in her fear to a wise dream-interpreter, who is unable to explain the wonderful dream before the end of three days. He then declares that the child she is carrying is destined to become a man of great importance; the dark cloud and the mountain of light signify that she and her son will at first have to undergo numerous trials, through tyrants and other enemies, but at last they will overcome all perils. Dughda at once returns to her home and informs Pourushacpa, her husband, of everything that has happened. Immediately after his birth, the boy was seen to laugh; this was the first miracle through which he drew attention to himself. *The magicians announce the birth of the child as a portent of disaster to the prince of the realm,* Durânsarûn, who betakes himself without delay to the dwelling of Pourushacpa, in order to stab the child. But his hand falls paralyzed, and he must leave with his errand undone; this was the second miracle. Soon after, the wicked demons steal the child from his mother and carry him into the desert, in order to kill him; but Dughda finds the unharmed child, calmly sleeping. This is the third miracle. Later on, Zoroaster was to be trampled upon, in a narrow passageway, by a herd of oxen, by command of the king.[55] But the largest of the cattle took the child between his feet and preserved it from harm. This was the fourth miracle. The fifth is merely a repetition of the preceding: what the cattle had refused to do, was to be accomplished by horses. But again the child was protected by a horse from the hoofs of the other horses. Durânsurûn thereupon had the cubs in a wolf's den killed during the absence of the old wolves, and Zoroaster was laid down in their place. But a god closed the jaws of the furious wolves, so that they could not harm the child. Two divine cows arrived instead and presented their udders to the child, giving it to drink. This was the sixth miracle through which Zoroaster's life was preserved.[56]

Related themes are also encountered in the history of Buddha (sixth century before Christ), such as the long sterility of the parents, the dream, the birth of the boy under the open sky, the death of the mother and her substitution by a foster mother, the announcing of the birth to the ruler of the realm, and later on the losing of the boy in the temple.[57]

Siegfried

The old Norse Thidreksaga, as recorded about the year 1250 by an Icelander, according to oral traditions and ancient songs, relates the history of the birth and youth of Siegfried.[58] King Sigmund of Tarlungaland, on his return from an expedition, banishes his wife Sisibe, the daughter of King Nidung of Hispania, who is *accused* by Count Hartvin, whose advances she has spurned, of having had *illicit relations with a menial*. The king's counselors advise him to mutilate the innocent queen, instead of killing her, and Hartvin is ordered to cut out her tongue in the forest, so as to bring it to the king as a pledge. His companion, Count Hermann, opposes the execution of the cruel command, and proposes to present the tongue of a dog to the king. While the two men are engaged in a violent quarrel, *Sisibe gives birth to a remarkably beautiful boy; she then took a glass vessel, and after having wrapped the boy in linens, she placed him in the glass vessel,* which she carefully closed again and placed beside her. Count Hartvin was conquered in the fight, and in falling kicked the glass vessel, *so that it fell into the river.* When the queen saw this she swooned, and died soon afterwards. Hermann went home, told the king everything, and was banished from the country. *The glass vessel meantime drifted downstream to the sea,* and it was not long before the tide turned. *Then the vessel floated onto a rocky cliff,* and the water ran off so that the place where the vessel was was perfectly dry. The boy inside had grown somewhat, and when the vessel struck the rock, it broke, and the child began to cry. The boy's wailing was heard *by a doe*, which seized him with her lips, and carried him to her litter, *where she nursed him together with her young*. After the child had lived twelve months in the den of the doe, he had grown to the height and strength of other boys four years of age. One day he ran into the forest, where dwelt the wise and skillful *smith Mimir, who had lived for nine years in childless wedlock*. He saw the boy, who was followed by the faithful doe, took him to his home, *and resolved to bring him up as his own son*. He gave him the name of Siegfried. In Mimir's home, Siegfried soon attained an enormous stature and strength, but his wilfulness caused Mimir *to get rid of him*. He sent the youth into the forest, where it had been arranged that the dragon Regin, Mimir's brother, was to kill him. But Siegfried conquers the dragon, and kills Mimir. He then proceeds to Brunhild, who names his parents to him.

Similar to the early history of Siegfried is an Austrasian saga that tells of the birth and youth of Wolfdietrich.[59] His mother is likewise accused of *unfaithfulness*, and of intercourse with the devil, by a vassal whom she had repulsed, and who speaks evil of her to the returning king, Hugdietrich of Constantinople.[60]

The king surrenders the child to the faithful Berchtung, who is to kill it, but exposes it instead in the forest, near the water, in the hope that it will fall in of its own accord and thus find its death. But the frolicking child remains unhurt, and even *the wild animals*—lions, bears, and wolves, which come at night to the water—*do not harm it*. The astonished Berchtung resolves to save the boy, and he *surrenders him to a gamekeeper* who, together with his wife, raises him and names him Wolfdietrich.[61]

Three later hero epics may also be quoted in this connection: First, there is the thirteenth-century French saga of Horn, the son of Aluf, who, after having been exposed on the sea, finally reaches the court of King Hunlaf; after numerous adventures, he wins the king's daughter, Rimhilt, for his wife. Secondly, a detail suggestive of Siegfried appears in the saga of the skillful smith Wieland, who, after avenging his foully murdered father, floats down the river Weser, artfully enclosed in the trunk of a tree, and loaded with the tools and treasures of his teachers.[62] Finally, the King Arthur legend contains the commingling of divine and human paternity, the exposure, and the early life with a lowly man.

Lohengrin

The widely distributed group of sagas that have been woven around the mythical Knight with the Swan (the old French *Chevalier au cigne*) can be traced back to very ancient Celtic traditions. The following is the version which has been made familiar by Wagner's dramatization of this theme—the story of Lohengrin, the Knight with the Swan, as transmitted by the medieval German epic (modernized by Junghaus) and briefly rendered by the Grimm brothers under the title "Lohengrin in Brabant."[63]

The Duke of Brabant and Limburg died, without leaving other heirs than a young daughter, Els, or Elsa by name; her he recommended on his deathbed to one of his retainers, Friedrich von Telramund. Friedrich, the intrepid warrior, became emboldened to demand the youthful duchess' hand and lands, under the false claim that she had promised to marry him. She steadfastly refused to do so. Friedrich complained to Emperor Henry I ("the Fowler"), and the verdict was that she must defend herself against him, through some hero, in a so-called divine judgment, in which God would accord the victory to the innocent, and defeat the guilty. As none were ready to take her part, the young duchess prayed ardently to God to save her; and far away in distant Montsalvatsch, in the Council of the Grail, the sound of the bell was heard, showing that there was someone in urgent need of help. The Grail therefore resolved to despatch as a rescuer, Lohengrin, the son of Parsifal. Just as he was about to place his foot in the stirrup *a swan came floating down the water drawing a skiff behind him.* As soon as Lohengrin set eyes upon the swan, he explained: "Take the steed back to the manger; I shall follow this bird wherever he may lead me." Having faith in God's omnipotence, he took no food with him in the skiff. After they had been afloat five days, the swan dipped his bill in the water, caught a fish, ate one half of it, and gave the other half to the prince to eat. *Thus the knight was fed by the swan.*

Meanwhile Elsa had summoned her chieftains and retainers to a meeting in Antwerp. Precisely on the day of the assembly, a swan was sighted swimming upstream (river Scheldt) and drawing behind him a skiff, in which Lohengrin lay asleep on his shield. The swan promptly came to land at the shore, and the prince was joyfully welcomed. Hardly had his helmet, shield, and sword been taken from the skiff, when the swan at once swam away again. Lohengrin heard of the wrong which had been done to the duchess and willingly consented to become her champion. Elsa then summoned all her relatives and subjects. A place was prepared in Mainz for Lohengrin and Friedrich to fight in the emperor's presence. The hero of the Grail defeated Friedrich, who confessed having lied to the duchess, and was executed with the axe. Elsa was awarded to Lohengrin, they having long been lovers; but he secretly *insisted upon her avoiding all questions as to his ancestry, or whence he had come*, saying that otherwise he would have to leave her instantaneously and she would never see him again.

For some time, the couple lived in peace and happiness. Lohengrin was a wise and mightly ruler over his land, and also served his emperor well in his expeditions against the Huns and the heathen. But it came to pass that one day in throwing the javelin he unhorsed the Duke of Cleve, so that the latter broke an arm. The Duchess of Cleve was angry, and spoke out amongst the women, saying, "Lohengrin may be brave enough, and he seems to be a good Christian; what a pity that his nobility is not of much account *for no one knows whence he has come floating to this land*." These words pierced the heart of the Duchess of Brabant, and she changed color with emotion. At night, when her spouse was holding her in his arms, she wept, and he said, "What is the matter, Elsa, my own?" She made answer, "The Duchess of Cleve has caused me sore pain." Lohengrin was silent and asked no more. The second night, the same came to pass. But in the third night, Elsa could no longer retain herself, and she spoke: "Lord, do not chide me!" *I wish to know, for our children's sake, whence you were born*; for my heart tells me that you are of high rank." When the day broke, Lohengrin declared in public whence he had come, that Parsifal was his father, and God had sent him from the Grail. He then asked for his two children, which the duchess had borne him, kissed them, told them to take good care of his horn and sword, which he would leave behind, and said: "Now, I must be gone." To the duchess he left a little ring which his mother had given him. Then the swan, his friend, came swimming swiftly, with the skiff behind him; the prince stepped in and crossed the water, back to the service of the Grail. Elsa sank down in a faint. The empress resolved *to keep the younger boy Lohengrin, for his father's sake, and to bring him up as her own child*. But the widow wept and mourned the rest of her life for her beloved spouse, who never came back to her.[64]

On inverting the Lohengrin saga in such a way that the end is placed first—on the basis of the rearrangement, or even transmutation of motifs, not uncommonly found in myths—we find the type of saga with which we have now become familiar: The infant Lohengrin, who is identical with his father of the same name, *floats in a vessel upon the sea and is carried ashore by a swan. The empress adopts him as her son, and he becomes a valorous hero.* Having married a noble maiden of the land, he forbids her to inquire as to his origin. When the command is broken he is obliged to reveal his miraculous descent and divine mission, after which the swan carries him back in his skiff to the Grail.

Other versions of the saga of the Knight with the Swan have retained this original arrangement of the motifs, although they appear commingled with elements of fairy tales. The saga of the Knight with the Swan, as related in the Flemish *People's Book*,[65] contains in the beginning the history of the birth of seven children,[66] borne by Beatrix, the wife of King Oriant of Flanders. Matabruna, the wicked mother of the absent king, order that the children be killed and the queen be given seven puppy dogs in their stead. But the servant contents himself with the exposure of the children, who are found by a hermit named Helias, and are nourished by a goat until they are grown. Beatrix is thrown into a dungeon. Later on, Matabruna learns that the children have been saved; her repeated command to kill them causes her hunter to bring her as a sign of apparent obedience the silver neck chains which the children already wore at the time of their birth. One of the boys—named Helias, after his foster father—alone keeps his chain, and is thereby saved from the fate of his brothers, who are transformed into swans as soon as their chains are removed. Matabruna volunteers to prove the relations of the queen with the dog, and upon her instigation, Beatrix is to be killed, unless a champion arises to defend her. In her need, she prays to God, who sends her son Helias as a rescuer. The brothers are also saved by means of the other chains, except one, whose chain has already been melted down. King Oriant now transfers the rulership to his son Helias, who causes the wicked Matabruna to be burned. One day, Helias sees his brother, the swan, drawing a skiff on the lake surrounding the castle. This he regards as a heavenly sign; he arms himself and mounts the skiff. The swan takes him through rivers and lakes to the place where God has ordained him to go. Next follows the liberation of an innocently accused duchess, in analogy with the Lohengrin saga; and his marriage to her daughter Clarissa, who is forbidden to ask about her husband's ancestry. In the seventh year of their marriage she disobeys and puts the question, after which Helias returns home in the swan's skiff. Finally, his lost brother swan is likewise released.

The characteristic features of the Lohengrin saga—the disappearance of the divine hero in the same mysterious fashion in which he has arrived; the transference of mythical motifs from the life of the older hero to a younger one bearing the same name (a universal process in myth formation)—are likewise embodied in the Anglo-Lombard saga of Sceaf, who reappears in the Prelude to the Anglo-Saxon *Beowulf*, the oldest Teutonic epic.[67] Here, he is called Scyld the Scefund (meaning "son of Sceaf") and his origin as a foundling is referred to. The older legend tells that he received his name because as a very young boy he was cast ashore, as a stranger, asleep in a boat on a sheaf of grain (Anglo-Saxon: *sceaf*). The waves of the sea carried him to the coast of the country he was destined to defend. The inhabitants welcomed his arrival as a miracle, raised him, and later on made him their king, considering him a divine emissary.[68] What was told of the father now is transferred in the Beowulf epic to his son, also called Scyld.[69] His body is exposed, as he had ordered before his death, surrounded by kingly splendor, upon a ship without a crew, which is sent out into the sea. Thus he vanished in the same mysterious manner in which his father arrived ashore, this trait being accounted for, in analogy with the Lohengrin saga, by the mythical identity of father and son.

Notes

1. Attention has been drawn to the great variability and wide distribution of the birth myths of the hero by the writings of Bauer, Schubert, and others referred to in the preceding pages. The comprehensive contents of the myths and their fine ramifications have been especially discussed by Hüsing, Lessmann, and other representatives of the modern trend.

2. *Editor's note*: More recent archaeological and other studies have cast some doubt on the traditional dating of the establishment of the Babylonian kingdom. Ceram places Sargon's reign as 2360–2306 B.C., and says, "The legend of his birth brings to mind Cyrus, Romulus, Krishna, Moses, and Perseus. . . . For a long time it was believed that Sharrunkên ("legitimate king," Sargon) had never really existed. Today the fact has been established that Sargon did live and wield a memorable historical influence." C. W. Ceram: *Gods, Graves, and Scholars* (New York: Alfred A. Knopf; 1951), pp. 303–4.

3. Innumerable fairy tales, stories, and poems of all times, up to the most recent dramatic and novelistic literature, show very distinct individual main motifs of this myth. The exposure-romance appears in the late Greek pastorals—Heliodorus' *Aethiopica*, Eustathius' *Ismenias and Ismene*, and Longus' story of the two exposed children, Daphnis and Chloe. The more recent Italian pastorals are likewise very frequently based upon the exposure of children, who are raised as shepherds by their foster parents, but are later recognized by the true parents, through identifying marks received at the time of their exposure. To the same set belong the family history in Grimmelshausen's *Limplizissimus* (1665), in Jean Paul's *Titan* (1800), as well as certain forms of the Robinson stories and Cavalier romances (compare Würzbach's Introduction to Hesse's edition of *Don Quixote*).

4. The various translations of the partly mutilated text differ only in unessential details. Compare Hommel: *History of Babylonia and Assyria* (Berlin, 1885), p. 302, where the sources of the tradition are likewise found; and A. Jeremias: *The Old Testament in the Light of the Ancient Orient*, 2d ed. (Leipzig, 1906), p. 410.

5. On account of these resemblances, a dependence of the Exodus tale from the Sargon legend has often been assumed, but apparently not enough attention has been paid to certain fundamental distinctions, which will be taken up in detail in the interpretation.

6. The parents of Moses were originally nameless, as were all persons in this, the oldest account. Their names were only conferred upon them by the priesthood. Chapter 6.20, says: "And Amram took him Jochebed his father's sister to wife; and she bare him Aaron and Moses"; Numbers 26.59 adds: ". . . and Miriam their sister." Also compare Winckler: *History of Israel*, Vol. II; and Jeremias, op. cit., p. 408.

7. The name, according to Winckler (*"Die babylonische Geisteskultur . . ."* loc. cit., p. 119), means "The Water-Drawer" (see also Winckler: *Ancient Oriental Studies*, Vol. III, pp. 468 ff.)—which would still further approach the Moses legend to the Sargon legend, for the name Akki signifies "I have drawn water."

8. Schemot Rabba 2.4 says concerning Exodus 1.22 that Pharaoh was told by the astrologers of a woman who was pregnant with the Redeemer of Israel.

9. After Bergel: *Mythology of the Hebrews* (Leipzig, 1882).

10. Compare Beer: *The Life of Abraham* (Leipzig, 1859), according to the interpretation of Jewish traditions; also August Wünsche: *From Israel's Temples of Learning* (Leipzig, 1907).

11. See chapters 20 and 21 of Genesis, and also Bergel, op. cit.

The sky flashes red and gold, and Ethan lifts his head from my shoulder. The red and gold make his eyes glitter like flames. The awe is plain to see on his face, even as the sky grows darker, and the time grows near.

"Why?" I ask after a moment.

"I dunno," Ethan says, and only then do I realize that I had spoken out loud. "But it's beautiful, right?"

I look back up at the sky, bright orange had joined the red and gold. "Yes, it is."

Ten minutes.

I close my eyes and tighten my arms around Ethan. Whispered declarations of love reach my ears from all around. I open my eyes again a moment later, when I feel Ethan burrow his head in the crook of my neck.

The sky is dark, almost black. No stars can be seen, and nothing can be heard but the deafening noise coming from the skies. Our story won't have a happy ending. Humanity will never fly amongst the stars. Our home will not be here for centuries to come. I don't look away; I don't close my eyes.

Our ten minutes are up.

12. The Hindu birth legend of the mythical king Vikramaditya must also be mentioned in this connection. Here again occur the barren marriage of the parents, the miraculous conception, ill-omened warnings, the exposure of the boy in the forest, his nourishment with honey, finally the acknowledgment by the father. See Jülg: *Mongolische Märche* (Innsbruck, 1868), pp. 73 ff.

13. *Indische Alterumskunde* (Karlsruhe, 1846).

14. Compare the detailed account in Lefmann: *History of Ancient India* (Berlin, 1890), pp. 181 ff.

15. See Röscher, concerning the *Ion* of Euripides. Where no other source is stated, all Greek and Roman myths are taken from the *Ausführliches Lexikon der griechischen und römischen Mythologie*, edited by W. H. Röscher, which also contains a list of all sources.

16. According to Bethe (*Thebanische Heldenlieder*), the exposure on the waters was the original rendering. According to other versions, the boy is found and raised by horseherds; according to a later myth, by a countryman, Melibios.

17. *Editor's note*: In 1912, three years after the appearance of this essay, Rank published *Das Inzestmotiv in Dichtung und Sage* ("The Incest Theme in Fiction and Legend"). A revised edition appeared in 1926, and a French translation in 1934. The cycle of Christian legends mentioned above has been discussed in detail in Chapter X of the book. Further references to this book will be abbreviated herein as *Inzestmotiv*.

18. Cholevicas: *History of German Poetry According to the Antique Elements*.

19. Firdausi: *Shah Namah* ("The Book of Kings"), as rendered by F. Spiegel: *Eranische Alterumskunde*, Vol. II, p. 584.

20. Ibid., translated by Schack.

21. *Editor's note*: Zal, a semi-divinity of Persian mythology, was the father of Rustam (the Hercules of Persia). A child born with white hair was then assumed to be the offspring of a deer.

22. In the version of Euripides, *Aleos caused the mother and the child to be thrown into the sea in a box*, but through the protection of Athena this box was carried to the end of the Mysian river Kaikos. There it was found by Teuthras who made Auge his wife and took her child into his house as his foster son.

23. Later authors, including Pindar, state that Danaë was impregnated, not by Zeus, but by the brother of her father.

24. Simonides of Ceos speaks of a casement strong as ore, in which Danaë is said to have been exposed. Geibel: *Klassisches Liederbuch*, p. 52.

25. According to Hüsing, the Perseus myth in several versions is also demonstrable in Japan. Compare also Sydney Hartland: *Legend of Perseus*, 3 vols. (London, 1894–6).

26. Claudius Aelianus: *Historia Animalium*, translated by F. Jacobs (Stuttgart, 1841), Vol. XII, p. 21. The same book tells of Ptolemy I, the son of Lagus and Arsinoë, that an eagle protected the exposed boy with his wings against the sunshine, the rain, and birds of prey.

27. F. E. Lange: *Herodots Geschichten* (Reclam edition), Vol. I, pp. 95, 107 ff. Compare also Duncker: *History of Antiquity* (Leipzig, 1880), p. 256,n. 5.

28. The same "playing king" is found in the Hindu myth of Chandragupta, the founder of the Maurya dynasty, whom his mother exposed after his birth, in a vessel at the gate of a cowshed, where a herder found him and raised him. Later on he came to a hunter, where he as cowherder played "king" with the other boys, and as king ordered that the hands and feet of the great criminals be chopped off. (The mutilation motif occurs also in the Cyrus saga, and is generally widely distributed.) At his command, the separated limbs returned to their proper position. Kanakja, who once looked on as they were at play, admired the boy, and bought him from the hunter for one thousand kârshâpana; at home he discovered that the boy was a Maurya. (After Lassen, op. cit., Vol. II, p. 196, n. 1.)

29. Justin (Marcus Junianus Justinus): *Extract from Pompeius Trogus' Philippian History*, Vol. I, pp. 4–7. Deinon's Persian tales (written in the first half of the fourth century before Christ) are presumably the sources of Trogus' narrative.

30. The words in parentheses are said to be lacking in certain manuscripts.

31. Nicol. Damasc. Frag. 66, Ctes.; Frag. Pers., II, 5.

32. This daughter's name is Amatyis (not Mandane) in the version of Ctesias.

33. Op. cit., Vol. I, pp. 581 ff.

34. On the basis of this motif of simulated dementia and certain other corresponding features, Jiriczek ("Hamlet in Iran," in the *Zeitschrift des Vereins für Volkskunde*, Vol. X [1900], p. 353) has represented the Hamlet saga as a variation of the Persian myth of Kaikhosrav. This idea was followed up by H. Lessmann (*"Die Kyrossage . . ."* loc. cit.), who shows that the Hamlet saga strikingly agrees in certain items—for example, in the simulated folly—with the sagas of Brutus and of Tell. (Compare also the protestations of Moses.) In another connection, the deeper roots of these relations have been more extensively discussed, especially with reference to the Tell saga. (See *Inzestmotiv*, Chapter vii.)

Attention is also directed to the story of David, as it is told in the books of Samuel. Here again, the royal scion, David, is made a shepherd, who gradually rises in the social scale up to the royal throne. He likewise is given the king's (Saul's) daughter in marriage, and the king seeks his life, but David is always saved by miraculous means from the greatest perils. He also evades persecution by simulating dementia and playing the fool. The relationship between the Hamlet saga and the David saga has already been pointed out by Jiriczek and Lessmann. The biblical character of this entire mythological cycle is also emphasized by Jiriczek, who finds in the tale of Siâvaksh's death certain features from the Passion of the Saviour.

35. Translated by Schack (op. cit.). The name Zohâk here is a mutilation of the original Zend Avesta expression *Ashi-dahaka* (*Azis-dahaka*), meaning "pernicious serpent." (See "The Myth of Feridun in India and Iran," by Dr. R. Roth, in the *Zeitschrift der Deutschen Morgenländischen Gesellschaft*, Vol. II., p. 216.) To the Persian Feridun corresponds the Hindu Trita, whose Avestian double is Thraetaona. The last-named form is the most predominantly authenticated; from it was formed, by transition of the aspired sounds, first Phrenduna, then Frêdûn or Afrêdun; Feridun is a more recent corruption. Compare Spiegel, op. cit., Vol. I, pp. 537 ff.

36. After Chop: *Erläuterungen zu Wagner's Tristan* (Reclam edition).

37. Compare Immermann: *Tristan und Isolde, Ein Gedicht in Romanzen* (Düsseldorf, 1841). Like the epic of Gottfried von Strassburg, his version begins with the preliminary history of the loves of Tristan's parents, King Riwalin Kannlengres of Parmenia and Mark's beautiful sister Blancheflur. The maiden never reveals her love, which is not sanctioned by her brother, but she visits the king, who is wounded unto death, in his chamber, and dying he procreates Tristan, "the son of the most daring and doleful love." Grown up as a foundling in the care of Rual and his wife, Florete, the winsome youth Tristan introduces himself to Mark in a stag hunt, as an expert huntsman, is recognized as his nephew by a ring, the king's gift to his beloved sister, and becomes his favorite.

38. *Wunscherfüllung und Symbolik im Märchen*, p. 56; from the Rittershaus collection of fairy tales (XXVII, p. 113). See translation by W. A. White, M.D., *Psychoanalytic Review*, Vol. I, No. 1.

39. Compare the substitution of the bride, through Brangäne.

40. Theodor Mommsen: *"Die echte und die falsche Acca Larentia"*; in *Festgaben für G. Homeyer* (Berlin, 1891), pp. 93 ff; and *Römische Forschungen* (Berlin, 1879), Vol. II, pp. 1 ff. Mommsen reconstructs the lost narrative of Fabius from the preserved reports of Dionysius (I, 79–831) and of Plutarch (*Romulus*).

41. The Capitoline She-Wolf is considered the work of very ancient Etruscan artists; it was erected at the Lupercal in the year 296 B.C., according to Livy (X, 231).

42. All these renderings were compiled by Schwegler, in his *Roman History*, Vol. I, pp. 384 ff.

43. Some Greek twin sagas are quoted by Schubert (op. cit. pp. 13 ff.) in their essential content. Concerning the extensive distribution of this legendary form, compare the somewhat confused book of J. H. Becker: *The Twin Saga as the Key to the Interpretation of Ancient Tradition* (Leipzig, 1891).

44. Mommsen: *Die Remus Legende* (Berlin, 1881).

45. After Preller: *Greek Mythology* (Leipzig, 1854), Vol. II, pp. 120 ff.

46. The same transformation of the divine procreator into the form of the human father is found in the birth history of the Egyptian queen, Hatshepsut (about 1500 B.C.), who believed that the god Amen, in the form of her father, Thothmes I, cohabited with her mother, Aahames. (See Budge: *A History of Egypt*.) Later on she married her brother, Thothmes II, after whose dishonorable death she endeavored to eradicate his memory, and herself assumed the rulership, in masculine fashion. (See *The Deuteronium*, edited by Schrader.)

47. A similar mingling of the divine and human posterity is related in the myth of Theseus, whose mother, Aethra, the beloved of Poseidon, was visited in one night by this god and by the childless King Aegeus of Athens, who had been brought under the influence of wine. The boy was raised in secret and in ignorance of his father. (See Röscher, op. cit., article "Aegeus.")

48. Alcmene bore Hercules as the son of Zeus, and Iphicles as the offspring of Amphitryon. According to Apollodorus, they were twin children, born at the same time; according to others, Iphicles was conceived and born one night later than Hercules. (See Röscher, op. cit., articles "Amphitryon" and "Alcmene.") The shadowy character of the twin brother, and his loose connection with the entire myth, is again evident. In a similar way, Telephus, the son of Auge, was exposed together with Parthenopaeus, the son of Atalanta, nursed by a doe, and taken by herders to King Corythos. The external subsequent insertion of the partner is here again quite obvious.

49. After Diodorus Siculus, Book IV, p. 9 of Wurm's German translation (Stuttgart, 1831).

50. After Preller, op. cit., Vol. II, p. 123.

51. For the formal demonstration of the entire identity with the other hero myths of the birth story and early history of Jesus, the author has presumed to rearrange the corresponding paragraphs from the different versions in the Gospels, irrespective of the traditional sequence and the originality of the individual parts. The age, origin, and genuineness of these parts are briefly summarized and discussed in W. Soltan: *Birth History of Jesus Christ* (Leipzig, 1902). The transmitted versions of the several Gospels—which according to

Usener: "The Birth and Childhood of Christ," in *Lectures and Essays* (Leipzig, 1907), contradict and even exclude each other—have been placed, or left, in juxtaposition, precisely for the reason that the apparently contradictory elements in these birth myths are to be elucidated in the present research, no matter if these contradictions be encountered within a single uniform saga, or in its different versions (as, for example, in the Cyrus myth).

52. Concerning the birth of Jesus in a cave, and the furnishing of the birthplace with the typical animals (ox and ass), compare Jeremias: *Babylonisches im Neuen Testament* (Leipzig, 1905), p. 56; and Preuschen, "*Jesu Geburt in einer Höhle,*" *Zeitschrift für die Neutest. Wissenschaften*, 1902, p. 359.

53. According to recent investigations, the birth history of Christ is said to have the greatest resemblance with the royal Egyptian myth, over five thousand years old, which relates the birth of Amenophis III. Here again recurs the divine prophecy of the birth of a son, to the waiting queen; her fertilization by the breath of heavenly fire; the divine cows, which nurse the newborn child; the homage of the kings; and so forth. In this connection, compare A. Malvert: *Wissenschaft und Religion* (Frankfort, 1904), pp. 49 ff.; also the suggestion of Professor Idleib of Bonn (*Feuilleton of Frankfurter Zeitung*, November 8, 1908).

54. *Editor's note*: More recent studies have resulted in new dates for many of the ancient heroes. Thus Zoroaster is now generally placed at one or another of several periods between 660 B.C., and Amenophis (Amenhotep) III, referred to in the preceding footnote, is now thought to have reigned about 1400 B.C.

55. Very similar traits are found in the Celtic saga of Habis, as transmitted by Justin. Born as the illegitimate son of a king's daughter, Habis is persecuted in all sorts of ways by his royal grandfather, Gargoris, but is always saved by divine providence, until he is finally recognized by his grandfather and assumes royal sway. As in the Zoroaster legend, there occurs an entire series of the most varied methods of persecution. He is at first exposed, but nursed by wild animals; then he was to be trampled upon by a herd in a narrow path; then he was cast before hungry beasts, but the again nursed him; and finally he is thrown into the sea, but is gently lapped ashore and nursed by a doe, near which he grows up.

56. Compare Spiegel, op. cit., Vol. I., pp. 688 ff.; also Brodbeck, op. cit.

57. As in the history of Jesus; compare Luke 2:41–49.

58. Compare August Rassmann: *Die deutsche Heldensage und ihre Heimat* (Hanover, 1857–8), Vol. II, pp. 7; for the sources, see Jiriczek: *Die deutsche Heldensage*, and Piper's introduction to the volume *Die Nibelungen*, in Kürschner's *German National Literature*.

59. Compare: *Deutsches Heldenbuch*, Vol. I, Part III (Berlin, 1871), edited by Amelung and Jaenicke, which also contains a second version of the Wolfdietrich saga.

60. The motive of calumniation of the wife by a rejected suitor, in combination with the exposure and nursing by an animal (doe), forms the nucleus of the story of Genovefa and her son Schmerzenreich, as told, for example, by the Grimm brothers: *Deutsche Sagen* (Berlin, 1818), Vol. II, pp. 280 ff. Here again the faithless calumniator proposes *to drown the countess and her child*. For literary and historical orientation, compare L. Zacher: *Die Historie von der Pfalzgräfin Genovefa* (Koenigsberg, 1860); and B. Seuffert: *Die Legende von der Pfalzgräfin Genovefa* (Wurzburg, 1877). Similar legends of wives suspected of infidelity and punished by exposure are discussed in Chapter xi of my *Inzestmotiv*.

61. The same accentuation of the animal motif is found in the saga of Schalû, the Hindu wolf-child. Compare Julg, op. cit.

62. *Editor's note*: Wieland, wonderful blacksmith of the Teutonic gods, appears in the Siegfried epic and in many Scandinavian, German, and English legends. The name is given variously as Volünd, Volunder, Wayland, and (in Scott's *Kenilworth*) as Wayland Smith.

63. Junghaus: *Lohengrin* (Reclam edition); Grimm brothers, op. cit., Vol. II, p. 306.

64. The Grimm brothers (op. cit., Vol. II., pp. 306 ff.) quote six further versions of the saga of the Knight with the Swan. Certain fairy tales of the Grimm brothers—such as "The Six Swans" (No. 49), "The Twelve Brothers" (No. 9), and the "Seven Ravens" (No. 25), with their parallels and variations, mentioned in the third volume of *Kinder- und Haus-märchen*—also belong to the same mythological cycle. Further material from this cycle may be found in H. Leo: *Beowulf* (Halle, 1839), and in Görre: *Introduction to Lohengrin* (Heidelberg, 1813).

65. Grimm: *Deutsche Sagen*, Vol. I., p. 29.

66. The ancient Lombard tale of the exposure of King Lamissio, related by Paulus Diaconus (L, 15), gives a similar incident. A public woman had thrown her seven newborn infants into a fishpond. King Agelmund passed by and looked curiously at the children, turning them around with his spear. But when one of the children took hold of the spear, the king considered this as a good augury; he ordered this boy to be taken out of the pond, and to be given to a wet nurse. As he had taken him from the pond, which in his language is called *lama*, he named the boy Lamissio. He grew up into a stalwart champion, and after Agelmund's death, became king of the Lombards.

67. *Editor's note*: In Norse mythology, Sceaf (or Scaf) is a descendant of

the great god Odin (Wodin, Wotan), father of Thor. In *Beowulf*, As Scyld and Scefing, he is the founder of the Danish royal house of the Scyldings (Skjoldungar)—his son is called in the poem, variously, Scyld, "son of Scyld," and Beowulf. This Beowulf was in turn the father of Beowulf the Great, hero of the Anglo-Saxon epic.

68. Compare Grimm: *Deutsche Sagen*, Vol. I, p. 306; Vol. III, p. 391; and Leo, op. cit., p. 24.

69. *Scaf* is the High German *Schaffing* ("barrel"), which leads Leo (op. cit.) to assume in connection with Scyld's being called Scefing, that he had no father Sceaf or Schaf at all, but was himself the boy cast ashore by the waves, and was named the "son of the barrel" (*Schaffing*). The name Beowulf itself, explained by Grimm as *Bienen-Wolf* ("bee-wolf"), seems to mean originally, according to H. von Wolzogen (translator into German of the Reclam edition of *Beowulf*), *Bärwelf*, namely *Jungbär* ("bear cub" or "bear whelp"), which is suggestive of the saga of the origin of the Guelphs (Grimm: *Deutsche Sagen*, Vol. II, p. 233), where the boys are to be thrown into the water as "whelps."

THE INTERPRETATION OF THE MYTHS

A CURSORY review of these variegated hero myths forcibly brings out a series of uniformly common features, with a typical groundwork, from which a standard saga, as it were, may be constructed. This schedule corresponds approximately to the ideal human skeleton that is constantly seen, with minor deviations, on transillumination of figures that outwardly differ from one another. The individual traits of the several myths, and especially the apparently crude variations from the prototype, can be entirely elucidated only by myth interpretation.

The standard saga itself may be formulated according to the following outline: The hero is the child of most distinguished parents, usually the son of a king. His origin is preceded by difficulties, such as continence, or prolonged barrenness, or secret intercourse of the parents due to external prohibition or obstacles. During or before the pregnancy, there is a prophecy, in the form of a dream or oracle, cautioning against his birth, and usually threatening danger to the father (or his representative). As a rule, he is surrendered to the water, in a box. He is then saved by animals, or by lowly people (shepherds), and is suckled by a female animal or by an humble woman. After he has grown up, he finds his distinguished parents, in a highly versatile fashion. He takes his revenge on his father, on the one hand, and is acknowledged, on the other. Finally he achieves rank and honors.[1]

Since the normal relations of the hero toward his father and his mother regularly appear impaired in all these myths, as shown by the outline, there is reason to assume that something in the nature of the hero must account for such a disturbance, and motives of this kind are not very difficult to discover. It is readily understood—and may be noted in the modern imitations of the heroic age—that for the hero, who is exposed to envy, jealousy, and calumny to a much higher degree than all others, the descent from his parents often becomes the source of the greatest distress and embarrassment. The old saying that "A prophet is not without honour, save in his own country and in his father's house," has no other meaning but that he whose parents, brothers and sisters, or playmates, are known to us, is not so readily conceded to be a prophet. There seems to be a certain necessity for the prophet to deny his parents; the well-known Meyerbeer opera is based upon the avowal that the prophetic hero is allowed, in favor of his mission, to abandon and repudiate even his tenderly loving mother.

A number of difficulties arise, however, as we proceed to a deeper inquiry into the motives which oblige the hero to sever his family relations. Numerous investigators have emphasized that the understanding of myth formation requires our going back to their ultimate source, namely the individual faculty of imagination.[2] The fact has also been pointed out that imaginative faculty is found in its active and unchecked exuberance only in childhood. Therefore, the imaginative life of the child should first be studied, in order to facilitate the understanding of the far more complex and also more handicapped mythological and artistic imagination in general.

Meanwhile, the investigation of the juvenile faculty of imagination has hardly commenced, instead of being sufficiently advanced to permit the utilization of the findings for the explanation of the more complicated psychic activities. The reason for this imperfect understanding of the psychic life of the child is traceable to the lack of a suitable instrument, as well as of a reliable avenue, leading into the intricacies of this very delicate and rather inaccessible domain. These juvenile emotions can by no means be studied in the normal human adult, and it may actually be charged, in view of certain psychic disturbances, that the normal psychic integrity of normal subjects consist precisely in their having overcome and forgotten their childish vagaries and imaginations; so that the way has become blocked. In children, on the other hand, empirical observation (which as a rule must remain merely superficial) fails in the investigation of psychic processes because we are not as yet enabled to trace all manifestations correctly to their motive forces; so that we are lacking the instrument. There is a certain class of persons, the so-called psychoneurotics, shown by the teachings of Freud to have remained children, in a sense, although otherwise appearing grown-up. These psychoneurotics may be said not to have given up their juvenile psychic life, which on the contrary, in the course of maturity has become strengthened and fixed, instead of modified. In psychoneurotics, the emotions of the child are preserved and exaggerated, thus becoming capable of pathological effects, in which these humble emotions appear broadened and enormously magnified. The fancies of neurotics are, as it were, the uniformly exaggerated reproductions of the childish imaginings. This would point the way to a solution of the problem. Unfortunately, however, access is still much more difficult to establish in these cases than to the child mind. There is only one known instrument which makes this road practicable, namely the psychoanalytic method, which has been developed through the work of Freud. Constant handling of this instrument will clear the observer's vision to such a degree that he will be enabled to discover the identical motive forces, only in delicately shaded manifestations, also in the psychic life of those who do not become neurotics later on.

Professor Freud had the kindness to place at the author's disposal his valuable experience with the psychology of the neuroses; and on this material are based the following comments on the imaginative faculty of the child as well as of the neurotic.

The detachment of the growing individual from the authority of the parents is one of the most necessary, but also one of the most painful achievements of evolution. It is absolutely necessary for this detachment to take place, and it may be assumed that all normal grown individuals have accomplished it to a certain extent. Social progress is essentially based upon this opposition between the two generations. On the other hand, there exists a class of neurotics whose condition indicates that they have failed to solve this very problem. For the young child, the parents are, in the first place, the sole authority and the source of all faith. To resemble them, i.e., the progenitor of the same sex—to grow up like father or mother—this is the most intense and portentous wish of the child's early years. Progressive intellectual development naturally brings it about that the child gradually becomes acquainted with the category to which the parents belong. Other parents become known to the child, who compares these with his own, and thereby becomes justified in doubting the incomparability and uniqueness with which he had invested them. Trifling occurrences in the life of the child, which induce a mood of dissatisfaction, lead up to a criticism of the parents; and the gathering conviction that other parents are preferable in certain ways is utilized for this attitude of the child toward the parents.

From the psychology of the neurosis, we have learned that very intense emotions of sexual rivalry are also involved in this connection. The causative factor evidently is the feeling of being neglected. Op-

"Less than five minutes," I say without looking at my watch.

"So soon…"

It's said so low that I almost miss it. I look at Ethan and see tears running down his cheeks. Without consciously thinking about it, I pull the kid onto my lap. He's so small that he fits easily.

"Sorry," Ethan mutters into my neck.

"It's fine."

Ethan shakes his head.

"I'm supposed to be strong. Dad said everything was going to be fine. Tomorrow's my birthday, and I'm gonna have pancakes and a skateboard, and I wanted an ice-cream cake, and Mom said okay even though it's winter."

The tears continue to fall, and I can do nothing but hold him. Honestly, what else can I do? He is too old to believe any lie I could come up with, and far too young to be prepared for what's coming. Even I'm not prepared for what's coming.

Ethan continues to cry into my shoulder, and several people look at us with so much pity, pain, and empathy, it almost breaks me. Is that the look I've been giving them?

The pregnant woman at the table near us leans against her husband, tears flowing freely down her cheeks, both hands over the tiny bump as if to shield it. I can't stand looking at it. Ethan stops shaking and I look down. Honey-brown eyes are gazing at me, so lost, so alone. My arms tighten around the small body.

No matter what, alone is something that Ethan won't be.

"Thank you for coming to sit with me," I say, smiling softly.

Ethan sits just a little bit straighter, a little bit taller. There are still tears in his eyes, but they don't fall, and I know that Ethan *is* strong. He is the strongest not-yet-ten-year-old I've ever seen, and his parents must be so damned proud of him. I know I am, and I've not even known the kid for ten minutes.

"Hey, Nick?"

"Hmm?"

"I love the little blue dot. I'm glad it's home."

My lips twitch again.

"So am I, kid."

portunities arise only too frequently when the child is neglected, or at least feels himself neglected, when he misses the entire love of the parents, or at least regrets having to share this with the other children of the family. The feeling that one's own inclinations are not entirely reciprocated seeks its relief in the idea—often consciously remembered from very early years—of being a stepchild, or an adopted child. Many persons who have not become neurotics very frequently remember occasions of this kind, when the hostile behavior of the parents was interpreted and reciprocated by them in this fashion, usually under the influence of storybooks. The influence of sex is already evident, is so far as the boy shows a far greater tendency to harbor hostile feelings against his father than his mother, with a much stronger inclination to emancipate himself from the father than from the mother. The imaginative faculty of girls is possibly much less active in this respect.

These consciously remembered psychic emotions of the years of childhood supply the factor which permits the interpretation of the myth. What is not often consciously remembered, but can almost invariably be demonstrated through psychoanalysis, is the next stage in the development of this incipient alienation from the parents, which may be designated by the term "family romance of neurotics." The essence of neurosis, and of all higher mental qualifications, comprises a special activity of the imagination that is primarily manifested in the play of the child, and which from about the period preceding puberty takes hold of the theme of the family relations. A characteristic example of this special imaginative faculty is represented by the familiar *daydreams*,[3] which are continued until long after puberty. Accurate observation of these daydreams shows that they serve for the fulfillment of wishes, for the righting of life, and that they have two essential objects, one erotic, the other of an ambitious nature (usually with the erotic factor concealed therein). About the time in question, the child's imagination is engaged upon the task of getting rid of the parents, who are now despised and are as a rule to be supplanted by others of a higher social rank. The child utilizes an accidental coincidence of actual happenings (meetings with the lord of the manor or the proprietor of the estate, in the country; with the reigning prince, in the city; in the United States, with some great statesman or millionaire). Accidental occurrences of this kind arouse the child's envy, and this finds its expression in fancy fabrics which replace the two parents by others of a higher rank. The technical elaboration of these two imaginings, which of course by this time have become conscious, depends upon the child's adroitness and also upon the material at his disposal. It is likewise a factor whether these fancies are elaborated with more or less claim to plausibility. This stage is reached at a time when the child is still lacking all knowledge of the sexual conditions of descent.

With the added knowledge of the manifold sexual relations of father and mother—with the child's realization of the fact that the father is always uncertain, whereas the mother is very certain—the family romance undergoes a peculiar restriction: it is satisfied with ennobling the father, while the descent from the mother is no longer questioned, but accepted as an unalterable fact. This second (or sexual) stage of the family romance is moreover supported by another motive, which did not exist in the first (or asexual) stage. Knowledge of sexual matters gives rise to the tendency to picture erotic situations and relations, impelled by the pleasurable emotion of placing the mother, or the subject of the greatest sexual curiosity, in the situation of secret unfaithfulness and clandestine love affairs. In this way the primary or asexual fantasies are raised to the standard of the improved later understanding.

The motive of revenge and retaliation, which was originally to the front, is again evident. These neurotic children are mostly those who were punished by the parents to break them of bad sexual habits, and they take their revenge upon their parents by their imaginings. The younger children of a family are particularly inclined to deprive their predecessors of their advantage by fables of this kind (exactly as in the intrigues of history). Frequently they do not hesitate in crediting the mother with as many love affairs as there are rivals. An interesting variation of this family romance restores the legitimacy of the plotting hero himself, while the other children are disposed of in this way as illegitimate. The family romance may be governed besides by a special interest, all sorts of inclinations being met by its adaptability and variegated character. The little romancer gets rid in this fashion, for example, of the kinship of a sister who may have attracted him sexually.

Those who turn aside with horror from this corruption of the child mind, or perhaps actually contest the possibility of such matters, should note that all these apparently hostile imaginings have not such a very bad significance after all, and that the original affection of the child for his parents is still preserved under their thin disguise. The faithlessness and ingratitude on the part of the child are only apparent, for on investigating in detail the most common of these romantic fancies—the substitution of both parents, or of the father alone, by more exalted personages—the discovery will be made that these new high-born parents are invested throughout with the qualities which are derived from real memories of the true lowly parents, so that the child does not actually remove his father but exalts him. *The entire endeavor to replace the real father by a more distinguished one is merely the expression of the child's longing for the vanished happy time, when his father still appeared to be the strongest and greatest man, and the mother seemed the dearest and most beautiful woman.* The child turns away from the father, as he now knows him, to the father in whom he believed in his earlier years, his imagination being in truth only the expression of regret for this happy time having passed away. *Thus the overvaluation of the earliest years of childhood again claims its own in these fancies.*[4] An interesting contribution to this subject is furnished by the study of dreams. Dream-interpretation teaches that even in later years, in the dreams of the emperor or the empress, these princely persons stand for the father and the mother.[5] Thus the infantile overvaluation of the parents is still preserved in the dream of the normal adult.

As we proceed to fit the above features into our scheme, we feel justified in analogizing the ego of the child with the hero of the myth, in view of the unanimous tendency of family romances and hero myths; keeping in mind that the myth throughout reveals an endeavor to get rid of the parents, and that the same wish arises in the fantasies of the individual child at the time when he is trying to establish his personal independence. The ego of the child behaves in this respect like the hero of the myth, and as a matter of fact, the hero should always be interpreted merely as a collective ego, which is equipped with all the excellences. In a similar manner, the hero in personal poetic fiction usually represents the poet himself, or at least one side of his character.

Summarizing the essentials of the hero myth, we find the descent from noble parents, the exposure in a river, and in a box, and the raising by lowly parents; followed in the further evolution of the story by the hero's return to his first parents, with or without punishment meted out to them. It is very evident that the two parent-couples of the myth correspond to the real and the imaginary parent-couple of the romantic fantasy. Closer inspection reveals the psychological identity of the humble and the noble parents, precisely as in the infantile and neurotic fantasies.

In conformity with the overvaluation of the parents in early childhood, the myth begins with the noble parents, exactly like the romantic fantasy, whereas in reality adults soon adapt themselves to the actual conditions. Thus the fantasy of the family romance is simply realized in the myth, with a bold reversal to the actual conditions. The hostility of the father, and the resulting exposure, accentuate the motive which has caused the ego to indulge in the entire fiction. The fictitious romance is the excuse, as it were, for the hostile feelings which the child harbors against his father, and which in this fiction are projected against the father. The exposure in the myth, therefore, is equivalent to the repudiation or nonrecognition in the romantic fantasy. The child simply gets rid of the father in the neurotic romance, while in the myth the father endeavors to lose the child. Rescue and revenge are the natural terminations, as demanded by the essence of the fantasy.

In order to establish the full value of this parallelization, as just sketched in its general outlines, it must enable us to interpret certain constantly recurring details of the myth which seem to require a special explanation. This demand would seem to acquire special importance in view of the fact that no satisfactory explanation of these details is forthcoming in the writings of even the most enthusiastic astral mythologists or natural philosophers. Such details are represented by the regular occurrence of dreams (or oracles) and by the mode of exposure in a box and in the water. These motifs do not at first glance seem to permit a psychological derivation. Fortunately the study of dream-symbolisms permits the elucidation of these elements of the hero myth. The utilization of the same material in the dreams of healthy persons and neurotics[6] indicates that the exposure in the water signifies no more and no less than the *symbolic expression of birth*. The children come out of the water.[7] The basket, box, or receptacle simply means the container, the womb;[8] so that the exposure directly signifies the process of birth, although it is represented by its opposite.

Those who object to his representation by opposites should remember how often the dream works with the same mechanism.[9] A confirmation of this interpretation of the exposure, as taken from the common human symbolism, is furnished by the material itself, in the dream by the grandfather (or still more convincingly by the mother herself)[10] in the Ctesian version of Cyrus before his birth; in this dream, so much water flows from the lap of the expectant mother as to inundate all Asia, like an enormous ocean.[11] It is remarkable that in both cases the Chaldeans correctly interpreted these water dreams as birth dreams. In all probability, these dreams themselves are constructed out of the knowledge of a very ancient and universally understood symbolism, with a dim foresight of the relations and connections which are appreciated and presented in Freud's teachings. There he says, in referring to a dream in which the dreamer hurls herself into the dark water of a lake: Dreams of this sort are birth dreams, and their interpretation is accomplished by reversing the fact as communicated in the manifest dream; namely, instead of hurling oneself into the water, it means emerging from the water, i.e., to be born.[12] The justice of this interpretation, which renders the water dream equivalent to the exposure, is again confirmed by the fact that precisely in the Cyrus saga, which contains the water dream, the theme of the exposure in the water is lacking, while only the basket, which does not occur in the dream, plays a part in the exposure.

In this interpretation of the exposure as the birth, we must not let ourselves be disturbed by the discrepancy between the succession of the individual elements of the symbolized materialization and the real birth process. This chronological rearrangement or even reversal has been explained by Freud as due to the general manner in which recollections are elaborated into fantasies; the same material reappears in the fantasies, but in an entirely novel arrangement, and no attention whatsoever is paid to the natural sequence of the acts.[13]

Besides this chronological reversal, the reversal of the contents requires special explanation. The first reason for the representation of the birth by its opposite—the life-threatening exposure in the water—is the accentuation of the parental hostility toward the future hero.[14] The creative influence of this tendency to represent the parents as the first and most powerful opponents of the hero will be appreciated when it is kept in mind that the entire family romance in general owes its origin to the feeling of being neglected—namely, the assumed hostility of the parents. In the myth, this hostility goes so far that the parents refuse to let the child be born, which is precisely the reason of the hero's lament; moreover, the myth plainly reveals the desire to enforce his materialization even against the will of the parents. The vital peril, thus concealed in the representation of birth through exposure, actually exists in the process of birth itself. The overcoming of all these obstacles also expresses the idea that the future hero has actually overcome the greatest difficulties by virtue of his birth, for he has victoriously thwarted all attempts to prevent it.[15] Or another interpretation may be admitted, according to which the youthful hero, foreseeing his destiny to taste more than his share of the bitterness of life, deplores in a pessimistic mood the inimical act which has called him to earth. He accuses the parents, as it were, for having exposed him to the struggle of life, for having allowed him to be born.[16] The refusal to let the son be born, which belongs especially to the father, is frequently concealed by the contrast motif, the wish for a child (as in Oedipus, Perseus, and others), while the hostile attitude toward the future successor on the throne and in the kingdom is projected to the outside—it is attributed to an oracular verdict, which is thereby revealed as the substitute of the ominous dream, or better, as the equivalent of its interpretation.

From another point of view, however, the family romance shows that the fantasies of the child, although apparently estranging the parents, have nothing else to say concerning them besides their confirmation as the real parents. The exposure myth, translated with the assistance of symbolism, likewise contains nothing but the assurance: this is my mother, who has borne me at the command of the father. But on account of the tendency of the myth, and the resulting transference of the hostile attitude from the child to the parents, this assurance of the real parentage can only be expressed as the repudiation of such parentage.

On closer inspection, it is noteworthy in the first place that the hostile attitude of the hero toward his parents concerns especially the father. Usually, as in the myth of Oedipus, Paris, and others, the royal father receives a prophecy of some disaster, threatening him through the expected son; then it is the father who causes the exposure of the boy and who pursues and menaces him in all sorts of ways after his unlooked-for rescue, but finally succumbs to his son, according to the prophecy. In order to understand this trait, which at first may appear somewhat startling, it is not necessary to explore the heavens for some process into which this trait might be laboriously fitted. Looking with open eyes and unprejudiced minds at the relations between parents and children, or between brothers, as these exist in reality,[17] a certain tension is frequently, if not regularly revealed between father and son, or still more distinctly a competition between brothers. Although this tension may not be obvious and permanent, it is lurking in the sphere of the unconscious, as it were, with periodic eruptions. Erotic factors are especially apt to be involved, and as a rule the deepest, generally unconscious root of the dislike of the son for the father, or of two brothers for each other, is related to be competition for the tender devotion and love of the mother. The Oedipus myth shows plainly, only in grosser dimensions, the accuracy of this interpretation, for the parricide is here followed by the incest with the mother. This erotic relation with the mother, which predominates in other mythological cycles, is relegated to the background in the myths of the birth of the hero, while the opposition against the father is more strongly accentuated.[18]

The fact that this infantile rebellion against the father is apparently provoked in the birth myths by the hostile behavior of the father, is due to a reversal of the relation, known as *projection*, which is brought about by very peculiar characteristics of the myth-forming psychic activity. The projection mechanism—which also bore its part in the re-interpretation of the birth act, as well as certain other characteristics of myth formation, to be discussed presently—necessitates the uniform characterization of the myth as a *paranoid* structure, in view of its resemblance to peculiar processes in the mechanism of certain psychic disturbances. Intimately connected with the paranoid character is the property of separating or dissociating what is fused in the imagination. This process, as illustrated by the two parent-couples, provides the foundation for the myth formation, and together with the projection mechanism supplies the key to the understanding of an entire series of otherwise inexplicable configurations of the myth. As the motor power for this projection of the hero's hostile attitude onto the father, there stands revealed the wish for its justification, arising from the troublesome realization of these feelings against the father. The displacement process that begins with the projection of the troublesome sensation is still further continued, however, and with the assistance of the mechanism of separation or dissociation, it has found a different expression of its gradual progress in very characteristic forms of the hero myth. In the original psychologic setting, the father is still identical with the king, the tyrannical persecutor. The first attenuation of this relation is manifested in those myths in which the separation of the tyrannical persecutor from the real father is already attempted, but not yet entirely accomplished, the former being still related to the hero, usually as his grandfather, for example in the Cyrus myth with all its versions, and in the majority of all hero myths in general. In the separation of the father's part from that of the king, this type signifies the first return step of the descent fantasy toward the actual conditions, and accordingly the hero's father appears in this type mostly as a lowly man (see Cyrus, Gilgamesh, and others). The hero thus arrives again at an approach toward his parents, the establishment of a certain kinship, which finds its expression in the fact that not only the hero himself, but also his father and his mother represent objects of the tyrant's persecution. The hero in this way acquires a more intimate connection with the mother—they are often exposed together (Perseus, Telephus, Feridun)—who is nearer to him on account of the erotic relation; while the renouncement of his hatred against the father here attains the expression of its most forcible reaction,[19] for the hero henceforth appears, as in the Hamlet saga, not as the persecutor of his father (or grandfather) but as the avenger of the persecuted father. This involves a deeper relation of the Hamlet saga with the Persian story of Kaikhosrav, where the hero likewise appears as the avenger of his murdered father (compare Feridun and others).

The person of the grandfather himself, who in certain sagas appears replaced by other relatives (the uncle, in the Hamlet saga), also possesses a deeper meaning.[20] The myth complex of the incest with the mother—and the related revolt against the father—is here combined with the second great complex, which has for its contents the erotic relations between father and daughter. Under this heading belongs, besides other widely ramified groups of sagas,[21] the story which is told in countless versions of a *newborn boy*, of whom it is *prophesied* that he is to become the *son-in-law* and *heir* of a certain ruler or potentate, and who finally does so in spite of all persecutions (exposure and so forth) on the part of the latter.[22] The father who refuses to give his daughter to any of her suitors, or who attaches to the winning of the daughter certain conditions difficult of fulfillment, does this because he really begrudges her to all others, for when all is told he wishes to possess her himself. He locks her up in some inaccessible spot, so as to safeguard her virginity (Perseus, Gilgamesh, Telephus, Romulus), and when his command is disobeyed he pursues the daughter and her offspring with insatiable hatred. However, the unconscious sexual motives of his hostile attitude, which is later on avenged by his grandson, render it evident that again the hero kills in him simply the man who is trying to rob him of the love of his mother; namely, the father.

Another attempt at a reversal to a more original type consists in the following theme: The return to the lowly father, which has been brought about through the separation of the father's rôle from that of the king, is again nullified through the lowly father's secondary elevation to the rank of a god, as in Perseus and the other sons of virgin mothers (Karna, Ion, Romulus, Jesus). The secondary character of this godly paternity is especially evident in those myths where the virgin who has been impregnated by divine conception later on marries a mortal (Jesus, Karna, Ion), who then appears as the real father, while the god as the father represents merely the most exalted childish idea of the magnitude, power, and perfection of the father.[23] At the same time, these myths strictly insist upon the motif of the virginity of the mother, which elsewhere is merely hinted at. The first impetus is perhaps supplied by the transcendental tendency, necessitated through the introduction of the god. At the same time, the birth from the virgin is the most abrupt repudiation of the father, the consummation of the entire myth, as illustrated by the Sargon legend, which does not admit any father besides the vestal mother.

The last stage of this progressive attenuation of the hostile relation to the father is represented by that form of the myth in which the person of the royal persecutor not only appears entirely detached from that of the father, but has even lost the remotest kinship with the hero's family, which he opposes in the most hostile manner, as its enemy (in Feridun, Abraham, King Herod against Jesus, and others). Although of his original threefold character as the father, the king, and the persecutor, he retains only the part of the royal persecutor or the tyrant, the entire plan of the myth conveys the impression that nothing had been changed—as if the designation "father" had been simply replaced by the term "tyrant." This interpretation of the father as a "tyrant," which is typical of the infantile ideation,[24] will be found later on to possess the greatest importance for the interpretation of certain abnormal constellations of this complex.

The prototype of this identification of the king with the father, which regularly recurs also in the dreams of adults, presumably is the origin of royalty from the patriarchate in the family, which is still attested by the use of identical words for king and father, in the Indo-Germanic languages (compare the German *Landesvater*, "father of his country," = king).[25] The reversal of the family romance to actual conditions is almost entirely accomplished in this type of myth. The lowly parents are acknowledged with a frankness which seems to be directly contradictory to the tendency of the entire myth.

Precisely this revelation of the real conditions, which hitherto had to be left to the interpretation, enables us to prove the accuracy of the latter from the material itself. The biblical legend of Moses has been selected as especially well adapted to this purpose.

Briefly summarizing the outcome of the previous interpretation-mechanism, to make matters plainer, we find the two parent-couples to be identical, after their splitting into the personalities of the father and the tyrannical persecutor has been connected—the highborn parents are the echo, as it were, of the exaggerated notions the child originally habored concerning his parents. The Moses legend actually shows the parents of the hero divested of all prominent attributes; they are simple people, devotedly attached to the child, and incapable of harming him. Meanwhile, the assertion of tender feelings for the child is a confirmation, here as well as everywhere, of the bodily parentage (compare the overseer in the Gilgamesh legend, the charioteer in the story of Karna, the fisherman in the Perseus myth, etc.). The amicable utilization of the exposure motif, which occurs in this type of myth, is referable to such a relationship. The child is surrendered in a basket to the water, but not with the object of killing him (as, for example, the hostile exposure of Oedipus and many other heroes), but for the purpose of saving him (compare also Abraham's early history, page 17). The danger-fraught warning to the exalted father becomes a hopeful prophecy for the lowly father—compare, in the birth story of Jesus, the oracle for Herod and Joseph's dream)—entirely corresponding to the expectations placed by most parents in the career of their offspring.

Retaining from the original tendency of the romance the fact that Pharaoh's daughter drew the child from the water, i.e., gave it birth, the outcome is the familiar theme (grandfather type) of the king whose daughter is to bear a son, but who, on being warned by the ill-omened interpretation of a dream, resolves to kill his forthcoming grandson. The handmaiden of his daughter (who in the biblical story draws the box from the water at the behest of the princess) is charged by the king with the exposure of the newborn child in a box, in the waters of the river Nile, that it may perish (the exposure motif, from the viewpoint of the highborn parents, here appearing in its original

"For a while everything was fine. Humanity grew and evolved, and space was within reach. Then, suddenly, space came to them. Hidden behind one of the bigger dots spread through the universe was a large chunk of rock. Because humans are such curious beings, they wanted to study it. It was then that they realized that the rock was getting closer and closer to their blue dot. At first, the humans were afraid. They knew what would happen if that rock hit their dot: their dot would be lost. That was when humans realized just how much Earth meant to them. Earth wasn't just a dot on the canvas of the universe. Earth was home, and home meant everything to humanity.

"So humanity came together, putting aside silly things like borders and race, and fought for their home. The brightest minds came together, and laid out a plan. They called for a group of brave souls to volunteer, and take flight up into space. Hundreds of people volunteered for the home they held so dear to their hearts, but ten were chosen. Those ten brave humans went up to space and did what now seems unthinkable: they placed their ship in the path of the asteroid speeding toward the planet, sacrificing themselves not just for their loved ones, but for all of humanity. Back on Earth, everyone looked up at the sky, praying for the brave souls that were giving everything for them, but they ultimately knew what would happen. They gazed at the sky breathlessly as the sky lit up in a rainbow of colors. The ten brave souls were lost, but Earth—home—was safe.

"Humanity continued to grow, to explore, and expand. They flew amongst the stars and discovered the mysteries that the universe had in store for them. But their little blue dot would always be their cherished home."

Another red streak flies across the sky, and I look back down towards Ethan. He stares at the sky, his eyes filled with tears.

"That's a happy story," Ethan whispers.

"Yeah."

"I wish it could be real."

"Yeah."

The sound of our voices doesn't go beyond our little table, but it still feels way too loud.

"It's darker now. How long?"

disastrous significance). The box with the child is then found by lowly people, and the poor woman raises the child (as his wet nurse); when he is grown up, he is recognized by the princess as her son. Just as in the prototype, the fantasy concludes with the recognition by the high-born parents.

If the Moses legend were placed before us in this more original form, as we have reconstructed it from the existing material,[26] the sum of this interpretation-mechanism would be approximately what is told in the myth as it is actually transmitted—namely, that his true mother was not a princess, but the poor woman who was introduced as his nurse, her husband being his father.

This interpretation is offered as the tradition, in the reconverted myth; and the fact that this tracing of the progressive mutation furnishes the familiar type of hero myth, is the proof of the correctness of our interpretation.

It has thus been our good fortune to show the full accuracy of our interpretative technique through the material itself, and it is now time to demonstrate the tenability of the general viewpoint upon which this entire technique is founded. Hitherto, the results of our interpretation have created the appearance that the entire myth formation started from the hero himself, that is, from the youthful hero. At the start we took this attitude in analogizing the hero of the myth with the ego of the child. Now we find ourselves confronted with the obligation to harmonize these assumptions and conclusions with the other conceptions of myth formation, which they seem to contradict directly.

The myths are certainly not constructed by the hero, least of all by the child hero, but they have long been known to be the product of a people of adults. The impetus is evidently supplied by the popular amazement at the apparition of the hero, whose extraordinary life history the people can only imagine as ushered in by a wonderful infancy. This extraordinary childhood of the hero, however, is constructed by the individual myth-makers—to whom the indefinite idea of the folk-mind must be ultimately traced—from the consciousness of their own infancy. In investing the hero with their own infantile history, they identify themselves with him, as it were, claiming to have been similar heroes in their own personality. The true hero of the romance is, therefore, the ego, which finds itself in the hero, by reverting to the time when the ego was itself a hero, through its first heroic act, i.e., the revolt against the father. The ego can only find its own heroism in the days of infancy, and it is therefore obliged to invest the hero with its own revolt, crediting him with the features which made the ego a hero. This object is achieved with infantile motives and materials, in reverting to the infantile romance and transferring it to the hero. Myths are, therefore, created by adults, by means of retrograde childhood fantasies,[27] the hero being credited with the mythmaker's personal infantile history. Meanwhile, the tendency of this entire process is the excuse of the individual units of the people for their own infantile revolt against the father.

Besides the excuse of the hero for his rebellion, the myth therefore contains also the excuse of the individual for his revolt against the father. This revolt has burdened him since his childhood, as he has failed to become a hero. He is now enabled to excuse himself by emphasizing that the father has given him grounds for his hostility. The affectionate feeling for the father is also manifested in the same fiction, as has been shown above. These myths have therefore sprung from two opposite motives, both of which are subordinate to the motive of vindication of the individual through the hero: on the one hand the motive of affection and gratitude toward the parents; and on the other hand, the motive of the revolt against the father. It is not stated outright in these myths, however, that the conflict with the father arises from the sexual rivalry for the mother, but is apparently suggested that this conflict dates back primarily to the concealment of the sexual processes (at childbirth), which in this way became an enigma for the child. This enigma finds its temporary and symbolical solution in the infantile sexual theory of the basket and the water.[28]

The profound participation of the incest motif in myth formation is discussed in the author's special investigation of the Lohengrin saga, which belongs to the myth of the birth of the hero. The cyclic character of the Lohengrin saga is referred by him to the *fantasy of being one's own son*, as revealed by Freud.[29] This accounts for the identity of father and son, in certain myths, and for the repetition of their careers; it explains the fact that the hero is sometimes not exposed until he has reached maturity, and also the intimate connection between birth and death in the exposure motif.[30] Jung, who regards the typical fate of the hero as the portrayal of the human libido and its typical vicissitudes, has made this theme the pivot of his interpretation, as the fantasy of being born again, to which the incest motif is subordinated. Not only the birth of the hero, which takes place under peculiar symbolic circumstances, but also the motif of the two mothers of the hero, are explained by Jung through the birth of the hero taking place under the mysterious ceremonials of a rebirth from the mother consort.[31]

Having thus outlined the contents of the birth myth of the hero it still remains for us to point out certain complications within the birth myth itself, which have been explained on the basis of its paranoid character, as "splits" of the personality of the royal father and persecutor. In some myths, however, and especially in the fairy tales that belong to this group,[32] the multiplication of mythical personages—and with them, of course, the multiplication of motifs, or even of entire stories—are carried so far that sometimes the original features are altogether overgrown by these addenda. The multiplication is so variegated and so exuberantly developed that the mechanism of the analysis no longer does it justice. Moreover, the new personalities here do not show the same independence, as it were, as the new personalities created by splitting, but they rather present the characteristics of a copy, a duplicate, or a "double," which is the proper mythological term. An apparently very complicated example, namely, Herodotus' version of the Cyrus saga, illustrates that there doubles are not inserted purely for ornamentation, or to give a semblance of historical veracity, but that they are insolubly connected with myth formation and its tendency. Also, in the Cyrus legend, as in the other myths, a confrontation occurs. The royal grandfather, Astyages, and his daughter, with her husband, are confronted by the cattle herder and his wife. A checkered gathering of other personalities which move around them, are readily grouped at sight: Between the highborn parent-couple and their child stand the administrator Harpagos with his wife and his son, and the noble Artembares with his legitimate offspring. Our trained sense for the peculiarities of myth structure recognizes at once the doubles of the parents in the intermediate parent-couples and all the participants are seen to be identical personalities of the parents and their child; this interpretation being suggested by certain features of the myth itself. Harpagos receives the child from the king, to expose it; he therefore acts precisely like the royal father and remains true to his fictitious parental part in his reluctance to kill the child himself—because it is related to him—but he delivers it instead to the herder Mithradates, who is thus again identified with Harpagos. The noble Artembares, whose son Cyrus causes to be whipped, is also identified with Harpagos; for when Artembares with his whipped boy stands before the king, to demand retribution, Harpagos at once is likewise seen standing before the king, to defend himself, and he also is obliged to present his son to the king. Then Artembares himself plays an episodal part as the hero's father, and this is fully confirmed by the Ctesian version, which tells us that the nobleman who adopted the herder's son, Cyrus, as his own son, was named Artembares.

Even more distinct than the identity of the different fathers is that of their children, which of course serves to confirm the identity of the fathers. In the first place, and this would seem to be conclusive, *the children are all of the same age*—not only the son of the princess, and the child of the herder, who are born at the same time; but Herodotus specially emphasizes that Cyrus played the game of "Kings" (in which he caused the son of Artembares to be whipped) with boys of the same age as Cyrus. He also points out, perhaps intentionally, that the *son of Harpagos*, destined to become the playmate of Cyrus, whom the king had recognized, was likewise apparently of the same age as Cyrus. Furthermore, the remains of this boy are placed before his father, Harpagos, in a basket; it was also a basket in which the newborn Cyrus was to have been exposed, and this actually happened to his substitute, the herder's son, whose identity with Cyrus is obvious and tangible in the version of Justin given on page 36. In this report, Cyrus is actually exchanged with the *living* child of the herder; but this paradoxical parental feeling is reconciled by the consciousness that in reality nothing at all has been altered by this exchange. It appears more intelligible, of course, that the herder's wife should wish to raise the living child of the king, instead of her own *stillborn* boy, as in the Herodotus version (page 24); but here the identity of the boys is again evident, for just as the herder's son suffered death instead of Cyrus in the past, twelve years later the son of Harpagos (also in a basket) is killed directly for Cyrus, whom Harpagos had allowed to live.[33]

The impression is thereby conveyed that all the multiplications of Cyrus, after having been created for a certain purpose, are again removed, as disturbing elements, once this purpose has been fulfilled. This purpose is undoubtedly the exalting tendency that is inherent in the family romance. The hero, in the various duplications of himself and his parents, ascends the social scale from the herder Mithradates, by way of the noble Artembares (who is high in the king's favor), and of the first administrator Harpagos (who is personally related to the king)—until he has himself become a prince; so his career is shown in the Ctesian version, where Cyrus advances from the herder's son to the king's administrator.[34] In this way, he constantly removes, as it were, the last traces of his ascent, the lower Cyrus being discarded after absolving the different stages of his career.[35]

This complicated myth with its promiscuous array of personages is thus simplified and reduced to three actors—the hero and his parents. Entirely similar conditions prevail in regard to the "cast" of many other myths. For example, the duplication may concern the daughter, as in the Moses myth, in which the princess-mother (in order to establish the identity of the two families)[36] appears among the poor people as the daughter Miriam, who is merely a split of the mother, the latter appearing divided into the princess and the poor woman. In case the duplication concerns the father, his doubles appear as a rule in the part of relatives, more particularly as his brother, as for example in the Hamlet saga, in distinction from the foreign personages created by the analysis. In a similar way, the grandfather, who is taking the place of the father, may also appear complemented by a brother, who is the hero's granduncle, and as such his opponent, as in the myths of Romulus, Perseus, and others. Other duplications, in apparently complicated mythological structures—as for example in Kaikhosrav, Feridun, and others—are easily recognized when envisaged from this angle.

The duplication of the fathers (or the grandfathers) by a brother may be continued in the next generation, and concern the hero himself, thus leading to the *brother myths*, which can only be hinted at in connection with the present theme. The prototypes of the boy (who in the Cyrus saga vanish into thin air after they have served their purpose, the exaltation of the hero's descent), if they were to assume a vitality of their own, would come to confront the hero as competitors with equal rights, namely, as his brothers. The original sequence is probably better preserved through the interpretation of the hero's strange doubles as shadowy brothers who, like the twin brother, must die for the hero's sake. Not only the father (who is in the way of the maturing son) is removed, but also the interfering competitor (the brother), in a naïve realization of the childish fantasies, for the simple reason that the hero does not want a family.

The complications of the hero legends with other myth cycles include (besides the myth of the hostile brothers, which has already been disposed of) also the actual incest myth, such as forms the nucleus of the Oedipus saga. The mother, and her relation to the hero, appear relegated to the background in the myth of the birth of the hero. But there is another conspicuous motif: the lowly mother is so often represented by an animal. This motif of the helpful animals[37] belongs in part to a series of foreign elements, the explanation of which would far exceed the scope of this essay.[38]

The animal motif may be fitted into the sequence of our interpretation, on the basis of the following reflections. Much as the projection onto the father justifies the hostile attitude on the part of the son, so the lowering of the mother into an animal is likewise meant to vindicate the ingratitude of the son who denies her. As the persecuting king is detached from the father, so the elusive rôle of wet nurse assigned to the mother—in this substitution by an animal—goes back to the separation of the mother into the parts of the child-bearer and the suckler. This cleavage is again subservient to the exalting tendency, in so far as the childbearing part is reserved for the highborn mother, whereas the lowly woman, who cannot be eradicated from the early history, must content herself with the function of nurse. Animals are especially appropriate substitutes, because the sexual processes are here plainly evident also to the child, while the concealment of these processes is presumably the root of the childish revolt against the parents. The exposure in the box and in the water asexualizes the birth process, as it were, in a child-like fashion; the children are fished out of the water by the stork, who takes them to the parents in a basket.[39] The animal fable improves upon this idea, by emphasizing the similarity between human birth and animal birth.

This introduction of the motif may possibly be interpreted from the parodistic point of view if we assume that the child accepts the story of the stork from his parents, feigning ignorance, but adding superciliously: If an animal has brought me, it may also have nursed me.[40]

When all is said and done, however, and when the cleavage is followed back, the separation of the childbearer from the suckler—which really endeavors to remove the bodily mother entirely, by means of her substitution through an animal or a strange nurse—does not express anything beyond the fact: The woman who has suckled me is my mother. This statement is found directly symbolized in the Moses legend, the retrogressive character of which we have already studied; for precisely the woman who is his own mother is chosen to be his nurse (similarly also in the myth of Hercules, and the Egyptian-Phoenician Osiris-Adonis myth—where Osiris, encased in a chest, floats down the river and is finally found under the name Adonis, by Isis, who is installed by Queen Astarte as the nurse of her own son).[41]

Only a brief reference can here be made to other motifs which seem to be more loosely related to the entire myth. Such themes include that of playing the fool, which is suggested in animal fables as the universal childish attitude toward grownups. They include, furthermore, the physical defects of certain heroes (Zal, Oedipus, Hephaestus), which are meant perhaps to serve for the vindication of individual imperfections, in such a way that the reproaches of the father for possible defects or shortcomings are incorporated into the myth, with the appropriate accentuation—the hero being endowed with the same weakness which burdens the self-respect of the individual.

This explanation of the psychological significance of the myth of the birth of the hero would not be complete without emphasizing its relations to certain mental diseases. Even readers without psychiatric training—or these perhaps more than any others—must have been struck with these relations. As a matter of fact, the hero myths are equivalent in many essential features to the delusional ideas of certain psychotic individuals who suffer from delusions of persecution and grandeur—the so-called paranoiacs. Their system of delusions is constructed very much like the hero myth, and therefore indicates the same psychogenic themes as the neurotic family romance, which is analyzable, whereas the system of delusions is inaccessible even for psychoanalytical approaches. For example, the paranoiac is apt to claim that the people whose name he bears are not his real parents, but that he is actually the son of a princely personage; he was to be removed for some mysterious reason, and was therefore surrendered to his "parents" as a foster child. His enemies, however, wish to maintain the fiction that he is of lowly descent, in order to suppress his legitimate claims to the crown or to enormous riches.[42] Cases of this kind often occupy alienists or tribunals.[43]

This intimate relationship between the hero myth and the delusional structure of paranoiacs has already been definitely established through the characterization of the myth as a paranoid structure, which is here confirmed by its contents. The remarkable fact that paranoiacs will frankly reveal their entire romance has ceased to be puzzling, since the profound investigations of Freud have shown that the contents of hysterical fantasies, which can often be made conscious through analysis, are identical up to the minutest details with the complaints of persecuted paranoiacs; moreover, the identical contents are also encountered as a reality in the arrangements of perverts for the gratification of their desires.[44]

The egotistical character of the entire system is distinctly revealed by the paranoiac, for whom the exaltation of the parents, as brought about by him, is merely the means for his own exaltation. As a rule the pivot for his entire system is simply the culmination of the family romance, in the apodictic statement: I am the emperor (or god). Reasoning in the symbolism of dreams and myths—which is also the symbolism of all fancies, including the "morbid" power of imagination—all he accomplishes thereby is to put himself in the place of the father, just as the hero terminates his revolt against the father. This can be done in both instances, because the conflict with the father—which dates back to the concealment of the sexual processes, as suggested by the latest discoveries—is nullified at the instant when the grown boy himself becomes a father. The persistence with which the paranoiac puts himself in the father's place, i.e., becomes a father himself, appears like an illustration to the common answers of little boys to a scolding or a putting off of their inquisitive curiosity: You just wait until I am a papa myself, and I'll know all about it!

Besides the paranoiac, his equally asocial counterpart must also be emphasized. In the expression of the identical fantasy contents, the hysterical individual, who has suppressed them, is offset by the pervert, who realizes them; and just so the diseased and passive paranoiac—who needs his delusion for the correction of the actuality, which to him is intolerable—is offset by the active criminal, who endeavors to change the actuality according to his mind. In this special sense, this type is represented by the anarchist. The hero himself, as shown by his detachment from the parents, begins his career in opposition to the older generation; he is at once a rebel, a renovator, and a revolutionary. However, every revolutionary is originally a disobedient son, a rebel against the father.[45] (Compare the suggestion of Freud, in connection with the interpretation of a "revolutionary dream.")[46]

But whereas the paranoiac, in conformity with his passive character, has to suffer persecutions and wrongs which ultimately proceed from the father—and which he endeavors to escape by putting himself in the place of the father or the emperor—the anarchist complies more faithfully with the heroic character, by promptly himself becoming the persecutor of kings, and finally killing the king, precisely like the hero. The remarkable similarity between the career of certain anarchistic criminals and the family romance of hero and child has been elsewhere illustrated by the author, through special instances.[47] The truly heroic element then consists only in the real justice or even necessity of the act, which is therefore generally endorsed and admired;[48] while the morbid trait, also in criminal cases, is the pathologic transference of the hatred from the father to the real king, or several kings, when more general and still more distorted.

As the hero is commended for the same deed, without asking for its psychic motivation, so the anarchist might claim indulgence from the severest penalties, for the reason that he has killed an entirely different person from the one he really intended to destroy, in spite of an apparently excellent (perhaps political) motivation of his act.[49]

For the present let us stop at the narrow boundary line where the contents of innocent infantile imaginings, suppressed and unconscious neurotic fantasies, poetical myth structures, and certain forms of mental disease and crime lie close together, although far apart as to their causes and dynamic forces. We resist the temptation to follow one of these divergent paths that lead to altogether different realms, but which are as yet unblazed trails in the wilderness.

Notes

1. The possibility of further specification of separate items of this outline will be seen from the compilation given by Lessmann at the conclusion of his "*Die Kyrossage in Europe*" (loc. cit.).

2. See also Wundt, who interprets the hero psychologically as a projection of human desires and aspirations (op. cit., p. 48).

3. Compare Freud: "Hysterical Fancies, and their Relation to Bisexuality," with references to the literature on this subject. The contribution is contained in the second series of *Sammlung kleiner Schriften zur Neurosenlehre* (Vienna and Leipzig, 1909).

4. For the idealizing of the parents by the children, compare Maeder's comments (*Jahrbuch für Psychoanalyse*, I (1909), p. 152, and *Zentralblatt für Psychoanalyse*, I, p. 51) on Varendonk's essay, "*Les idéals d'enfant.*"

5. *Interpretation of Dreams.*

6. Compare the "birth dreams" in Freud's *Interpretation of Dreams*, also the examples quoted by the author in *Die Lohengrin Saga* (Vienna, 1911), pp. 27 ff.

7. In fairy tales, which are adapted to infantile ideation, and especially to the infantile sexual theories (compare Freud in the December, 1908, number of *Sexuelle Probleme*), the birth of man is frequently represented as a lifting of the child from a well or a lake (Thimme, op. cit. p. 157). The story of "Dame Holle's Pond" (Grimm: *Deutsche Sagen*, Vol. I, p. 7) relates that the newborn children come from her well, whence she brings them forth. The same interpretation is apparently expressed in certain national rites; for example, when a Celt had reason to doubt his paternity, he placed the newborn child on a large shield and put it adrift in the nearest river. If the waves carried it ashore, it was considered as legitimate, but if the child drowned, this was proof of the contrary, and the mother was also put to death (see Franz Helbing: *History of Feminine Infidelity*). Additional ethnological material from folklore has been compiled by the author in *Die Lohengrin Saga*, pp. 20 ff.

8. The "box" in certain myths is represented by the *cave*, which also distinctly symbolizes the womb; aside from statements in Abraham, Ion, and others, a noteworthy case is that of Zeus, who is born in a cave on Mount Ida and nourished by the goat Amalthea, his mother concealing him for fear of her husband, the Titan Cronus. According to Homer's *Iliad* (XVIII, 396 ff.), Hephaestus is also cast into the water by his mother, on account of his lameness, and remains hidden for nine years in a cave surrounded by water. By exchanging the reversal, the birth (the fall into the water) is here plainly represented as the termination of the nine months of the intra-uterine life. More common than the cave birth is the exposure in a box, which is likewise told in the Babylonian Marduk-Tammuz myth, as well as in the Egyptian-Phoenician Osiris-Adonis myth (compare Winckler: *Die Weltanschauung des alten Orients*, *Ex Oriente Lux*, Vol. I., p. 43; and Jeremias, *Die Babylonisches* . . . , p. 41). Bacchus, according to Pausanius (III, 24), is also removed from the persecution of the king through exposure in a chest on the Nile, and is saved at the age of three months by a king's daughter, which is remarkably suggestive of the Moses legend. A similar story is told of Tennes, the son of Cycnus (Siecke: "*Hermes* . . ." loc. cit., p. 48) and of many others.

The occurrence of the same symbolic representation among the aborigines is illustrated by the following examples: Stucken (op. cit.) relates the New Zealand tale of the Polynesian Fire (and Seed) Robber, Mani-tiki-tiki, who is exposed directly after his birth, his mother throwing him into the sea, wrapped in an apron (chest, box). A similar story is reported by Frobenius (op. cit., p. 379) from the Betsimisaraka of Madagascar, where the child is people sitting here. Waiting, just waiting. I'm still as stunned as I was yesterday. I don't really know what I was expecting when I first heard the news, but this calm acceptance hadn't been it.

They're probably thinking the same thing about me, what with me sitting here, chatting with a kid. I'm not accepting, though. I hate this. Every fiber of my being is telling me to stand up and rage. I want to rage and scream and curse. I want to shake these people and tell them to stand up and fight, to not give up. I want to do something, anything, that tells me that I'm still here. That I'm still standing. I want so much, and these ten minutes are killing me.

"Nick?"

I turn away from the people around me, and look at Ethan.

"Tell me a story?"

My eyes widen a little, and I stay still for a moment.

"A story?" I say. Ethan nods.

"A happy one."

"A happy story?" I say, thinking. "It will have to be a short one."

We look at the sky again as another deep crimson streak crosses over us.

"I know," Ethan says, and there's no hiding the tears in his eyes.

I close my own for a moment, but only for a moment. I can't waste time.

"All right, a happy short story," I say. I take a deep breath while keeping my eyes on the sky—it's getting darker by the second.

"There once was a small blue dot. It was surrounded by millions of other dots, some smaller, but most of them larger, in various colors. All of these dots were special in their own way, but this small blue dot held a secret. This dot was actually a planet called Earth, and on it lived a race called humans. As far as species go, humans were young—barely out of their infancy—but they had something that made them strive. They were curious. They always wanted to know what would come next. They always wanted to go one step further, and the final frontier was space. The human race dreamed of flying amongst the stars, of leaving behind their little blue dot and discovering what mysteries the universe had in store for them. And humans, driven by their curiosity, did just that.

exposed on the water, is found and raised by a rich, childless woman, but finally resolves to discover his actual parents. According to a report of Bab (*Zeitschrift für Ethnologie*, 1906, p. 281), the wife of the Raja Besurjay was presented with a child floating on a bubble of water-foam (from Singapore).

9. Compare Freud: *Interpretation of Dreams.*

10. Abraham (op. cit. pp. 22–3) contains the analysis of a very similar although more complicated birth dream, corresponding to the actual conditions: the dreamer, a young pregnant woman awaiting her delivery, not without fear, dreamed of the birth of her son, and the water appeared directly as the amniotic fluid.

11. This fantasy of an enormous water is extremely suggestive of the large and widespread group of the flood myths, which actually seem to be no more than the universal expression of the exposure myth. The hero is here represented by humanity at large. The wrathful father is the god; the destruction and the rescue of humanity follow each other in immediate succession. In this parallelization, it is of interest to note that the ark, or pitched house, in which Noah floats upon the water is designated in the Old Testament by the same word (*tebah*) is the receptacle in which the infant Moses is exposed (Jeremias: *The Old Testament* . . . , p. 250). For the motif of the great flood, compare Jeremias, p. 226, and Lessmann, at the close of his treatise, "*Die Kyrossage* . . . ," loc. cit., where the flood is described as a possible digression of the exposure in the water. A transition instance is illustrated by the flood saga told by Bader, in his Baden folk legends: When the Sunken Valley was inundated once upon a time by a cloudburst, a little boy was seen floating upon the waters in a cradle, and was miraculously saved by a cat (Gustav Friedrich, op. cit., p. 265).

Translator's note: The author has endeavored to explain the psychological relations of the exposure myth, the flood legend, and the devouring myth in his article on the "Overlying Symbols in Dreams Awakening, and Their Recurrence in Mythical Ideation"—"*Die Symbolschichtung in Wecktraum und ihre Wiederkehr im mythischen Denken,*" *Jahrbuch für Psychoanalyse*, V (1912).

12. *Interpretation of Dreams.* Compare the same reversal of the meanings in Winckler's interpretation of the etymology of the name of Moses, on page 16, footnote 7.

13. The same conditions remain in the formation of dreams and in the transformation of hysterical fantasies into seizures. See p. 238 (and the annotation on that page) of Freud's *Traumdeutung* (the German edition of *Interpretation of Dreams*); see also his "*Allgemeines über den hysterischen Anfall* ("Gen-

eral Remarks on Hysterical Seizures") in *Sammlung kleiner Schriften* . . . , 2d series, pp. 146 ff.

14. According to a pointed remark of Jung's, this reversal in its further mythical sublimation permits the approximation of the hero's life to the solar cycle. Carl G. Jung: *"Wandlungen und Symbole der Libido,"* *Jahrbuch für Psychoanalyse,* V (1912), p. 253.

15. The second item of the schedule here enters into consideration: the voluntary continence or prolonged separation of the parents, which naturally induces the miraculous conception and virgin birth of the mother. The abortion fantasies, which are especially distinct in the Zoroaster legend, also belong under this heading.

16. The comparison of birth with a shipwreck, by the Roman poet Lucretius, seems to be in perfect harmony with this symbolism: "Behold the infant: Like a shipwrecked sailor, cast ashore by the fury of the billows, the poor child lies naked on the ground, bereft of all means for existence, after Nature has dragged him in pain from the mother's womb. With plaintive wailing he filleth the place of his birth, and he is right, for many evils await him in life" (*De Natura Rerum,* V, 222–7). Similarly, the first version of Schiller's *Robbers,* in speaking of Nature, says: "She endowed us with the spirit of invention, when she exposed us naked and helpless on the shore of the great Ocean, the World. Let him swim who may, and let the clumsy perish!"

17. Compare the representation of this relation and its psychic consequences, in Freud's *Interpretation of Dreams.*

18. Some myths convey the impression that the love relation with the mother had been removed, as being too objectionable to the consciousness of certain periods or peoples. Traces of this suppression are still evident in a comparison of different myths or different versions of the same myth. For example, in the version of Herodotus, Cyrus is a son of the daughter of Astyages; but according to the report of Ctesias, he makes the daughter of Astyages, whom he conquers, his wife, and kills her husband (who in the rendering of Herodotus is his father). See Hüsing, op. cit. Also a comparison of the saga of Darab with the very similar legend of St. Gregory serves to show that in the Darab story the incest with the mother which otherwise precedes the recognition of the son is simply omitted; here, on the contrary, the recognition prevents the incest. This attenuation may be studied in the nascent state, as it were, in the myth of Telephus, where the hero is married to his mother but recognizes her before the consummation of the incest. The fairy-tale-like setting of the Tristan legend, which makes Isolde draw the little Tristan from

the water (i.e., give him birth), thereby suggests the fundamental incest theme, which is likewise manifested in the adultery with the wife of the uncle.

Translator's note: The reader is referred to *Inzestmotiv*, in which the incest theme, which is here merely mentioned, is discussed in detail, picking up the many threads which lead to this theme, but which have been dropped at the present time.

19. The mechanism of this defense is discussed in Freud's "Hamlet Analysis," in his *Interpretation of Dreams*. Ernest Jones has also discussed this is an article (1911) in the *American Journal of Psychology*.

20. In regard to further meanings of the grandfather, see Freud's "Analysis of a Phobia in a Five-Year-Old Boy," *Jahrbuch für Psychoanalyse*, I (1909); also the contributions of Jones, Abraham, and Ferenczi in the March, 1913, issue of *Internationale Zeitschrift für ärtzliche Psychoanalyse*.

21. See Chapter xi, *Inzestmotiv*.

22. Detailed literary references concerning the wide distribution of this story are found in R. Köhler: *Kleiner Schriften*, Vol. II, p. 357.

23. A similar identification of the father with God ("Heavenly Father," etc.) occurs, according to Freud, with the same regularity in the fantasies of normal and pathological psychic activity as the identification of the emperor with the father. It is also noteworthy in this connection that almost all peoples derive their origin from their god (Abraham, op. cit.).

24. An amusing example of unconscious humor in children recently appeared in the daily press: A politician had explained to his little son that a tyrant is a man who forces others to do what he commands, without heeding their wishes in the matter, "Well," said the child, "then you and Mama are also tyrants!"

25. See Max Müller, op. cit., pp. 20 ff. Concerning the various psychological contingencies of this setting, compare pp. 83 ff. of *Inzestmotiv*.

26. Compare Eduard Meyer: *"Die Mosessagen und die Lewiten,"* in *Sitzungsberichte der königlich preussischen Akademie der Wissenschaften*, XXXI (1905), p. 640: "Presumably Moses was originally the son of the tyrant's daughter (who is now his foster mother), and probably of divine origin." The subsequent elaboration into the present form is probably referable to national motives.

27. This idea, which is derived from the knowledge of the neurotic fantasy and symptom construction, was applied by Professor Freud to the interpretation of the romantic and mythical work of poetic imagination, in a lecture

entitled "Der Dichter und das Phantasieren" ("Poets and Imaginings"), reprinted in *Sammlung kleiner Schriften* . . . , 2d series.

28. For ethno-psychologic parallels and other infantile sexual theories which throw some light upon the supplementary myth of the hero's procreation, compare the author's treatise in *Zentralblatt für Psychoanalyse*, II (1911), pp. 392–425.

29. Rank: *Die Lohengrin Saga.*

30. Concerning the water as the "water of death," compare especially ibid., Chapter iv.

31. Loc. cit., p. 356.

32. The fairy tales, which have been left out of consideration in the context, precisely on account of these complications, include especially: "The Devil with the Three Golden Hairs" (Grimm, No. 29), and the very similar "Saga of Emperor Henry III" (Grimm, *Deutsche Sagen*, Vol. II, p. 177); "Water-Peter," with numerous variations (Grimm, Vol. III, p. 103); "Fundevogel," No. 51; "The Three Birdies" (No. 96); "The King of the Golden Mountain" (No. 92), with its parallels; as well as some foreign fairy tales, which are quoted by Bauer, at the end of his article (loc. cit.). Compare also, in Hahn: *Greek and Albanese Fairy Tales* (Leipzig, 1864), the review of the exposure stories and myths, especially No. 20 and No. 69.

33. A connection is here supplied with the theme of the twins, in which we seem to recognize the two boys born at the same time—one of which dies for the sake of the other, be it directly after birth, or later—and whose parents appear divided in our myths into two or more parent-couples. Concerning the probable significance of this shadowy twin brother as the afterbirth, compare the author's discussion in his *Inzestmotiv* (pp. 459 ff).

34. The early history of Sigurd, as it is related in the Völsungasaga (compare Rassmann, op. cit., Vol. I, p. 99), closely resembles the Ctesian version of the Cyrus saga, giving us the tradition of another hero's wonderful career, together with its rational rearrangement. For particulars, see Bauer, loc. cit., p. 554. Also the biblical history of Joseph (Exodus 37–50)—with the exposure, the animal sacrifice, the dreams, the sketchy brethren, and the fabulous career of this hero—seems to belong to this type of myth.

35. In order to avoid misunderstandings, it appears necessary to emphasize at this point the historical nucleus of certain hero myths. Cyrus, as is shown by the inscriptions which have been discovered (compare Duncker, op. cit., p. 289; and Bauer, loc. cit., p. 498) was descended from an old hereditary royal house. It could not be the object of the myth to elevate the descent of

Cyrus, nor must the above interpretation be regarded as an attempt to establish a lowly descent. Similar conditions prevail in the case of Sargon, whose royal father is also known (compare Jeremias: *The Old Testament* . . . , p. 410 *n.*). Nevertheless a historian writes about Sargon as follows (Ungnad: *"Die Anfänge der Staatenbildung in Babylonien,"* *Deutsche Rundschau,* July 1905): "He was evidently of noble descent, or no such saga could have been woven about his birth and his youth." It would be a gross error to consider our interpretation as an argument in this sense. Again, the apparent contradiction which might be held up against our explanation, under another mode of interpretation, becomes the proof of its correctness, through the reflection that it is not the hero but the average man who makes the myth and wishes to vindicate himself in it. The people imagine the hero in this manner, investing him with their own infantile fantasies, irrespective of their actual compatibility or incompatibility with historical facts. This also serves to explain the transference of the typical motifs, be it to several generations of the same hero-family, or be it to historical personalities in general (concerning Caesar, Augustus and others, compare Usener, *Rhein. Mus.,* LV, p. 271).

36. This identification of the families is carried through to the minutest detail in certain myths, as for example in the Oedipus myth, where one royal couple is offset by another, and where even the herdsman who receives the infant for exposure has his exact counterpart in the herdsman to whom he entrusts the rescue of the boy.

37. Compare Gubernatis: *Zoological Mythology* (London, 1872); and Hartmann: *Die Tiere in der indogermanischen Mythologie* (Leipzig, 1874). Concerning the significance of animals in exposure myths, see also the contributions by Bauer (loc. cit., pp. 574 ff.); Goldziher (op. cit., p. 274); and Liebrecht: *Zur Volkskunde, Romulus und die Welfen* (Heilbronn, 1879).

38. Compare Freud's article on the infantile recurrence of totemism, in *Imago,* Vol. II (1913). Concerning the totemistic foundation of the Roman she-wolf, see Jones's writings on nightmares (*Älptraume*). The woodpecker of the Romulus saga was discussed by Jung (loc. cit., pp. 382 ff.).

39. The stork is known also in mythology as the bringer of children. Siecke (*Liebesgeschichten des Himmels*, p. 26) points out the swan as the player of this part in certain regions and countries. The rescue and further protection of the hero by a bird is not uncommon; compare Gilgamesh, Zal, and Cycnus (who is exposed by his mother near the sea and is nourished by a swan, while his son Tennes floats in a chest upon the water). The interpretation of the leading motif of the Lohengrin saga also enters into present consideration. Its most important motifs belong to this mythical cycle: Lohengrin

floats in a skiff upon the water, and is brought ashore by a swan. No one may ask whence he has come; the sexual mystery of the origin of man must not be revealed, but it is replaced by the suggestion of the stork fable; the children are fished from the water by the swan and are taken to the parents in a box. Corresponding to the prohibition of all inquiries in the Lohengrin saga, we find in other myths (for example, the Oedipus myth), a *command to investigate,* or a riddle that must be *solved.* For the psychological significance of the stork fable, compare Freud: *Infantile Sexual Theories.* Concerning the hero myth, see also the author's *Die Lohengrin Saga.*

40. Compare Freud: "Analysis of a Phobia in a Five-Year-Old Boy," loc. cit.

41. Usener (*Stoff des griechischen Epos,* p. 53) says that the controversy between the earlier and the later Greek sagas concerning the mother of a divinity is usually reconciled by the formula that the mother of the general Greek saga is recognized as such, while the mother of the local tradition is lowered to the rank of a nurse. Thero may therefore be unhesitatingly regarded as the mother, not merely the nurse, of the god Ares.

42. Abraham, loc. cit., p. 40; Riklin, op. cit., p. 74.

43. Brief mention is made of a case concerning a Frau von Hervay, because of a few subtle psychological comments upon the same by A. Berger (*Feuilleton der Neue Freie Presse,* Nov. 6, 1904), which in part touch upon our interpretation of the hero myth. Berger writes as follows: "I am convinced that she seriously believes herself to be the illegitimate daughter of an aristocratic Russian lady. The desire to belong through birth to more distinguished and brilliant circles than her own surroundings probably dates back to her early years; and her wish to be a princess gave rise to the delusion that she was not the daughter of her parents, but the child of a noblewoman who had concealed her illegitimate offspring from the world by letting her grow up as the daughter of a sleight-of-hand man. Having once become entangled in these fancies, it was natural for her to interpret any harsh word that offended her, or any accidental ambiguous remark that she happened to hear, but especially her reluctance to be the daughter of this couple, as a confirmation of her romantic delusion. She therefore made it the task of her life to regain the social position of which she felt herself to have been defrauded. Her biography manifests the strenuous insistence upon this idea, with a tragic outcome."

The female type of the family romance, as it confronts us in this case from the asocial side, has also been transmitted as a hero myth in isolated instances. The story goes of the later Queen Semiramis (in Diodorus, II, 4) that her mother, the goddess Derceto, being ashamed of her, exposed the child in a barren and rocky land, where she was fed by doves and found by shepherds, who gave the infant to the overseer of the royal flocks, the childless Simnas, who raised her as his own daughter. He named her Semiramis, which meant "dove" in the ancient Syrian language. Her further career and autocratic rulership, thanks to her masculine energy, is a matter of "history."

Other exposure myths are told of Atalanta, Cybele, and Aërope (see Röscher, op. cit.).

44. Freud: *Three Contributions to the Theory of Sex*; also *Psychopathologie des Altagslebens*; and *Hysterische Phantasien und ihre Beziehung zur Bisexualität*.

45. This is especially evident in the myths of the Greek gods, where the son (Cronus, Zeus) must first remove the father, before he can enter upon his rulership. The form of the removal, namely through castration—obviously the strongest expression of the revolt against the father—is at the same time the proof of its sexual provenance. Concerning the revenge character of this castration, as well as the infantile significance of the entire complex, compare Freud: "Infantile Sexual Theories," and "Analysis of a Phobia in a Five-Year-Old Boy (loc. cit.).

46. Freud: *Tramdeutung* (German edition of *Interpretation of Dreams*), 2d edition, p. 153.

47. "*Belege zur Rettungsphantasie*," *Zentralblatt für Psychoanalyse*, I (1911), p. 331; also "*Die Rolle des Familienromans in der Psychologie des Attentäters*," *Internationale Zeitschrift für ärtzliche Psychoanalyse*, I (1913).

48. Compare the contrast between Tell and Parricida, in Schiller's *Wilhelm Tell*, which is discussed in detail in the author's *Inzestmotiv*.

49. Compare in this connection the unsuccessful homicidal attempt of Tatjana Leontiew, and its subtle psychological illumination, in Wittels: *Die sexuelle Not* (Vienna and Leipzig, 1909).

PART II

THE HERO:

A STUDY IN TRADITION, MYTH, AND DRAMA

by Lord Raglan

THE GENESIS OF MYTH

WE have seen in the preceding chapters that there are no valid grounds for believing in the historicity of tradition, and I have suggested that some distinguished heroes of tradition are really heroes of myth, and that a saga, far from being a record of fact, is really a novel based chiefly upon myth.

Those who have made any study of myths have realized that a myth is not merely an untrue story; they have, however, given very different explanations of myth, explanations which fall into three main classes. What, as I shall try to show, are the wrong explanations are firstly that a myth is a statement of historical fact clothed in more or less obscure language, and secondly that it is a fanciful or speculative explanation of a natural phenomenon. Having dealt with these, I shall show that what a myth really is is a narrative linked with a rite.

Let us begin with the theory of what is known as the "historic myth." This theory is, or seems to be, that people who lived in ages more or less remote from our own felt an urge to transmit to their descendants the facts of their tribal or local history; for some obscure reason, however, they were unable to do this in straightforward language, and therefore had recourse to allegory. These old peoples, it is supposed, carefully transmitted the allegories, or myths, to their descendants, who have continued to repeat them ever since. As the myth-makers omitted to transmit the key, however, the purpose that they had in mind has been frustrated, and the recipients of these myths invariably misunderstood them, either taking them literally or regarding them as a kind of sacred fairy-tale.

It seems to follow from this theory that if our ancestors had acquired the "historic myth" habit, we should now have no account of the Norman Conquest except a story of how a Frenchman married an English heiress against her will and took possession of her estate, and our only version of the Hundred Years' War would be a story of how one of our ancestors kept on jumping over a brook into his neighbour's garden.

In criticizing this theory, as put forward by Sir William Ridgeway and others, Mr. Alfred Nutt asked:[1] "Is there such a thing as an historic myth at all? Do men commemorate tribal wanderings, settle-

"Are you ready?" he asks.

"Yes," I lie.

"Are you afraid?"

"No." Lying is becoming my go-to thing, it seems.

"Are you lying?"

I snort. I can't help myself. Ethan's lips twitch.

"Brat," I mutter, losing the fight against the small grin that has been threatening to appear on my lips. "Why do you wanna know?"

Ethan shrugs, his slumped-over position makes the action a little awkward. He looks as sour as most ten-year-olds look when they're not getting their way.

"Dad lied, too. I don't like it. I'm not a kid."

I raise an eyebrow, and Ethan does that glower-pout thing again.

"I'm not. I know what's happening."

The small smile that had been playing on my lips vanishes in a heartbeat. Of course he knows. I sigh, slumping in my seat.

"I know. I'm sorry."

The kid sits back up, eyes never leaving me.

"Here's the truth: no, I'm not ready for this. Yes, I'm afraid. I think," I say, looking him in the eye. "At this point, everyone is."

"Dad, too?"

I nod. Especially parents. I don't even want to think about how frightened parents must be. I've always wanted kids. I was even looking forward to settling down and having a couple little devils to call my own, but now I'm so freaking glad I don't have any.

I startle when his small hand touches mine.

"It's okay," he says, and I almost laugh.

Okay? *Okay?* It was far from okay. It was everything *but* okay, but what could we do?

I look away from him again, cursing my luck. I was perfectly fine by myself. The last thing I need is this not-yet-ten-year-old kid telling me his birthday is tomorrow and that the red sky is beautiful.

Not long now.

An elderly couple by the window catches my attention. They're looking at pictures, probably of their grandkids, small smiles on their lips even as tears fill their eyes. I continue to look around at all the

ments, conquests, subjugations, acquisitions of new forms of culture, or any of the other incidents in the collective life of a people in the form of stories about individual men and women? I do not deny the possibility of their doing so; all I ask for is evidence of the fact."

I cannot learn that anyone ever gave Mr. Nutt the evidence for which he asked, no doubt for the very good reason that there is no such evidence, but the theory is still widely held. It is a very convenient theory, since any scholar who has views of his own on the early age of Greece, or of Tahiti, is able to produce what he can regard as convincing evidence in their favour by dubbing some local myth a "historic myth" and placing his own interpretation upon it. Now, to take incidents from myth and represent them as literal history is bad enough, since, as I must continue to point out, there is no good reason to believe that a myth or any other traditional narrative has ever embodied a historic fact, but to take portions of myths and to represent them as saying something which they do not say, and which those who relate them have never supposed them to say, is infinitely worse. That such procedure is considered compatible with sound scholarship indicates the gulf which separates scholarship from science.

Let us start with Professor Gilbert Murray. He tells us that he strongly suspects the lists of men slain by the heroes of the *Iliad* to be tribal records condensed and, "of course," transferred from their original context. He has already given us one of these "tribal records." In the *Iliad* it is said that Phaestus was slain by Idomeneus, and fell from his chariot with a crash. On this Professor Murray comments: "Idomeneus is the King of Knossos in Crete, and Phaestus is only known to history as the next most important town in the same island. That is to say, Phaestus *is* the town, or the eponymous hero of the town. . . . We may well have in this passage a record of a local battle or conquest in Crete, torn up from its surroundings and used to fill up some details of slaughter in a great battle before Troy." Even if we admitted the possibility of historic myth, it would be difficult to explain why a town should be represented as falling from a chariot; why an eponymous hero should be invented for one town but not for the other; and why the poet should have recourse to Cretan records to fill in details of a battle before Troy, since he has imagination enough to enable him to make "mythological changes and false identifications." Professor Murray has succumbed to the temptation to treat those portions of the *Iliad* which fit in with his theories as "real history," and those which do not as "the emptiest kind of fiction."[2]

Dr. W. J. Perry tells us[3] that traditions are to be treated as something ranking as fact, and that if not forced to support any *a priori* view, but allowed to tell their own tale in their own time, they frequently serve to throw a flood of light on dark places. We soon find, however, that the traditions are not allowed to tell their tale in their own time, but must tell it in Dr. Perry's. In his view, tales of gods and culture heroes are reminiscences of real individuals, the first bringers of Egyptian culture to the area where the tales are told, and when people say that they were civilized by a man who came from the sky, we must read instead of "sky" whatever place Dr. Perry supposes that their culture came from. When a tribe claims that its culture is due to certain supernatural beings who, among other feats told the sun to go down and give them rest, instead of staying up all the time, we are told that "the claim of the natives that certain beings originated their civilization is apparently trustworthy."[4] Yet why should their history be more trustworthy than their astronomy?

Believers in the historic myth are fond of telling us how easily such myths arise, but never produce any evidence to show that they have so arisen. Thus Mr. M. E. Lord assures us[5] that "a labyrinthine palace in which Athenian slaves were killed in a fight with the king's bulls would easily give rise to the story of the Athenian captives devoured by a monster half man and half bull." For many centuries men have been killed every year in the bull-rings of Spain, yet their death has given rise to no such myth; this is not surprising, since nobody who had seen a bull could suppose that fighting bulls have human bodies. The early Greek vase-painters represent the Minotaur not as a man-devouring monster but as a helpless-looking creature being stabbed unresistingly—no doubt a sacrificial victim wearing a mask.

"Into the ten days' Battle of Dunheath," says Professor R. W. Chambers,[6] "Norse poetry has probably compressed the century-long struggle of Goth and Hun. . . . For popular tradition will easily turn a desultory conflict into a single dramatic encounter, but hardly the reverse." The wars of the Saxons with the Welsh and the Danes were desultory conflicts, but tradition has not turned them into a single dramatic encounter, and there seems no reason to believe that what Professor Chambers describes as easy is in fact possible.

If a process cannot actually be proved to occur, it is surely the duty of those who postulate it to give some reason for believing in its occurrence, yet the two examples that I have just quoted, in which scholars describe as "easy" processes the very possibility of which they have attempted neither to demonstrate nor to explain, are unfortunately typical. It seems to be regarded as the privilege of a professor of classics or literature to guess the origin of a particular story and then elevate his guess to the status of a universal rule. What is needed is a comparative study of history and myth, and this, so far as I have been able to carry it, seem to show clearly that the "historic myth" is a fiction.

The same applies to the "nature myth," the theory, that is to say, that myths are fanciful or speculative explanations of natural phenomena. According to Max Müller and his school, all myths are sun myths. "The siege of Troy is but a repetition of the siege of the East by the solar powers that every evening are robbed of their brightest treasures in the West."[7] Alternatively, it is a repetition of the contest between summer and winter, in which summer is defeated every autumn, but revives and becomes victorious every spring.

As a fact, however, there is not contest, either between night and day or between summer and winter, and it never occurs to us to imagine that there is. We say: "It is getting rather dark," and not "Day is giving ground before the blows of Night," and when we feel the first frost it never occurs to us to suggest that the life-blood of summer is oozing away. The latter are the ideas of court poetry, not of everyday life. Mr. Tiddy says that "the people naturally conceive of the Old and New Year as combatants,"[8] but the very idea of a New Year is highly artificial. In nature the year has no beginning.

The sun-myth, in its earlier form, is now out of fashion, and has been replaced by a revised version in which myth is represented as "primitive science." The believers in this theory suppose that primitive man was consumed by a thirst for knowledge, and spent much of his time in speculating on the origin of the heavenly bodies, of the seasons, and of life and death. In default of a better explanation, he explained all these phenomena in terms of his own experience, and that is why in the myths the stars and the seasons are represented as human beings.

Thus Andrew Lang thought that "the origin of the world and of man is naturally a problem which has excited the curiosity of the least developed minds,"[9] and Sir Laurence Gomme believed that "everywhere, almost, man has stood apart for a moment and asked himself the question, Whence am I?"[10]

Professor Halliday similarly supposes that "myths represent the answers given by the human imagination to the problem of how things came to be. How were Earth and Sky created or how did evil enter the world?"[11] and Professor H. J. Rose alleges that "in the myth proper, imagination plays freely, poetically also it may be, or grotesquely, upon some striking phenomenon . . . or the nature and activities of a superhuman being."[12]

Professor Rose's myth-maker must have been a very remarkable person. On the one hand, he could not have been an atheist, for then supernatural beings would have had no existence for him, and on the other hand he could not have been a believer, for then the freedom of his imagination must have been trammelled by the nature of his belief. This is no quibble; if a man believes in the supernatural, he must have some beliefs about it, and if he has beliefs he cannot give free rein to his imagination. All men, both savage or civilized, are bound to accept, or possibly to reject, the beliefs of their day; to only the tiniest minority is it given to go even an inch beyond them. Half a dozen of the Greek philosophers might qualify as myth-makers under Professor Roses's definition, and in modern times perhaps Spinoza and Kant, but did the latter compose myths? Certainly not, and those philosophers who have speculated about the origin of evil have not, to my knowledge, produced a rival myth to that of Eve and the Serpent. All these theories are based upon the supposition that illiterate savages live in a state of highly intellectual agnosticism, in the luxuriant soil of which, owing to the lack of scientific cultivation, weeds monstrous or strangely beautiful are continually springing up.

This picture is an utterly false one. The savage is interested in nothing which does not impinge upon his senses, and never has a new idea even about the most familiar things. In this he is like our own illiterates. At the elementary schools some knowledge of more remote subjects is impressed upon them with the aid of books, but as soon as their school days are over, the majority relapse into the mental state in which savages remain permanently. It has been held that the curiosity which is displayed in some degree by all human beings is evidence of ability to speculate;[13] is the interest that a herd of cattle displays in a strange dog evidence of ability to speculate? Professor Halliday's myth-makers are filled with curiosity about the origin of the universe and of evil in it, but such curiosity is not merely unknown among savages, it is extremely rare among the civilized. How many of us have tried seriously to understand the theory of relativity or the doctrine of the Atonement? I wonder whether Professor Halliday can explain why the grass is green, and whether Professor Rose has reflected imaginatively upon the causes of volcanic activity. Anyhow, the savage attempts nothing of the kind. In discussing the mythology of the Bantus, Dr. Lindblom[15] expresses surprise at "their great lack of feeling that the origin of the most important phenomena of existence need explanation." We may safely accept the fact from a most competent observer; his surprise is due to his failure to realize that it is a question not of feeling but of *thinking*. Thinking, in the sense in which we use the word when we say that a man is a "thinker," is a skilled occupation, requiring not merely a long apprenticeship but a highly specialized set of tools. Even the simplest speculation about cosmic origins or moral principles requires a vocabulary of abstract terms, and such terms are lacking in savage, and even in semi-civilized languages. In our discussion of the simplest scientific or philosophical questions we use such terms as *cause, effect, creation, origin, result, nature, reason, idea, image, theory, problem*—terms which it is difficult to translate into Anglo-Saxon, and impossible to translate into any unwritten language. We can say with confidence that myths are not the result of speculation, firstly because they are never expressed in the only forms of language in which speculation is possible, and secondly because illiterates never speculate, and the speculations of literate communities lead not to mythology but to philosophy and science.

Professor Malinowski[15] quotes *Notes and Queries in Anthropology* as saying that "myths are stories which, however marvellous and improbable to use, are nevertheless related in all good faith, because they are intended, or believed by the teller, to explain by means of something concrete and intelligible an abstract idea or such vague and difficult conceptions as Creation, Death . . . ," and asks: "Would our Melanesians agree with this opinion? Certainly not. They do not want to 'explain,' to make 'intelligible,' anything which happens in their myths—above all an abstract idea. Of that there can be found to my knowledge no instance in Melanesia or in any other savage community. . . . Nor would a Trobriander agree with the view that 'Creation, Death . . .' are vague and difficult conceptions." He could not possibly do so, since there is no word for "to create," or even "to make," in any Melanesian language.[16]

In putting forward a view of myth very different from that which Professor Malinowski criticizes, I find myself in the unusual position of being able to quote in its support a number of distinguished writers, including Professor Malinowski himself. I shall begin with Professor Hooke, who defines myth as "the spoken part of a ritual; the story which the ritual enacts."[17]

"A *mythos* to the Greeks," says Miss Harrison,[18] "was primarily just a thing spoken, uttered by the *mouth*. Its antithesis or rather correlative is the thing done, enacted.... The primary meaning of myth in religion is just the same as in early literature; it is the spoken correlative of the acted rite.... Its object is not at first to give a reason; that notion is part of the old rationalist fallacy which saw in primitive man the leisured and eager inquirer bent on research."

"We shall probably not err," says Sir James Frazer, "in assuming that many myths, which we now know only as myths, had once their counterpart in magic; in other words, that they used to be acted as a means of producing in fact the events which they describe in figurative language. Ceremonies often die out while myths survive, and thus we are left to infer the dead ceremony from the living myth."[19]

Even Professor Rose, whose definition of myth I have criticized above, when dealing with the mythical quarrel of Zeus and Hera and the Plataean rite which "commemorated" it, says that "the legend has pretty certainly grown out of the rite, as usually happens";[20] and Professor A. B. Cook[21] says that "behind the myth [of the Minotaur], as is so often the case, we may detect a ritual performance."

"And not only is the Myth the explanation of the rite," says Professor Thomson,[22] "it is at the same time, in part at least, the explanation of the god. To primitive minds it is a matter of such transcendant importance to get the ritual exactly right (for the slightest deviation from the rules will ruin everything) that the worshippers will not proceed one step without authority. And who is their authority? In normal circumstances the oldest man in the tribe, the worshipper who has been most frequently through this particular ceremony before. And his authority? Well, the oldest tribesman within his memory. And so the tradition goes back and back.... But it must end somewhere, and it ends, as a thousand instances show, in an imaginary divine founder of the rite, who becomes the centre of the Myth."

"We must always look for an explanation," says Professor Hocart,[23] "not to the survival, but to the living custom or belief. If we turn to the living myth, that is the myth that is believed in, we find that it has no existence apart from the ritual. The ritual is always derived from someone, and its validity must be established by its derivation. The actors are merely impersonating the supposed inventors of the ritual, and this impersonation has to be expressed in words. Knowledge of the myth is essential to the ritual, because it has to be recited at the ritual."

"Psychologists like Wundt," says Professor Malinowski,[24] "sociologists like Durkheim, Hubert and Mauss, anthropologists like Crawley, classical scholars like Miss Jane Harrison, have all understood the intimate association between myth and ritual, between sacred tradition and the norms of social structure. . . . Myth as it exists in a savage community, that is, in its living primitive form, is not merely a story told but a reality lived. It is not of the nature of fiction, such as we read to-day in a novel, but it is a living reality, believed to have once happened in primeval times, and continuing ever since to influence the world and human destinies. This myth is to the savage what, to a fully believing Christian, is the Biblical story of Creation, of the Fall, of the Redemption." Discussing myths of origin, he says: "We can certainly discard all explanatory as well as all symbolic ex-interpretations of these myths of origin. The personages and beings which we find in them are what they appear to be on the surface, and not symbols of hidden realities. As to any explanatory function of these myths, there is no problem which they cover, no curiosity which they satisfy, no theory which they contain."

The myth, then, has nothing to do with speculations or explanations, any more than it has with historical facts. Strictly speaking, it is nothing but the form of words which is associated with a rite. To give a simple example—when we part from a friend, we shake him by the hand and say "Good-bye." The handshake is the rite; and the expression "good-bye," which is a shortened form of "God be with you," is the myth. By calling upon God to be with our friend, we give strength and validity to the bond which the handshake sets up, and which will draw us together again. In this case, however, the myth has probably been truncated, as it has certainly been contracted. It has now no direct connection with the rite. If, however, when shaking hands on parting, we were in the habit of saying: "King Solomon, when he parted from the Queen of Sheba, shook her by the hand and said: 'God be with you,' " we should give a sacramental character to the rite by attributing its foundation to an ancient and sacred personage; this is what a myth normally does.

The purpose of ritual is to confer benefits on, or avert misfortunes from, those by whom or on whose behalf the ritual is performed, by means of actions and words which from a scientific point of view are entirely ineffective, except in so far as they produce a psychological effect upon the participants themselves. This is, of course, not the view of the ritualists, who usually judge the efficacy of the ritual not by its effect upon themselves, but by its supposed effect upon the forces of nature. Many Africans believe that rain will not fall unless there has been a proper rain-making ceremony; if the rain follows the ceremony, then it is clear that the ceremony has been properly performed, and if rain does not follow, it is equally clear that the ceremony has not been properly performed. Where the ritual can be so easily judged by its apparent results, there is no need of a myth.

Usually, however, the supposed effects of the ritual are far less clearly apparent, so that, if belief in its efficacy is to be maintained, a more complex type of faith is required. This is induced by the myth, which not merely links the ritual of the present with the ritual of the past, but actually identifies the present, in its ritual aspect, with a past conceived solely in terms of ritual—a past, that is to say, in which superhuman figures devote themselves to the performance of acts which are the prototypes of the ritual. The stories of their activities, the myths, then perform the dual function of sanctifying and of standardizing the ritual. This standardization of myth is never complete, however, before the introduction of writing, when those myths which are closely associated with rites become scriptures; other myths become "folklore," as I shall now try to show.

Notes

1. *Folk-Lore*, vol. xii, p. 339.
2. *The Rise of the Greek Epic*, pp. 220–3.
3. *The Children of the Sun*, p. 104.
4. Ibid., pp. 123–4.
5. *Classical Journal*, 1923–4, p. 269.
6. *Widsith*, p. 48.
7. Max Müller: *The Science of Language*, vol. i, p. 515.
8. R.J.E. Tiddy: *The Mummers' Play*, p. 108.
9. *Myth, Ritual, and Religion*, vol. i, p. 162.
10. Op. cit., p. 130.
11. *Indo-European Folktales and Greek Legend*, p. 5.

12. *Folk-Lore*, vol. xlvi, p. 11.

13. A. Lang, op. cit., vol. i, p. 87.

14. G. Lindblom: *The Akamba*, p. 252.

15. In the *Frazer Lectures*, ed. W. R. Dawson, p. 81.

16. A. M. Hocart: *Kingship*, p. 197.

17. S. H. Hooke: *Myth and Ritual*, p. 3.

18. J. E. Harrison: *Themis*, p. 328.

19. Op. cit., vol. ix, p. 274. It must be admitted that Sir James elsewhere expresses views difficult to reconcile with this.

20. Op. cit., p. 104.

21. Op. cit., vol. i, p. 522.

22. J.A.K. Thomson: *Studies in the Odyssey*, p. 54.

23. A. M. Hocart: *The Progress of Man*, p. 223.

24. Op. cit., pp. 70, 72, 98.

THE FOLK-TALE

CERTAIN folklorists have divided, or attempted to divide, the traditional prose narrative into three completely distinct classes: the myth, the saga, and the folk-tale or *Märchen*. We saw in the last chapter that the myth is a narrative linked with ritual, and in Chapter V that a saga, though it may sometimes include matter drawn from chronicles or from contemporary history, is a form of novel based chiefly upon myth. Let us now see what the folk-tale really is.

Spence, in his definition of a folk-tale, says that it may be of mythical origin,[1] and Andrew Lang, in the course of a few pages, describes the story of a Jason as a myth, a legend, and a saga, and refer to its parallels as fairy-tales and as popular tales,[2] but other writers, as I said just now, have attempted to draw a hard-and-fast line between the folk-tale or *Märchen* and other types of traditional narrative, and have supposed that the former is a type of fiction, composed by and for the folk—that is to say, the illiterate.

Thus MacCulloch says that all over the world simple stories were invented, and that "as time went on, and man's inventive and imaginative faculties developed, these simple stories . . . became incidents in longer tales. New episodes were invented; the growth of custom and belief would furnish ever new material."[3]

Hartland tells us that in the *Märchen* or fairy-tale "the reins are thrown upon the neck of the imagination," and of uncivilized man that "his imagination predominates over his reason and his hypotheses about the origin of things take the shape of tales originating in unbounded draughts upon his own emotions."[4]

Krappe assures us that "it is certainly excusable to take the common-sense view and to regard the fairy-tale as a definite type of popular fiction, primarily designed to please and to entertain,"[5] and Professor H. J. Rose defines a *Märchen* as "primitive fiction told merely to amuse or interest the audience and without ulterior purpose. It follows certain well-worn lines, as popular imagination is very limited."

"We'll have a front row seat." My smile is brittle, a showing of teeth more than anything else, but Ethan doesn't seem to mind. "Were you able to talk to your parents?"

I almost kick myself as soon as the question is out of my mouth. I sit stiffly waiting for the waterfalls to start, but Ethan just nods his head.

"Mom was crying and saying sorry. Dad said everything was going to be all right."

It took everything in me not to snort. Judging by the look Ethan threw me, I didn't do as good of a job as I thought.

"Dad never lies to me," Ethan said with a stare, daring me to contradict him.

Does it make me a bad person, if, for a fraction of a second, I want to do it? That I want to look into those teary, honey-brown eyes and tell him: yes, he does.

I look away.

My gaze flickers to the couple sitting at the table beside mine. They are completely absorbed in each other. Slowly, his hand goes to rest on her belly, and only then do I notice a small bump. It's tiny, barely there, and I bite my lip while tearing my gaze away. God, why?

I look at Ethan again and notice that he's people-watching, too. His eyes are fixed on a small family. The boy has a small smile on his lips, the mother has tears in her eyes, and the father is a rock at their side, shielding them from any harm that could come their way.

Ethan looks away when he notices me watching.

"You sure you don't wanna go home?" I ask.

Ethan nods his head.

"They live longer than ten minutes away."

I'm about to open my mouth to say something—I don't even really know what—when there is a sudden red flare. Everyone present looks up and out of the cafe, our eyes fixed on the red streak across the sky.

"It's beautiful," Ethan whispers. I can't help but envy him in that moment. While he sees the beauty, I can only see the end. The sky goes back to blue, darker than before, and we look away. It's almost time.

Never have ten minutes felt so long. Never have they felt so short, either. Ethan sighs and lets his head fall onto the table.

These views are, I think, demonstrably incorrect. The facts are:

1. No popular story-teller has ever been known to invent anything.

2. Not only are the incidents in folk-tales the same all over the world, but in areas of the same language they are commonly narrated in the same actual words.

3. Folk-tales deal as a rule with subjects of which the folk can have no knowledge.

4. The exercise of the imagination consists not in creating something out of nothing, but in the transmutation of matter already present in the mind.

I shall deal with these seriatim, and shall begin by quoting Hartland against himself. He expatiates upon the imagination of uncivilized man, but is nevertheless at pains to show that the popular story-teller never displays any imagination whatever. He tells us that "the dislike of voluntary change forbids amendment of formularies which have long ceased to be understood. . . . It is by no means an uncommon thing for the rustic story-teller to be unable to explain . . . episodes in any other way than Uncle Remus—'She wuz in de tale, en de tale I give you like hit were gun to me.' " He cites Dr. Steere as saying that the Swahili story-tellers scarcely understood the sung parts of their tales, and Dr. Rink as saying of the Eskimo that "the art requires the ancient tales to be related as nearly as possible in the words of the original version." He also tells us that "in these [Campbell's] tales words were often used which had dropped out of ordinary parlance, giving proof of careful adherence to the ancient forms. . . . To sum up," he concludes, "it would appear that national differences in the manner of story-telling are for the most part superficial. Whether told by men to men in the bazaar or coffee-house of the East, or by old men or women to children in the sacred recesses of the European home, or by men to a mixed assembly during the endless nights of the Arctic Circle, or in the huts of the tropical forest, and notwithstanding the license often taken by the professional reciter, the endeavour to render to the audience just what the speaker has himself received from his predecessors is paramount."[6]

"As a rule," says Professor Halliday,[7] "the pride of the professional is rather in the preservation of the old tale; both he and his hearers put a high premium on conservatism." According to Sir John Rhys, the Welsh story-tellers were not inventors but merely editors, and their stories echoes of ancient myths,[8] and we are told that the Irish story-teller "never chose his own words—he always had the story by heart, and recited the words from memory."[9]

The rustic or savage story-teller may seem to be improvising his stories, just as to one who visits a theatre for the first time the funny man may seem to be improvising his jokes. Investigation, however, shows that in illiterate communities not merely do the people as a whole not invent stories, but they do not even tell stories. The telling of stories may only be done by recognized story-tellers, and not only is it incumbent on these to tell the stories in the traditional manner and with the traditional words, but among many tribes they may tell only the particular stories that they have a recognized right to tell.

These being the facts, we are faced with two possible explanations. We must conclude either that savages once possessed a faculty of imagination and invention which has unaccountably disappeared, or that the attribution of imagination and inventiveness to savages is erroneous.

We now come to the second point, which is that the same tales are told in many parts of the world. Professor Rose explains this, as we saw, by the limitations of the popular imagination, but while this might conceivably explain the similarity in the incidents, it cannot possibly explain the similarity in the wording and the names. We find, for example, that the fairy-tales of England and France contain not merely the same incidents, but the same or equivalent names. How does Professor Rose account for this? Does he really believe that an English rustic, trying to think of a name for a man who murders his wives, is restricted by his imagination to "Bluebeard," and that a French rustic is similarly restricted to "*Barbebleue*"? Or that an Englishman and a Frenchman, devising a name for a girl who meets a wolf, have no possible alternatives to "Little Red Riding Hood" and "*Le Petit Chaperon rouge*"? Unless we form so extravagant a hypothesis, we must conclude that one set of tales is a translation. The argument could be carried much farther, but the above seems enough to show that the fairy-tales of one country are not of popular origin, and this being so, we have no reason to assume that the fairy-tales of another country are of popular origin.

Like the fairy-tale, the folk-play is alleged to be of popular origin. The fact that all over England and a great part of Europe the incidents of the folk-play are very similar might again be accounted for by the limitations of the popular imagination, but what are we to say when we find the couplet:

"Here comes I, old Beelzebub,
Over my shoulder I carry my club,"

with trifling variations in the folk-plays of Lincolnshire, Gloucestershire, Sussex, Cornwall, and other English counties, and of Belfast?[10] Are we to suppose that these words spring inevitably to the lips of a rustic playwright?

It should be quite clear that to say that a story, song, or play is of popular origin means nothing unless we assume that it actually originated with the people among whom it is now found, or their ancestors. If we find reason to believe that a folk-story has been borrowed, even from the next village, its popular origin becomes suspect, for if one community borrows instead of inventing, another may well do the same, and if one item of what passes as folklore is borrowed, it is at least possible that all is borrowed.

It is, of course, difficult to prove that no folk-tales are of popular origin, but a study not merely of the wording and names, but of the incidents in detail, may be sufficient to show that their popular origin is at least highly improbable. It is often alleged, for example, that the Celtic peasantry are highly imaginative people, and that their imagination expresses itself in fairy-tales, but a detailed comparison of the fairy-tales of Brittany with those of Italy led Coote to the conclusion that none of the Breton tales could be of Celtic origin.[11]

Let us take a story that is found all over the world, the details of which, though they cannot of course prove that it has been diffused from a common source, at any rate strongly suggest it. The story has been discussed by Andrew Lang[12] and by Professor Saintyves,[13] and in its simplest form goes as follows: A youth somehow finds his way to the house of a giant or ogre, who lives in a remote part of the world or in the sky. The ogre has a beautiful daughter, and she and the youth fall in love. The ogre finds the youth and sets him a succession of impossible tasks, such as emptying a large lake with a bucket or cleaning an Augean stable, but the ogre's daughter has magic at her disposal, by means of which the youth is enabled to perform the tasks, to the ogre's intense annoyance. The youth and the girl then decide to elope; the ogre pursues them, but he is delayed by magic obstacles that the girl places in his path until a river is reached which allows the lovers to cross, but drowns the ogre.

"The Greeks have the tale," Lang tells us, "the people of Madagascar have it, the Lowland Scotch, the Celts, the Russians, the Italians, the Algonquins, the Finns, and the Samoans have it . . . while many scattered incidents occur in even more widely severed races, such as Zulus, Bushmen, Japanese, Eskimo, Samoyeds." Other versions have come to light since he wrote, and, as he points out,[14] it is not merely the main features that are the same in the most remote parts of the world, but even the details. In many of the versions, for example, the girl throws her comb to the ground, whereupon it turns into a forest or thicket, which delays the ogre's pursuit. We may conclude with Dr. Krappe[15] that "it is unthinkable that a tale with a plot as complicated . . . should have arisen independently."

There are other tales with a plot as complicated and a distribution as wide as that just cited. Lang discusses another of them, that of which the story of Jason is the type; "we must suppose," he says,[16] "either that all wits jumped and invented the same romantic series of situations by accident, or that all men spread from one centre, where the story was known, or that the story, once invented, has drifted all round the world." He inclined, as might be expected, to the last explanation, and we must again insist that if one story which a savage tells is derived from an alien source, it is possible, and even probable, that the other stories which he tells have a similar origin.

Having seen that the manner in which the folk-tales are told, and the manner in which they are distributed, render it at least highly improbable that they are of popular origin, we have next to consider their matter. If folk-tales were really composed by the folk, we should expect them to deal with subjects with which the folk are familiar— matters of village courtship and marriage, of quarrels and revenges, of seed-time and harvest, of plenty and dearth, of hunting and fishing— in short, of such material as were used by Mary Webb in *Precious Bane*, or Pearl Buck in *The Good Earth*—but we should be disappointed. These stories are novels written by and for highly sophisticated people, and the material of folk-tales is of a very different character. It is very seldom that peasants appear in the tales at all. The *dramatis personae*, when they are not supernatural beings, are kings, queens, princes, and princesses, or other potentates, with their ministers and attendants.

The scenes are laid, not in the farmyard or the harvest field, but in palaces, castles, and courts; the plots are concerned not with rural life, but with heroic feats of arms and the succession to kingdoms; and the accessories consist largely of magic jewels, helmets of invisibility, and other objects quite outside the range of a peasant's ideas.

Even when the characters are supposed to be peasants, the situations and incidents are quite unreal. Take, for example, the story of Red Riding Hood: bedridden old women do not really live alone in the heart of wolf-haunted forests; wolves cannot really gobble people up without leaving a trace, and girls do not really mistake wolves, however conversational, for their grandparents. The story was obviously composed neither by nor for people who really lived in danger of wolves, and the father is represented as a wood-cutter merely in order that he may be at hand with a weapon at the proper moment.

In many stories in which the hero ends by ascending the throne and reigning as if to the manner born, he is represented as starting life as a pauper, but this is done, as I shall try to show later, to explain the fact that in the typical myth the hero has to pass through a period of adversity. It is usually found that, though ostensibly the son of a peasant, he is really a prince who in early infancy was either stolen by an enemy or hidden from a tyrant by his friends.

It seems to be supposed, though I have nowhere seen this clearly stated, that the peasant and the savage, though they are great hands at making up stories, are nevertheless incapable of making up the simplest story of the doings of ordinary human beings, and are therefore obliged to have recourse to ogres, fairies, talking animals, and people endowed with supernatural powers, to which conceptions they are led by some mysterious but universal force. It has been suggested that this force operates by means of dreams and hallucinations, but those who make this suggestion fail to realize that dreams and hallucinations cannot put new ideas into the mind.

This brings me to my next point, that concerning the widespread superstition that the imagination is capable of making something out of nothing, or, in other words, that there can come out of a man's mind ideas, whether of fact or fiction, which bear no relation to anything that has gone into it. Most theories of the origin of folklore, though they do not state this definitely, nevertheless imply that savages and rustics possess such powers of the imagination as in reality the most brilliant literary genius has never possessed.

An architect cannot design a new type of house unless he has in his mind or on his desk recollections or records of a large number of existing houses, unless he understands thoroughly the purpose of the different parts of a house, and the means of making access from one to another, and unless he has a thorough knowledge of the materials out of which houses are constructed, and of the means employed for putting them together. In exactly the same way, nobody can hope to be a successful poet or composer of stories unless he has familiarized himself with a large number of poems or stories of different types, both in their general outlines and in the details of their construction; and the better the writers whose works he studies, the better are his own writings likely to be. This simple fact is, of course, the basis of all literary education. In addition, our budding author must, if he is to produce anything possessing the least degree of originality, observe and read a good deal, and thus acquire a large fund of ideas. By drawing upon these he will be able to vary the form and content of his writings; this is the most that he will be able to do, since imagination at its highest is no more than the combination of two or more old ideas to form a new idea. The "wild fancy" of the savage, of which we hear so much, could rise to no greater heights than that of imagining an orgy of meat and beer lasting two or three days instead of one, and to suppose the unlettered rustic capable of composing the story of Cinderella is as absurd as to suppose him capable of designing the palace in which she left her slipper.

The belief that folk-tales are the product of "popular imagination" is due to a confused use of the word *imagination*. Anyone who has seen elephants, or pictures of elephants, can "imagine" an elephant; that is to say, he can form a mental picture of an elephant, which will be more or less accurate according as his memory is more or less retentive, but which will add nothing to his or anyone else's ideas on the subject of elephants, or on any other subject. Compare with this the picture of a pterodactyl as imagined by a scientist. Out of some bones and other fossil remains, together with a wide knowledge of the appearance and anatomy of birds and of reptiles, he "imagines" a picture of a pterodactyl which definitely adds to the stock of human ideas. Imagination of the first type could not invent a folk-tale, since it can invent nothing, and even the second type, the infinitely rarer creative imagination, could invent a folk-tale only if the elements out of which it was to be composed were present in its possessor's mind.

In his masterly work *The Road to Xanadu*, Professor Lowes has taken a portion of Coleridge's *Ancient Mariner* and has traced every idea, and almost every phrase, in it to something that Coleridge can be shown to have read. Professor Lowes says that the poem is a work of pure imagination, but that "a work of pure imagination is not something fabricated by a *tour de force* from nothing, and suspended, without anchorage in fact, in the impalpable ether of a visionary world. No conception could run more sharply counter to the truth."[17] He later speaks of "a strange but widely prevalent idea" that "the shaping spirit of imagination sits aloof, like God as he is commonly conceived, creating in some thaumaturgic fashion out of nothing its visionary world. That and that only is deemed to be 'originality'—that, and not the imperial moulding of old matter into imperishably new forms."[18]

It is very few writers, however, who have even devised new forms; literary conventions are universal, especially poetic conventions. These conventions apply just as strictly to ballads and other forms of what are known as "folk-poetry" as they do to literary products. When, for example, Countess Cesaresco describes how "a herdsman or tiller of the soil strings together a few verses embodying some simple thought which came into his head whilst he looked at the green fields or the blue skies," and how "one or two friends get them by heart,"[19] she forgets not only that such a process has never actually been known to occur, but that bucolic poetry is perhaps the most sophisticated form of poetry, and that its successful composers, from Theocritus to Wordsworth, have been men of the highest education.

Even so great a poet as Theocritus is less original than is commonly supposed. Speaking of his *Festival of Adonis*, perhaps the most admired of his idylls, Dr. Tyrrell says that he himself had always regarded it as a triumphantly successful piece of character-painting. "But I own," he continues, "that I was grieved to find what seems to me clear evidence that such scenes, in which women inveigh against their absent spouses, were part of the stock in trade of the mimographer, and were constantly reproduced. So also the reviling of servants by their mistresses, which also appears in this idyll. I am sure that Theocritus has handled these scenes with an art altogether transcending that of his rivals, but I had thought that they were the fruits of his own genius and invention."[20] Far from ploughing a lonely furrow, Theocritus was, in fact, rather the winner of a ploughing competition, and if the greatness of a great poet consists merely in improving upon the efforts of his predecessors or rivals, how can it be supposed that an unlettered rustic could invent themes and metres for himself?

Hundreds of English poets have dealt on conventional lines with mountains, primroses, and love's young dream, and the range of non-European poets is even more limited. "Everybody knows," says Bain,[21] that classical Sanscrit authors have no originality. They do not rhetorically reset and embellish notorious themes; such originality as they possess lying not in their subject but in its treatment." In China, so Mr. Waley tells us, "innumerable poems record 'Reflections on visiting a ruin,' or on the 'Site of an old city.' The details are ingeniously varied, but the sentiments are in each case identical." Innumerable Arabic poems are supposed to be written on the deserted camp site of the loved one's tribe; at first the hearer is apt to take for an expression of genuine emotion what he later learns to recognize as an exhibition of virtuosity.

It is the same with stories; every literary community has certain types of story outside which none but exceptional geniuses can venture. As for the folk, they may make minor alterations, mostly for the worse, in existing poems, stories, or plays, but they never compose them for themselves.

This fact, like negatives in general, is difficult to prove. We may note that though the French Canadians have been in Canada for over three centuries, the songs that they sing are those which they brought from France. The editors of a collection of these songs "sought in vain for evidences of song-creation among the Canadian population."[22] There seems to be nothing in the *Uncle Remus* stories, except the language, which the Negroes did not bring from Africa. The English folk-play, which I discussed a few pages back, is not merely much the same, both in incidents and in language, all over the country, but some versions embody long quotations from the works of Congreve and Addison.[23] This is a striking illustration of the fact that the literature of the folk is not their own production, but comes down to them from above.

Notes

1. L. Spence: *An Introduction to Mythology*, p. 12.
2. *Custom and Myth*, pp. 94, 99.

3. J. A. MacCulloch: *The Childhood of Fiction*, p. 457.

4. E. S. Hartland: *The Science of Fairy Tales*, pp. 23, 33.

5. A. H. Krappe: *The Science of Folklore*, p. 11.

6. Op. cit., pp. 6, 18–21.

7. Op. cit., p. 23.

8. *Studies in the Arthurian Legend*, p. 175.

9. P. W. Joyce: *Old Celtic Romances*, p. ix.

10. R.J.E. Tiddy, op. cit.

11. H. C. Coote, in *Folk-Lore*, vol. i, p. 212.

12. *Custom and Myth*, pp. 87 ff.

13. *Les Contes de Perrault*, p. 272.

14. Op. cit., p. 92.

15. Op. cit., p. 8.

16. Op. cit., p. 101.

17. *The Road to Xanadu*, p. 241.

18. Op. cit., p. 428.

19. Countess Martinengo-Cesaresco: *The Study of Folk-Songs*, p. 59.

20. *The Idylls of Theocritus*, tr. Calverley, ed. R. Y. Tyrrell, p. xvi.

21. F. W. Bain: *A Digit of the Moon*, p. x.

22. *Folk-Lore*, vol. xxxvii, p. 102.

23. R.J.E. Tiddy, op. cit., pp. 82, 85.

MYTH AND RITUAL

THE position which we have now reached is that the folk-tale is never of popular origin, but is merely one form of the traditional narrative; that the traditional narrative has no basis either in history or in philosophical speculation, but is derived from the myth; and that the myth is a narrative connected with a rite.

The theory that all traditional narratives are myths—that is to say, that they are connected with ritual—may be maintained upon five grounds:

1. That there is no other satisfactory way in which they can be explained. As the whole of this book is intended to establish this proposition, I shall not refer to it in particular here.

2. That these narratives are concerned primarily and chiefly with supernatural beings, kings, and heroes.

3. That miracles play a large part in them.

4. That the same scenes and incidents appear in many parts of the world.

5. That many of these scenes and incidents are explicable in terms of known rituals.

It was once supposed that the idea of a god or of gods was innate, but thinking persons have realized, since the days of Locke, that there are no innate ideas. The idea that it is natural to believe in the supernatural has only to be so stated to show its absurdity. Apart from innate ideas, we have inspiration and revelation, but even if all the claims made for these were admitted, they would still fail to provide an explanation for at least three quarters of the phenomena connected with the belief in supernatural beings. Nobody, so far as I know, has claimed that the quarrels of the gods in the *Iliad* were divinely revealed to Homer.

Passing over the kings and heroes for a moment, we come to the miraculous elements in our narratives. It may be said that miracles never happen, but that does not explain the important fact, which is at the final moments of the human race. You'll also find the story that formed the origin of this book. Whether told through words, images, or any combination of the two, all of these stories go beyond the individual who created them. They're about all of us, and the experiences we all share.

At Radix Media, we want to publish stories that get to the root of the human experience, and want those stories to reflect the complex beauty of our experiences. *AFTERMATH: Explorations of Loss & Grief* weaves together the struggles and joys of many. It's a reminder that we're all connected, regardless of how different our day-to-day lives are. We hope that this sets the stage for bringing many more stories to print. It's our way of helping to make the world a better place.

We're so incredibly happy to have you on this journey with us.

Radix Media
January 2018

Silence stretches between us, and I'm not too keen to break it. Turns out I don't need to. Ethan, who is still staring at me, asks, "Where were you when you found out?"

"At a bar with a few friends," I say after thinking about it. I don't know what makes me answer. I thought that these ten minutes would be spent in silence.

"I was with Grandpa Joe and Grandma Edith. Dad and Mom are away for work. They were supposed to come back today. Dad promised chocolate chip pancakes for my birthday."

I wince again. Does the kid need to bring up his birthday every other sentence? It's hard enough to know just how young he is. God, I don't even want to think about the parents that have to explain everything to their children. What could they possibly say to make it better? Is there any way to make it better?

"Chocolate chip pancakes are my favorite," I say. Really, the award for most awkward conversation had with a ten-year-old goes to me. I should be proud of that achievement.

"Mom makes the best," Ethan says, and I have to look away when tears come to his eyes. I'm no good with tears; I could hardly comfort Mom when I stumbled home a couple of days ago. Seeing me made her cry even more, and I did nothing but stand there while she broke down on our living room couch. She only calmed down when she was able to contact Mark. She begged him to come home—she wanted both of her boys with her—but it was impossible. Mark was too far, and there was too little time. He would never make it by car, and planes were out of the question.

"Why aren't you with your grandparents?" I ask, still looking away but trying to distract the boy. I think it works because there is no trace of tears in his voice when he speaks.

"They wanted to stay home."

"You didn't?" I raise an eyebrow and look back at Ethan.

"I wanted to see."

I hum, reclining a little in my chair. Many want to see; it's why most of us are outside. Others just want the company. I suppose being alone isn't really something that one looks forward to in a moment like this.

that they are believed to happen. Further than that, an occurrence is never considered miraculous unless it is believed to be due to the action either of a supernatural being or of a human being endowed with supernatural power, and unless it is believed to have a significant effect upon the fortunes of human beings. An earthquake is in itself not a miracle; it becomes a miracle when it destroys the ungodly, or when the godly have a narrow escape. In religious literature it is used interchangeably with the word *sign*, and we often hear of "signs and wonders." Now, a sign is essentially a preparatory act, a minor wonder performed as a preliminary to a major wonder. In my view, this sign is the ritual act. It seems to me, that is to say, that when an African rainmaker pours beer upon the sacred rain-stones with the appropriate ceremonies, he is making a sign or signal to the rain to fall.

We find here all the characteristics of a miracle; firstly, it is performed by a person believed to be endowed with super-human power; secondly, the end proposed is recognized as a proper one for super-human action; and, thirdly, the ritual is the recognized means of bringing about such action.

When we use the expression "to perform a miracle," we normally confuse the action of the miracle-worker with the supposed result of that action. We are apt to think of the miracle-worker as performing some quite impossible action, such as turning a person into a pig. If we study the narratives, however, we shall see that what he really does is some quite simple action. The conjurer, the sham miracle-worker, pretends to perform his feats by waving a wand and saying: "Hey, presto!" but this is all that the real miracle-worker, the ritualist, does, as a study of the stories will show. The miracle takes place not as a direct result of the miracle-worker's act, but as the result of a ceremony in which the miracle-worker's act is the culminating rite.

If we take the story of Cinderella and examine its miracles, we find exactly the same features present as in the rain-making rite mentioned above. In the first place the miracle-worker is a being endowed with supernatural power, the fairy godmother; second, the object—that is, the provision of suitable equipment for one who is herself to be a queen, a person endowed with supernatural power—is a proper object for supernatural intervention; thirdly, the fairy godmother is not supposed to be able to make something out of nothing, but most go through the proper ritual. What the beer and the sacred stones are to the rain-maker, the magic wand and the pumpkin are to her. She is, in fact, a ritual personage using ritual objects to perform ritual acts. In the same way we find that the hero, whether of myth, saga, or fairy-tale, cannot injure the monster without the magic weapons; and that nobody else can use the magic weapons to injure the monster. Against the hero with the magic weapons the monster is powerless; he falls at the first blow. That is because the hero is a ritual personage using ritual weapons to deliver a ritual blow. The machinery of the traditional miracle, far from suggesting that it is either the product of an unfettered imagination or the embellished version of a historical incident, bears witness to its ritual origin.

It is not merely myths and fairy-tales that contain these reminiscences of ritual, but the sagas, romances, and even novels which are based upon them, not to mention their verse forms, the epic, the ballad, and even the nursery rhyme. It is proper to use these terms as long as they are understood to refer to the form of the stories, and not their contents, but if people claim, as certain folklorists do, that they can tell from the form of a story whether it originated in fact, fiction, or philosophical speculation, then they have left the realm of science, if they ever were in it, for that of prejudice.

The manner in which traditional stories are transformed in romance is well described by Professor Kittredge, who shows how "supernatural creatures of the most various kinds exchange rôles with bewildering nonchalance, or are reduced to the status of robbers, knights, ladies, or other classes of ordinary mortals. The other World may appear as an island, or a castle, or a cave, or an orchard, or a fair meadow, or even the Christian hell."[1] He later tells us that the substitution of enchanted for supernatural beings is due to rationalization; "it brings the supernatural personages down to the level of humanity, and makes them thoroughly reasonable and natural creatures. . . . The process, then, is of the same kind as that by which gods became heroes, or by which animal spouses became, not real animals, but men transformed for the time into brute shape. As time goes on, however, the very idea of enchantment may itself come to seem unreasonable, and therefore an attempt is sometimes made by the story-teller to represent the strange events as due to natural causes, or to tell them as facts, with no mention of the super-human. This kind of rationalizing is extremely common in Arthurian romance, and it frequently results in contradiction or sheer incomprehensibility."[2] The same may be said for the rationalizing of our euhemerists.

Professor Gruffydd, dealing with the story of Lleu or Llew, says that the four stages through which it has grown to its present form in the *mabinogi* can be set down as follows:

First stage: Mythology . . . —of Lugh-Lleu as a god we have consider-able evidence.
Second stage: Mythology becomes history.
Third stage: Mythological history becomes folklore.
Fourth stage: Folklore is utilized to form literary tales.[3]

It is pretty certain that every old story has passed through a series of vicissitudes, and it is clearly impossible to reconstruct the original form by the aid of taste alone. We can, however, say with some confidence that where we have two or more versions of the same story, the older is likely to be nearer to the mythical—that is, the ritual—type. This applies not merely to stories, but also to folk-songs and folk-customs. Dr. C. B. Lewis, after making a study of the nursery rhyme: "Where are you going to, my pretty maid?" and then of the folk-customs connected with May-day, summarizes the question as follows:

"The conclusion, then, is the same as the one we reached with re-gard to our nursery rhyme: the folk has neither part nor lot in the making of folklore. The source of our folksong and folk customs is religion: on the one hand Christian religion; on the other pagan. At what date in history these elements of religion turned, the one into folksong, the other into folklore, it is difficult to affirm, and indeed it is a different date in each case; but one may perhaps venture to say that it was then the religious origin of the themes in question was finally forgotten. From that moment on, the theme of our song and the details of our customs changed more rapidly than before, were even simplified or whittled down by this or that trait falling into oblivion, until they now appear as pearls of such pure loveliness that only the folk, it is thought, in a far-distant past could have conceived them. Thus folklore and folk-song, at least in the cases we have considered, turn out to be the last stage of all in an age-long evolution, and not by any means the first beginnings."[4]

This age-long evolution probably began, like most of the earlier ele-ments of our culture, in the valleys of the Nile, the Euphrates, or the Indus. Dr. Lewis traces the songs and customs with which he deals back to southwestern Asia, the culture of which was largely influenced by that of the great agricultural civilizations. In these countries the livelihood of the people depended upon the river flood, and we have good reason to believe that from very early times they were ruled, or perhaps rather reigned over, by kings whose principal duty it was to ensure by means of ritual that the floods should be punctual and adequate. The flood myths probably originated as descriptions of this ritual. But the functions of the kings were by no means limited to the production of floods; they had also to ensure the fertility of women and animals, success in war, hunting, and fishing, freedom from disease—in fact, the general prosperity of the community. This duty they discharged by means of a complex ritual, in which they pretended to destroy the old world and create a new one; the descriptions of this ritual are the creation myths, in which the flood myths are included.[5] It is obvious that the kings could not be uniformly successful, and that people would remember years in which the crops or the hunting had been better than last year or the year before. Even among ourselves vague memories of certain facts combined with misconceptions of others readily coalesce into a belief in "good old days," in which things in general were much better than they are now. Such "good old days" among ourselves are often associated with "Good Queen Bess" or "Good King Charles," but in a community without records that very small modicum of fact which among most English people passes for the history of these monarchs would be completely lost, and the Golden Age might be believed to be much more recent and much more golden.

And what do we mean when we say that Charles was a good king? We certainly do not mean that he was a good man; a good king is one whose subjects prosper, whether he is himself virtuous and kindly or not. This applies much more fully in the case of a king whose duties are purely ritual. Just as the good rain-maker is the one who induced good rain, so the good king is the king who induces good crops, good hunting, and so on. The ideal is one, not of supreme moral perfection, but of supreme functional efficiency. Vague memories of especially good kings may lead to the belief in the supremely good king. This king becomes the originator of the ritual, but not in a historical sense, because, it must be repeated, the idea of history is meaningless to the ritualist. History is what happens once, but things that happen once only are nothing to the ritualist, who is concerned only with things that are done again and again. Myth is ritual projected back into the past, not a historical past of time, but a ritual past of eternity. It is a description of what should be done by a king (priest, chief, or magician) in order to secure and maintain the prosperity of his people, told in the form of a narrative of what a hero—that is, an ideal king, etc.— once did. And not only a hero, but a heroine, for in ritual the queen is as important, or nearly as important, as the king, and a queen can ensure prosperity and also victory, though she may never go near a battle. Myths are concerned almost entirely with gods and heroes, or goddesses and heroines, because they are accounts of royal ritual.

It may be urged that if all myths are derived from the royal ritual of the Nile-Indus region, then all myths should be alike. In fact, many myths are extremely widespread; this fact has been generally realized, except by exponents of the "Aryan" theory, but has been attributed to the alleged similar working of the human mind. This theory breaks down, however, when it is realized that however widespread certain features of myth and ritual may be, other myths and rites have a distribution comparable, let us say, to that of the Moslem religion. Nobody asserts that, because we find in Java and in Nigeria men who marry four wives and pray five times a day, the human mind works naturally in the direction of four wives and five daily prayers. No belief or practice can be claimed as natural unless it is universal, and even the most widespread myths and rites are not that.

The myth varies with the ritual, and both, especially among the illiterate, tend to reflect political and economic conditions. A ritual developed among a people who both kept cattle and cultivated the soil might spread on the one hand to pastoral nomads, and on the other to cultivators who kept no cattle. One part of the ritual would then die out, and as it would, of course, not be the same part, it might come to be supposed that the two rituals were quite independent. The beliefs that the sun drives in a chariot and that the moon sails in a boat are both derived from ritual, and tend to die out among people who have no chariots or no boats, though they usually leave traces.

But the political environment is, perhaps, more important than the economic in the development or retention of myth and ritual. The original ritual, so far as can be judged from the general pattern, was based on the existence of a king who was killed and replaced annually. A hundred myths describe his death and the installation of his successor. Such a system suggests a centralized kingdom with not more than a trinity of gods, gods who represent the old king, the new king, and the queen. Extended polytheism might be due to the rise of empires, in which the god of the capital reigns over the gods of the other cities, or to the existence of loose confederations, such as that of Greece, in which Zeus is supposed to reign rather uncertainly over a large number of other deities, just as Agamemnon is supposed to reign rather uncertainly over a large number of other kings and chiefs.

Thus myth and ritual, though probably derived, like logarithms, from a common source, are, so long as they are alive, and especially so long as they remain unwritten, continually subject to changes induced by local conditions. That they have remained in general so similar is evidence, not of the similar working of the human mind, but of that inertia which is in general its most salient characteristic.

Notes

1. G. L. Kittredge: *Gawaine and the Green Knight*, p. 77.
2. Ibid., p. 239.
3. W. J. Gruffydd: *Math vab Mathonwy*, p. 81; the examples which he cites are very interesting, but too long to quote.
4. *Folk-Lore*, vol. xlvi, p. 74.
5. For these see A. M. Hocart: *Kingship*, ch. xvi, and my *Jocasta's Crime*, pp. 141 ff.

MYTH AND RITUAL
(CONTINUED)

THE theory put forward in the last chapter is part of the general theory of the diffusion of culture, over which there has been so much discussion. The protagonists have been on the one hand those who refuse to admit the possibility of diffusion, except where, as in the case of the diffusion of the Christian religion, it cannot be denied, and on the other those who have maintained that all culture was diffused in the same manner, and from the same centre.

"It would be wrong," says Sir E. A. Wallis Budge,[1] "to say that the Egyptians borrowed from the Sumerians or the Sumerians from the Egyptians, but it may be submitted that the litterati of both peoples borrowed their theological systems from some common but exceedingly ancient source." He has told us that "the similarity between the two Companies of gods is too close to be accidental," but we are bound to agree with him that the present state of our knowledge does not enable us to point to any one definite source. That there are many more similarities in the religious systems of Egypt, Mesopotamia, and Palestine, especially in connection with the divine kingship, has been shown by Professor Hooke and his colleagues in *Myth and Ritual* and *The Labyrinth*, in which a dozen learned writers show that the religious systems of those countries "possessed certain fundamental characteristics in common. They were essentially ritual religions aiming at securing the well-being of the community by the due performance of ritual actions. Each of these religions had certain rituals of central importance, and in each the central figure was the king, in whose person the fortune of the state was, so to speak, incarnate. In each religion these rituals presented the same general pattern.

"This pattern consisted of a dramatic ritual representing the death and resurrection of the king, who was also the god, performed by priests and members of the royal family. It comprised a sacred combat, in which was enacted the victory of the god over his enemies, a triumphal procession in which the neighbouring gods took part, an enthronement, a ceremony by which the destinies of the state for the coming year were determined, and a sacred marriage.

"Together with the ritual and as an essential part of it there was always found, in some form or other, the recitation of the story whose outlines were enacted in the ritual. This was the myth, and its repetition had equal potency with the performance of the ritual. In the beginning the thing said and the thing done was inseparably united, although in the course of time they were divorced and gave rise to widely differing literary, artistic, and religious forms."[2]

I have quoted this passage here in order again to emphasize the close connection which exists between myth and ritual, and I shall now attempt to show that the myths of other countries, especially of Greece, are inexplicable except in terms of ritual, that many of them are actual descriptions of such a ritual as Professor Hooke describes, and that the accounts of the heroes are really accounts of the rites which the divine king had to perform. But whereas the existing accounts of the ritual of Egypt and Mesopotamia provide only for a pretence of killing the king, the traditions of Greece and less civilized countries point to a ritual in which the king was actually killed, either annually, at the end of some longer term, or when his strength fails, as in some parts of the world he still is.[3]

While the separation of Greek myth from Greek ritual may be due in part to the ancient philosophers, who composed allegories which, though in myth form, had no connection with ritual, it is due chiefly to modern classical scholars, who have failed to realize the close connection between Greek poetry and Greek religion, and to note that the Greek descriptive writers, such as Herodotus and Pausanias, never cite a myth except with reference to some rite or some sacred site. The completely fallacious ideas of myth which scholars derived from their purely literary studies of Homer have been extended over the world; scholars naturally "approached the myths of Egypt, Babylonia, and India in the spirit they had imbibed from their classical studies. They picked out the myths from the texts in which they were embedded, arranged them into neat systems of mythology after the fashion of Hellenistic mythologists, and threw the rest of the texts on the rubbish heap."[4]

Leaving them to be rescued by other hands, I shall now examine some of the myths of Greece, and shall begin with perhaps the best-known, that of Helen.

The story of Helen is as follows: she is the daughter of Zeus and Leda, or of Oceanus and Tethyak, or of Tyndareus, or of Nemesis. She is the sister of Castor and Polydeuces, the Heavenly Twins, and is hatched from a swan's egg. She is born in various places. As a girl she is carried off by Theseus, but is rescued by her brothers while Theseus is on a visit to the underworld. On her return to Sparta she is wooed by all the great chiefs of Greece, and chooses Menelaus, in favour of whom her father or stepfather Tyndareus resigns his throne. By Menelaus she has a daughter, Hermione, who is old enough to be betrothed before the Trojan War. Helen elopes with Paris and goes with him to Troy, though in some accounts it is only her phantom that goes to Troy, while she herself remains in Egypt. After the ten years' siege and the death of Paris, she marries Deiphobus, who is killed by Menelaus. After many adventures she returns with Menelaus to Sparta, where they reign splendidly and uneventfully. Of her end there are various accounts. In one version she and Menelaus are transported alive to the Elysian Fields; in another she is expelled by her stepson and flees to Rhodes, where she is put to death; a third makes her end her days as the wife of Achilles.[5]

Many attempts have, of course, been made to euhemerize the story. Dr. Leaf says that Helen is "more than half mythical,"[6] by which he means that he can believe that whatever suits his theories is historically true, and treat the rest as fanciful additions. Dr. Farnell,[7] with the incurable romanticism of most classical scholars, finds no difficulty in believing that "a love episode should be the cause of a great war," and speaks of lovers running away together as if the elopement of a queen was an everyday occurrence. I can, however, find in history no instance in which a queen has eloped with a foreign prince, or anyone else. He fails to notice that she was carried off at least four times, by Hermes and by a robber as well as by Theseus and Paris.[8] The only queens who elope are the queens of myth, such as Etain, wife of Eochaidh, King of Ireland, and Guinevere, wife of King Arthur. The latter, like Helen, is said to have been carried off at least four times.[9]

There can be no reasonable doubt that this story, with all its miracles, improbabilities, and inconsistencies, is a myth; that is to say, it is a story which in its earlier forms described, and in its later forms tries to combine and explain, the various features and incidents in the worship of Helen, as it was carried on in different parts of Greece.

Perhaps the most important centre of her worship was at Sparta. There she had a great festival at which the maidens rode to her temple in chariots, and wore lotus flowers in her honor. Herodotus[10] tells us how an ugly and deformed little girl was taken to the temple of Helen by her nurse, who stood before the image and entreated the goddess to free the child from its deformity. A woman appeared, stroked the child, and said that she should surpass all the women of Sparta in beauty, which duly came to pass.

At Rhodes she was worshipped as Helen of the Tree, and a story was told of how she had been captured by the women of Rhodes and hanged from a tree.

In Egypt, according to Herodotus,[11] she was worshipped as the foreign Aphrodite, and a story was told of how she had been taken from Paris by an Egyptian king and later handed back to Menelaus.

At Therapnae she had a temple, where her grave was shown, and in many places trees and wells were sacred to her. She caused the appearance of light round ships (St. Elmo's fire), and was identified with a star. She also seems to have been the moon, since there are grounds for equating Helene with Selene. Further than that, it is probably from her, rather than from the insignificant Hellen, that the Hellenes get their name.

Those who think that a woman could arrive at such a pitch of glory merely because she was exceptionally beautiful and fascinating should reflect upon Cleopatra, the most beautiful and fascinating woman in history. No miracles were performed on her behalf, no temples were erected in her honour, and she owes her fame chiefly to her suicide.

It was not merely Helen, however, and other Greek heroes and heroines of the Tale of Troy who were worshipped as gods or goddesses in Greece, but in Trojan heroes and heroines as well. Hector was worshipped at Thebes, a striking fact to which we shall return later, and Kassandra, the Trojan prophetess, was worshipped at the Spartan cities of Leuctra, Amyclae, and Therapnae, as well as in Apulia.[12] Dr. Farnell accounts for these and many other facts connected with the worship of the Homeric heroes by supposing that the Greeks derived a large part of their religion from the *Iliad*, and cites as a parallel the development of Christian saint-worship under the influence of the sacred books.[13] But his whole case for the historicity of Homer is based on the assumption that the *Iliad* started as the purely secular account pulling at the corners of their lips. I've lived in New York all my life, and I've never heard the city so silent, so peaceful. Ironic, if one really thought about it.

"Yeah, kid, sure."

The boy pulls up a chair. The scraping of its feet across the floor is unbearably loud in the cafe.

"I'm Ethan," the kid tells me, holding out his tiny hand.

My lips twitch at the gesture. Trying to act all grown up and strong.

"Nick." I shake his hand, hating just how small it feels in mine.

There's silence for a moment, and now I feel awkward, when I hadn't before. I've never dealt well with being the center of attention, and the kid has been staring at me for what feels like ages. It wasn't, of course. Not even a full minute has passed since he sat down.

"I didn't wanna be alone," Ethan says. "You were alone, too."

"Ah," I say, because what else could I say? I look around the room again. The kid could have picked any other person.

I don't have a large family, and I lost track of my mom a few hours ago. My brother isn't even in the same state, and my dad died a couple of years back. There's no one else I count as family. I think, for a second—because time isn't something we can waste, now—of looking for my mom, but what's the point?

"It's my birthday tomorrow," Ethan says. "I'll be ten."

"Really?" I say, wincing at the thought. Weren't ten-year-olds supposed to be taller? I was taller, wasn't I? I don't remember being that small. Ethan glares at me—or pouts, it's really hard to tell the difference, with the pink cheeks and the messy blond curls that fall over his honey-brown eyes.

"I'm not small."

"Never said you were."

The pouty glare doesn't ease up.

"Ten, huh? That's an important milestone."

"Yeah," Ethan says quietly. "Dad promised me a skateboard."

I don't know what makes me do it, but I reach over and ruffle the feather-soft locks of hair, gaining a small smile from the boy. It doesn't reach his eyes, but I wasn't really expecting it to. I don't believe that anyone could be capable of a true smile now. I certainly can't muster the strength.

of a purely secular war. I know of no reason for supposing that anyone has ever derived his religion from a military chronicle, however skilfully versified.

In order to explain these facts, and the facts of Greek mythology in general, we shall have to get far from the romantic rationalizations of Dr. Farnell and his school, into the atmosphere of ritual. I shall try to convey an idea of what this atmosphere really is by quoting Professor Gronbech, who by his exposition of the Norse myths gives us perhaps as good an idea as possible of what the Homeric poems originally were.

"The poet," he says, "gives his narrative in the past form as if it were something over and done with. . . . But the literary form which the myths acquired in the hands of the poets during the Viking Age and later obscures the actual meaning that was plain to the listeners, when the legends were recited at the feast, and illustrated, or rather supplemented, by rites and ceremonial observances. . . . The legends will not tell us what happened in some year or other according to chronology; in our craving for a kernel of historical truth in the myths, we naïvely insinuate that the myth-makers ought to think in a system unknown to them for the benefit of our annalistic studies. . . . Time is, in our experience, a stream of events descending from the unknown mists of beginning and running in a continuous flow down the future into the unknown; to the men of the classical ages the actual life is the result of a recurrent beginning and has its source in the religious feast. The festival consists of a creation or new birth outside time, eternal it might be called if the word were not as misleading as all others and as inadequate to describe an experience of a totally alien character. When the priest or chieftain ploughs the ritual furrow, when the first seed is sown while the story of the origin of corn is recited, when the warriors act the war game, they make history, do the real work, fight the real battle, and when the men sally forth with the plough or the seed or the weapons, they are only realizing what was created in the ritual act.

"Ceremonial forms are the stream of life itself, not narrowing banks against which life grinds its passage. They are solemn because they are necessary. . . . To go with the sun, to grow and let grow with the moon, to carry out the ritual whereby kinship, whether with men or with nature, is strengthened and renewed, shereby the sun is held to its course and earth and heaven preserve their youth and strength, to effect honour and luck, to give the child its name-gift, to drink the cup of brotherhood—this is to live. It is forms which divide the living from the dead.

"Not only the future needed creation, the past too had to be renewed in the *blot* [sacrifice] to retain its reality. The eternity of life lay not in the fact that it had once begun, but solely in the fact that it was constantly being begun, so that the blotman's sacrifice points back as well as forward. In order to do justice to the meaning of the *blot* we must say that it not only condenses and renews the past, but in true earnest creates it over and over again. . . . Now we shall be able to look for the gods where they are really to be found. They are present as power in the events and power in the sacrificers. . . . The reciter and the ritual agent is no less the subject of the poem than the original hero himself, and no less responsible for the happy issue of his enterprise. . . .

"In the history of the sacrifical hall, the indivdual warrior is sunk in the god, or, which is the same thing, in the ideal personification of the clan, the hero. This form of history causes endless confusion among later historians, when they try their best to arrange the mythical traditions into chronological happenings, and the deeds of the clan into annals and lists of kings, and the confusion grows to absurdity when rationalistic logicians strive by the light of sound sense to extricate the kernel of history from the husks of superstition."[14]

This view was not confined to the Norse, but was, according to Professor Hooke,[15] general in the ancient world. The cyclic movement of the seasons and the heavenly bodies, together with the ritual system associated with them, "inevitably tended to produce a view of Time as a vast circle in which the pattern of the individual life and of the course of history was a recurring cyclic process." This view of time as a ritual circle seems to have been carried over into Christianity, since, according to Professor James;[16] "in the Eucharistic sacrifice the redemptive work of Christ was celebrated, not as a mere commemoration of a historical event, for in the liturgy the past became the present, and the birth at Bethlehem and the death on Calvary were apprehended as ever-present realities independent of time and space."

It is difficult for those who regard rites and ceremonies as desirable but not indispensable aids to the attainment of certain religious or social ends to understand the attitude of those to whom ritual means life, life in the social as well as in the religious sense. Ritual is far more to millions today than history has ever been to anyone. To all savages religion is ritual, and nothing more, and to most members of the higher religions ritual is far more important than either belief or ethics. People become, and remain, members of religious bodies (and social bodies such as the Freemasons) by performing ritual acts and uttering ritual words. As long as there is nothing novel about these acts and words, nobody troubles about their meaning. That is theology, a matter for the priests; and the chief, almost the sole, object of *their* study is to convince themselves that what they do or direct is right; that is to say, that the ritual and myth are in perfect agreement. Belief in the unity of myth and ritual is what we now call Fundamentalism, and a Fundamentalist is a person to whom the historical past is of no importance compared with the ritual past that is described in the myth. Adam really lived because he lives now—in the ritual. Criticism of the myth implies criticism of the ritual; hence the indignation of the Fundamentalists at anyone who fails to begin his history of the world with the myth of Adam. The ancient Greeks, who were, with the exception of a handful of philosophers, all Fundamentalists, had no cause to complain of their historians, since these all started their works by paying due respect to the myths, particularly the myth of Troy. They then made a big jump; according to the usual theories it was a jump of six or seven centuries, but it was really a jump from pure myth to history, though their history is not free from mythical elements. The reasons for this are firstly that there were no records upon which they could rely, and secondly that their object was not to build up a solid structure of knowledge of the past which should be available for the future, but merely interest and edify their contemporaries.[17]

The object of the poets was different. It was to combine into more or less coherent stories, and to make available for large audiences, the myths that were periodically enacted or otherwise handed on at the myriad temples and shrines of Greece. Professor Nilsson complains of "that disregard for history and geography which is peculiar to epic poetry,"[18] but they were not concerned with history at all, and as for geography, it was merely a question of what would pass muster; their audiences would accept Ithaca as a large and fertile island, just as Shakespeare's would accept Bohemia as a country on the sea coast.

As for the temple myths, out of which, in all probability, the epics were composed, even those who believe in the historicity of tradition realize their ritual origin. Thus Professor Halliday says that "the story of Lycaon, connected as it undoubtedly was with some form of human sacrifice which seems to have persisted up to the time of Pausanias, is an hieratic legend connected with the savage ritual of Lycaean Zeus, appears to me almost certain. The story of the serving up of Pelops by Tantalus may also have had a ritual origin and have been in the first place connected with some rite of human sacrifice and sacrament."[19]

Professor Cook refers the legend of Ixion, who was bound to a wheel, to a ritual in which a man was bound to a wheel and sacrificed in the character of the sun-god, and the legend of Triptolemus, who was borne over the earth in a winged chariot, from which he introduced the blessings of corn, to a rite at Eleusis; "the *protégé* of the goddess, mounting his winged seat, was swung aloft by means of a *géranos* or scenic crane."[20] And Professor Hooke[21] says that "both the Minotaur and Perseus myths involve an underlying pattern of human sacrifice, and take us back to a stage when myth and ritual were united."

In spite of his views on Lycaon and the Lycaean Zeus, Professor Halliday assures us that "we may assume with some certainty that a person about whom a legend was told was not a fictitious character, but a real person who once existed."[22] This is a striking example of the self-contradictions into which those who seek to establish the historicity of tradition inevitably fall. These contradictions can be resolved only by supposing that the Greeks were meticulous antiquaries who preserved through the centuries the facts of their history with the most scrupulous accuracy, and at the same time that they were people of the wildest imagination, who invented the most ridiculous stories about their ancestors, and believed in them as soon as they had invented them. And through all this haze of pseudo-history and pseudo-fiction we can see, not clearly, yet clearly enough, the Greeks for what they really were: a highly religious people, for whom the past existed, as for the vast majority of the human race it still exists, solely in the ritual. In the light of this fact, for I venture to assert categorically that it is a fact, let us return to the Tale of Troy.

Notes

1. *From Fetish to God in Ancient Egypt*, p. 155.

2. S. H. Hooke in *The Labyrinth*, p. v.

3. J. G. Frazer, op. cit., vol. iv, pp. 104, etc.; C. G. Seligman: *Egypt and Negro Africa*, pp. 21 ff.

4. A. M. Hocart in *The Labyrinth*, p. 264.

5. Smith: *Classical Dictionary*; H. J. Rose, op. cit.; G. Murray, op. cit., p. 205.

6. *Troy*, p. 329.

7. *Greek Hero Cults*, p. 325.

8. G. Murray, op. cit., p. 206.

9. E. K. Chambers: *Arthur of Britain*, p. 213.

10. Ch. vi, p. 61.

11. Ch. ii, p. 112.

12. L. R. Farnell, op. cit., pp. 410–11.

13. L. R. Farnell, op. cit., p. 340.

14. W. Gronbech: *The Culture of the Teutons*, vol. i, p. 249; vol. ii, pp. 106–7, 222, 223, 226, 240, 261.

15. *The Labyrinth*, p. 215.

16. *Christian Myth and Ritual*, p. 268.

17. G. G. Murray, op. cit., p. 2.

18. Op. cit., p. 118.

19. Op. cit., p. 103.

20. Op. cit., vol. i, pp. 211, 218.

21. In *Myth and Ritual*, p. 6.

22. Op. cit., p. 61.

MYTH AND RITUAL:
THE TALE OF TROY

THE scientific, as contrasted with the literary, study of the Homeric poems has hardly yet begun, and cannot take us very far until a sufficient number of students has realized that the poems have no historical foundation, but that as documents illustrating the development of religious ideas and beliefs they are of the highest importance. It is impossible for one who, like myself, is neither a Greek nor a German scholar (for there is much untranslated matter on this subject in German) to do more than try to point out the direction that in my belief these studies will take.

We must first try to form a picture of Greece as it really was about 700 B.C. It was in some respects analogous to England in A.D. 600; that is to say, it was occupied by tribes of barbarians who had blotted out an ancient civilization and were themselves beginning to be civilized through alien influence. Of the Greeks, as of the Saxons, we know nothing from historical, and little from archaeological, sources of the origin and history of these tribes, but of the Greeks we know much less than we do of the Saxons, for the period of darkness is much longer, and we have nothing to correspond with the late classical literature. There is this other difference: that whereas the Saxons never progressed very far along the path of civilization, a very small porportion of the Greeks rapidly reached a pitch of intellectual eminence which has rarely been rivalled. That this progress was extremely rapid, and that it was based upon alien elements, are shown not merely by the known facts of contemporary and earlier Asiatic culture, but by the manners and customs of the generality of Greeks, which up to the end of the classical period were still almost incredibly barbarous.

About 700 B.C., then, when we first begin to know something of the Greeks, we find a small educated class making, under the most favourable social and political conditions, the most phenomenal progress from a foundation of thought and knowledge which was entirely non-Greek, and a vast majority of illiterates, who knew nothing, and could know nothing, of their past history, but who were largely absorbed in their religion. This religion, though one in origin, and generally similar in ritual, had retained or acquired varying features in the more or less isolated cities, islands, and rural valleys; it consisted in the sacrificial worship of "heroes" at local shrines, combined with group meetings at highly sacred sites for the periodical performance of more important or more generalized rites. There were in historical times a number of these group meetings, at Delphi, at Olympia, at Delos, at Dodona, at Mycale, and elsewhere, the rites at which, especially the games and contests, suggest developments or survivals from a different state of society, a state in which the kingship played a highly important part. The type of kingship suggested by these rites, and by the survivals of the kingship in historical Greece, such as that of the archon at Athens, who was called the "king," and the extremely limited monarchy at Sparta, is a kingship of a purely ritual character. There is a great deal to suggest that the winners at the games were the successors of kings who became kings as the result of success in a ritual contest, and that in prehistoric Greece—that is, Greece before about 700 B.C.—kings were purely ritual figures, regarded as the personification of Zeus, and liable to be sacrificed at the end of a fixed period, which Sir James Frazer finds grounds for believing to have been eight years.[1] This aspect of the kingship, as I hope to show, is implicit in Homer and the rest of the myths, but taken as historical documents, they give a very different picture.

The kings of Homer, taken literally, are not in the Greek sense kings at all, but tyrants who gain their thrones by successful adventure and whose powers are limited only by their capacity for exercising them. Now, the ritual kingship as we find it in the fifth century B.C. is merely a survival represented by a number of rites and institutions, all of them more or less in a state of decay. If Homer wrote history, we must then suppose that after his time the type of kingship which was familiar to him disappeared and was succeeded by a very different type, which had time to rise, thrive, and decay before the fifth century; and that the Greeks of the latter period had forgotten almost everything about the later type of kingship, but had preserved a vivid recollection of the earlier.

All the difficulties, including those set out in Chapter IX, disappear when we realize that the Homeric poems, or rather the songs and stories out of which they were composed, are myths—that is, ritual narratives, connected with one or more of the group meetings mentioned above—and that the ritual performed at these meetings was very similar to, if not identical with, the ritual pattern described by Professor Hooke.[2] It may be remembered that the principal features of this ritual are the death and resurrection of the king, a sacred combat, a triumphal procession and enthronement, and a sacred marriage; and the difference I suggested was that in Greece the actual killing of the king survived longer than in the more civilized countries to the south and east. However this may be, there is, as we have seen, evidence that the kingship in prehistoric Greece was a temporary office, and that the kings were either actually killed or else reinstated after a pretended death, at the end of eight years. Now, in Greek the eight-year period was called a nine-year period, since both the first and last years were included,[3] and we find that in the Tale of Troy all the important incidents take place in the first and tenth years of the siege, and that in the mythological cycles, especially those of Troy and Thebes, all the important events are represented as taking place at intervals of about ten years. But if the ritual king's reign is eight years, his ritual life is longer, since, as we shall see later, the most important events in it take place before he is actually installed. This may explain the discrepancy between the eight- and the nine- or ten-year periods, since, as we must always bear in mind, these periods are ritual—that is to say, recurrent and not historical.

The question now arises whether these rites were actually performed at Troy and at Thebes, and the probability on the whole seems to be that they were, and that the two rituals were identical. There are many resemblances between the stories of Troy and Thebes. Both were built where a cow lay down. Both were unsuccessfully attacked, but ten years later stormed and razed to the ground. According to Hesiod, all the heroes of Greece were killed at one or the other. The Greek fleet that is to attack Troy meets at Aulis, a place most inconvenient for this purpose, but most convenient for an attack on Thebes, of which it is the port. Hector is a leading hero of both cities. Whether these and other resemblances are due to the partial combination of two different stories or the splitting up of what was one original story is not certain, but the latter seems more probable when we realize how easily mythical incidents can be located at actual places, and also transferred from one place to another. There is no difficulty about this, for, as we have seen in the stories of Robin Hood and other heroes, the place where the ritual is performed becomes the place where the incidents of the myth originally occurred.

We find a good example of this in Java. The war of the *Pandawa*, which forms the subject of the great Indian epic, the *Mahabharata*, is also the subject of the most popular Javanese poem, and the war is believed by the Javanese to have taken place in Java; "not only the countries mentioned in that war, but the dwelling-places and temples of the different heroes who distinguished themselves in it, are at the present day pointed out in Java."[4] The ritualistic attitude towards the past which could transfer all the sites and incidents of a mythical war from India to Java could transfer all the sites and incidents of a mythical war from Asia to Troy to Thebes.

What probably happened was that when the later forms of this kingship ritual were introduced into Greece, they were at first associated by the small independent tribes with the myths of their own gods or heroes, and that later attempts were made to combine these myths into one story. This seems to have happened in Palestine, where the origin of circumcision ritual was attributed to three different heroes, Abraham, Moses, and Joshua.[5]

The principal attempt to combine the myths of Greece into one story was, of course, made by Homer. And who was Homer? Homer, so Professor J.A.K. Thomson tells us, was the title given to the victor in the conquest of minstrelsy held at the festival of Apollo at Delos. He was the eponymous hero of the hymn-singers and sacred dancers, and was originally identical with the Delian Apollo.[6] "The hymn," Professor Thomson continues,[7] "has given birth to the heroic epos. For these 'men and women' are the old local Daimones—Achilles, Helen, and the rest. Their legends have combined to form one great legend recited at the Delian festival in honour of Apollo the Father god of all the Ionians. . . . The hymn gradually added to itself more and more of the inherited or borrowed legends of the Ionian race until it grew into the proportions of all 'Homer.' And as Homer was the traditional author of the original hymn, so he remained the traditional author of all the rest."

Yet although the Homeric poems are concerned almost entirely with the doings of gods and worshipped heroes, and although in classical times the poems were, as Professor Thomson shows, sacred poems recited at sacred festivals, yet most classical scholars are so obsessed by their literary aspect that they become quite incapable of realizing their religious character. Thus Professor Nilsson holds that "the return and vengeance of Odysseus is not an heroic legend but a novel,"[8] and even Professor Gilbert Murray regards the poems as "elaborate works of fiction."[9] As usual, these writers hover precariously between the fact theory and the fiction theory, but can they really believe that people compose fictitious tales about the gods they worship, and recite these tales at sacred festivals?

Mr. Burn[10] says that "Andromache is almost certainly a creation of the poet's brain. Her and her husband's function in the poem is simply to supply a foil to the other characters." But again let us turn to Java, and there we find in the sacred epic, which is of Hindu origin, a general similarity to the Tale of Troy, and parallels to many of its characters and incidents. In particular the account of the parting of Salia from his wife Satia Wati and his subsequent death bears a striking resemblance to the account of Hector's parting from Andromache and his subsequent death.[11]

That the hero king, at the conclusion of his tenure of office, normally goes out of the city to be killed we shall see in the next chapter; it may well be that a ceremonial parting from his consort formed part of the ritual in Greece and Java as it did in Mexico, where the man who took the part of the "god of gods" bade farewell to his consorts at a fixed spot before ascending the pyramid at the top of which he was to meet his doom.[12] Here again we must emphasize that what has to be explained is not the fact that a man should bid farewell to his wife before going to his death, but that such an incident should form part of a sacred poem. The idea that the subject-matter of hymns is drawn from domestic scenes, real or fictitious, is erroneous.

Let us now try to get a more general idea of the ritual of which this scene formed a part. Mr. W.F.J. Knight[13] notes that the name of Troy is widely associated with mazes or labyrinths, and that various incidents in the *Iliad* correspond with known features of a once widespread maze ritual, and says that "the goddess or one of the heroines of Troy corresponds to the maiden who stays in the nucleus of a maze during a maze ritual, or to the princess who is united to a hero in northern myths after he has penetrated to the heart of a mountain, sometimes by the aid of a magic horse." He goes on to show that ring magic and armed dances are connected both with fertility and with military de-

TEN MINUTES

A.G. Lopes

IT'S STRANGE, TEN MINUTES NEVER MEANT MUCH TO ME. SURE, there had been those moments before an exam started or ended, where it felt as if those ten minutes would make or break me. But once it was over, that was it—it was done, and life went on. For that moment in time, those ten minutes felt like the most important of my life. Then they were swallowed by all the other minutes that had also felt life-altering but weren't.

This, though... this is different. I'm just twenty-four. I'm not ready. Then again, I don't think any of us are.

"Mister?"

I look down at the little boy pulling my sleeve. He can't be older than seven; he's tiny.

"Yes?"

"Can I stay with you?"

There is no point in asking about his parents; what would it matter now? I glance at the few people around us. Most of them are silent, waiting, while others are talking in quiet voices, tiny smiles fence. The wooden horse is then a ritual beast akin to Pegasus and Sigurd's horse Grani, and is not, as has been absurdly supposed, a genuine military stratagem.

The *Iliad* is, then, on Mr. Knight's showing, an account of a ritual that includes a sacred combat and a sacred marriage. But there is much more in the Homeric poems than this. Professor Hocart gives a list of twenty-six features that characterize the ceremonies attendant on the installation of kings in all parts of the world. I believe that all of these are to be found in the Homeric poems, but the search would occupy a large volume, and I shall be content to touch on two which he includes in his list and one which he does not. He begins his list with "(A) The theory is "that the King (1) dies; (2) is reborn, (3) as a god."[14] In Fiji during a chief's installation the same ceremonies are observed as at his death, and after his installation he is nursed as a new-born babe for four days. In ancient India, according to the scriptures, the officiating priest invested the new king with garments called "the caul of sovereignty" and "the womb of sovereignty," and "thereby caused him to be born." In Egypt the Pharaoh is shown on monuments being suckled by his wife of the principal god.[15] In these cases the ceremonies of death and resurrection and rebirth are symbolized, but at Umundri, in Nigeria, the rite is performed more literally. There, according to Mr. Jeffreys,[16] the officiating priest says to the candidate for the kingship: "You are about to enter the grave; rise up again with a vivid and shining body." The candidate is then prepared for burial in the usual way, and buried in a grave dug outside his own house. His wives wail and the usual mourning ceremonies are performed. At sunset he is dug up, washed, and whitened all over with clay, and thus fulfils the prayer that he should rise with a white and shining body. Henceforth he is regarded as a god. We can now understand why heroes visit the underworld, the dwelling-place of the dead. They do so in order that they may return from the dead as gods. Odysseus, therefore, visits the dead as part of his progress to the divine kingship, and Heracles, Theseus, Orpheus, and Dionysos do the same. I may add that according to Mr. Knight[17] "the Latin word *inire*, the origin of our word 'initiation,' has been thought with reason to have been directly used for ritual entry into the earth, as in sacrificial burials."

After the king has been installed, he makes a tour of his dominions, always starting from the east and following the course of the sun, and at each of the four quarters receiving the homage of vassals. According to the Buddhist scriptures, a king, when he has performed this rite, becomes a "wheel monarch."[18] In the other rituals discussed by Professor Hocart the rite has become a mere procession round the city, like our Lord Mayor's Show, which, of course, follows his installation. It would seem, however, that Dhu'l Qarnein, the Two-horned One of the Qurân, was also a "wheel-monarch,"[19] as was Dermot, King of Ireland, who "on his regal circuit travelled right-handed round Ireland," and after visiting the four provinces returned to Tara.[20] These were inland kings, but the king of the Ægean must have made his progress by sea, and the Odyssey, though it has had other ritual features incorporated in it, would seem to be in the main an account of such a progress. The story of Sinbad the Sailor perhaps embodies a similar myth, the ritual aspect of which seems to have found its last expression in the voyages of the Areoi, the guilds of sacred actors of Polynesia.

One of the most important duties of the divine king is to rekindle the sacred fire. This rite is still performed annually at Jerusalem, though not by the normal method, which is to rotate a pointed piece of hard wood in a hole made in a piece of soft wood. In this form the rite is almost world-wide. Professor A. B. Cook[21] adduces much evidence to suggest that the story of how Odysseus plunged his heated bar into the Cyclops' eye is derived from a fire-making rite, and that his title of "Ithakos," which has led to the belief that he came from the island of Ithaka, may be equivalent to "Ithax," which is an alternative name for Prometheus, and means "the fiery one." Just as "Odysseus" is the king's cult title in his character of the wolf-god,[22] so may "Ithakos" be his cult title in his capacity as kindler of the sacred fire.

It would be possible, and indeed easy, to find parallels in myth and ritual for every incident in the Odyssey, but those given should be enough to convince any person of open mind that there is a great deal more in it than meets the eye. No argument can make any impression on the minds of the orthodox scholars, who refuse to look outside the text and are content to believe that Odysseus was a real man, whose exploits gave rise to his fame, and whose fame stimulated a blind man to invent his exploits.

There is one phenomenon that actually connects "the holy town of Ilium," which, though a foreign town, was loved by Zeus, the god of the Greeks, "above all cities and all nations of the earth,"[23] but which he nevertheless allowed to be destroyed, with the historic city near the entrance to the Hellespont—the affair of the Locrian maidens.

Every year, from prehistoric times down to 200 B.C., and probably later, the Locrians, a people whose chief town was Opous, about twenty miles north of Thebes, sent a tribute of two noble maidens to Troy, or Ilium as it was then known. The citizens of Ilium met them and attempted to kill them, but usually without success, since they were guarded by a body of their fellow countrymen, who smuggled them through an underground passage into the Temple of Athena. Once there, they were safe, but lived for a year a despised and degraded life as temple slaves, after which they were replaced, but were condemned to perpetual celibacy. On the rare occasions when one of the maidens was slain, her slayer received the thanks of the citizens, and her body was destroyed by a particular ritual. The Locrians made frequent attempts to rid themselves of this burden, but were always threatened by the Delphic oracle with disaster.

The explanation of this remarkable proceeding given in classical times was that it was a punishment imposed upon the Locrians for the conduct of their great cult-hero, Aias Oileus, who at the sack of Troy had violated Kassandra in the Temple of Athena. Dr. Farnell, of course, accepts this story as historically true, and in so doing misses its whole point. "No incident was more likely," he says,[24] "than that a certain Greek leader should have violated the purity of a temple." But the incident, far from being "likely," is represented as unparalleled; that is why, according to the story, it received a unique punishment. Professor Nilsson also fails to realize that the whole proceeding was unique, since he suggests[25] that Locris was a colony of Troy, and appears to suppose that annual tribute of maidens from a colony to the mother city was normal.

Now we must note in the first place that the whole procedure was sacrificial; the maidens, if not killed, went through a rite of pretence burial, from which they emerged as vestals. This rite has no connection whatever with the alleged crime of Aias, but is connected with another myth, that of the theft of the Palladium by Odysseus and Diomedes, who were said to have entered Troy by the same underground passage.[26] Secondly, it seems that the name "Oileus" is closely connected with "Ilion,"[27] so that Aias, whose second name it was, may be suspected of being the eponymous hero of Ilium, while Kassandra, like Athens, was a city-goddess, and may be identical with her. It may be added that Pausanias describes a very similar ritual at Athens.[28]

We know from what Professor Hocart[29] tells us that the installation of a king normally includes a sacred marriage and a human sacrifice, and I suggest that of the two maidens, who were always drawn from the alleged descendants of Aias, one was originally the divine bride and the other the divine victim. Anyhow, we know that Aias had an elaborate cult in Locris, and on the supposition that he was a real man we must conclude that the Locrians, looking back through the long centuries of their history, could find no citizen worthy of honour except a second-rate buccaneer whose infamous conduct had brought upon them eternal injury and disgrace.

Dr. Farnell's belief that personalities can be vividly remembered for eight hundred years or more is astonishing, since he must have realized how little we know, even assuming tradition to be true, of Greek prehistory. Did he really believe that during a period of at least four centuries there was nobody in Greece who possessed a personality? Of course he could not have, but like most classical scholars he had been so thoroughly soaked in the belief that tradition is history that any other view of it was inconceivable. And even those scholars who have realized that tradition in its main features in myth are ready to jump back to pseudo-history on the smallest provocation. Thus Miss Jessie Weston, in her *From Ritual to Romance*, after dealing with a large group of Grail stories, concludes that these stories "repose eventually," not upon a poet's imagination, but upon the ruins of an august and ancient ritual, a ritual which once claimed to be the accredited guardian of the deepest secrets of life."[30] Yet she supposes that certain historical incidents have crept into these narratives. For example, the story of how King Amangens outraged one of the Grail maidens and took her golden Cup from her, in which action he was imitated by his knights, may be the record "of an outrage offered by some, probably local, chieftain to a priestess of the cult."[31] Yet this story is clearly analogous to that of Aias and Kassandra, which we have just been discussing. And the story of how Ghaus, a squire of King Arthur, dreams of taking a golden candlestick from a chapel in the forest, and of being attacked by an ugly black man, and awakes to find himself mortally wounded, may have "made a profound impression on the popular imagination owing to the youth and possible social position of the victim."[32] Victim of what? Miss Weston failed to realize that accounts of isolated outrages do not find their way into ancient and august rituals, and that successful breaches of taboo, far from being recorded, are ignored and their very possibility denied.

Mr. Nutt tells us that "the development of the mythical literature connected with the Tuatha de Danann may now be safely sketched. Originally, it doubtless consisted wholly of chants forming part of the ritual, and of legends accounting for and interpreting ritual acts."[33] Yet even Mr. Nutt, as we saw,[34] thought that there might be some historical foundations for the Irish myths. How could legends that account for and interpret ritual acts have a historical basis?

Hartland, again, realized that "the ceremony at Coventry is a survival of an annual rite in honour of a heathen goddess, from which men were excluded."[35] The ceremony to which he refers is, of course, that associated with the name of Lady Godiva, and was probably similar to that at Banbury, where a fine lady rode on a white horse. Yet he postulates a different origin for many stories of the same type.

Similarly MacCulloch, who, as we saw,[36] attributes so many traditional tales to imagination, realizes that some myths are connected with ritual. "Some of these," he says of the Algonquin stories,[37] "are myths, and in this group we have those which are recited at the initiation of candidates . . . as well as some which are not now recited, but are believed to have formed part of the sacred ritual long ago. All form part of a mythological cycle dealing with the life of the hero-divinity. Manabush." The Homeric poems are also mythological cycles dealing with the lives of hero-divinities, but nothing arouses the fury of our scholars so much as the suggestion that these cycles are founded upon ritual. It is scarcely an exaggeration to say that in their view the Tale of Troy is a sober record of historic fact, composed entirely of scraps of picturesque fiction.

There is nothing in Homer that we cannot find elsewhere; "in other poems we observe the ancient ritual underlying poetical composition, as the substratum on which the poets have moulded a literary form; when for instance the Eddaic description of Sigurd's dragon-killing and wooing of the sleeping woman in armour culminates in a ritual toast . . . the succession of the scenes is probably governed by the procedure of the feast. . . . Thor's voyage to the giant Geirrod is really a descriptive of the ritual journey of the sacrificer and his assistants to the cattle-fold, and their procedure there."[38]

With this we may compare the opinion of Professor Saintyves, who holds that the magical transformations in Hop-o'-My-Thumb and similar tales are really *étapes coutumières* in the initiation ceremony, and that ogre, giant, devil, dragon, troll, sorcerer, and cannibal are merely titles for a liturgical personage, the tempter or terrifying devil of the initiations.[39]

As in the myth, the epic, the saga, and the fairy-tale, so also in the ballad we find that the basis is ritual. "The earliest form of the ballad in France seems to have been a little wooing-dance acted as a sort of May-game and originating in the ritual wedding. There are great numbers of such wooing-dances in Sweden and Denmark. . . . A Danish ballad even remembers the significance of the ritual; Ridder Stig drinks to his lady-love so that 'field and the wood blossom there at.' "[40]

Notes

1. Op. cit., vol. iv, pp. 58, 87; also vol. ii, p. 177.

2. *Supra*, p. 117.

3. J. G. Frazer, op. cit., vol. iv, p. 59 n.

4. T. S. Raffles: *History of Java*, vol. ii, p. 76.

5. E. O. James in *Myth and Ritual*, p. 152. A similar phenomenon in America is described by Professor R. H. Lowie in the *American Anthropologist*, vol. 16, p. 107.

6. *Studies in the Odyssey*, pp. 205, 207, 224.

7. Ibid., p. 229.

8. Op. cit., p. 137.

9. Op. cit., p. 231.

10. Op. cit., p. 18.

11. R. S. Raffles, op. cit., vol. i, p. 510. The parallel is mine.

12. J. G. Frazer, op. cit., vol. ix, p. 279.

13. In *Folk-Lore*, vol. xlvi, p. 106.

14. *Kingship*, p. 70.

15. Ibid., pp. 74, 77, 84.

16. M.D.W. Jeffreys, in a paper read to the International Congress of Anthropology, 1934.

17. Loc. cit., p. 107.

18. A. M. Hocart, *Kingship*, p. 23.

19. Qurân, sura xviii, 83 ff.

20. S. H. O'Grady: *Silva Gadelica*, p. 86.

21. Op. cit., vol. i, p. 327.

22. J.A.K. Thomson, op. cit., p. 16.

23. *Iliad*, vi, p. 448.

24. Op. cit., p. 301.

25. *Iliad*, vi, p. 46.

26. W.F.J. Knight in *Folk-Lore*, vol. xlvi, p. 101 n.

27. L. R. Farnell, op. cit., p. 302.

28. I. xxvii, 3.

29. Op. cit., p. 71.

30. J. Weston: *From Ritual to Romance*, p. 176.

31. Ibid., p. 163.

32. Ibid., p. 171.

33. A. Nutt: *The Voyage of Bran*, vol. ii, p. 194.

34. Raglan: *The Hero: A Study in Tradition, Myth, and Ritual*, Part I, p. 95.

35. Op. cit., p. 92.

36. *Supra*, p. 99.

37. Op. cit., p. 460.

38. W. Gronbech, op. cit., vol. ii, pp. 229, 274.

39. Op. cit., pp. 275, 303.

40. B. S. Phillpotts, op. cit., pp. 200, 202.

THE HERO

IN the earlier chapters of this book I took a succession of well-known heroes of tradition, and attempted to show that there is no justification for believing that any of these heroes were real persons, or that any of the stories of their exploits had any historical foundation. In the course of the discussion I had frequent occasion to suggest that these heroes, if they were genuinely heroes of tradition, were originally not men but gods, and that the stories were accounts not of fact but of ritual—that is, myths. As my chief object in those chapters was, however, to show that the heroes had no claim to historicity, I made no attempt to link them, or the beliefs connected with them, to any general ritual scheme. Before so doing, it seemed desirable to demonstrate, both theoretically and by examples, the intimate association of myth with ritual, an association that has been recognized by many leading students of these subjects, and upon which depends the validity of the conclusions I have reached.

Some years ago I had occasion to study the myth of Œdipus, and to try to analyse it,[1] and I was struck by the similarity of many of the incidents in it to incidents in the stories of Theseus and Romulus. I then examined the stories of a number of other traditional heroes of Greece, and found that when these stories were split up into separate incidents, there were certain types of incident which ran through all the stories.

Whether these parallels have any significance, or whether they are merely coincidences, the sort of thing that might happen to or be readily invented about any hero, are questions to which we shall come later. My first task is to show that the parallels exist, and for that purpose it is necessary to tabulate and number them. What I have done is to take a dozen heroes whose stories are narrated in sufficient detail, to tabulate the incidents in their careers, and to regard as typical such incidents as occur in the majority of the stories. By tabulating these typical incidents, I have arrived at what appears to be a pattern, in which I include all incidents, whether they are miraculous or whether they seem insignificant, which occur with sufficient regularity. I have often then fitted the pattern back on to my dozen heroes and, finding that it fits, have extended it to a number of heroes from outside the classical area, with what have been to me surprising results.

I should like it to be quite clear that in the potted biographies which follow there is no intention of giving a complete account of the heroes. Irrelevant incidents and alternative versions are omitted, and no attempt is made to distinguish between genuine mythology—that is, mythology connected with ritual—and the imitation mythology which probably forms a large part of the stories of Arthur and of Romulus. The wearing of an imitation sword may be just as significant as the wearing of a real one, and it is with the uniform of the heroes and not with their outfitters that I am at present concerned.

The pattern, then, is as follows:

    (1) The hero's mother is a royal virgin;

    (2) His father is a king, and

    (3) Often a near relative of his mother, but

    (4) The circumstances of his conception are unusual, and

    (5) He is also reputed to be the son of a god.

    (6) At birth an attempt is made, usually by his father or his maternal grandfather, to kill him, but

    (7) He is spirited away, and

    (8) Reared by foster-parents in a far country.

    (9) We are told nothing of his childhood, but

    (10) On reaching manhood he returns or goes to his future kingdom.

    (11) After a victory over the king and/or a giant, dragon, or wild beast,

    (12) He marries a princess, often the daughter of his predecessor, and

    (13) Becomes king.

    (14) For a time he reigns uneventfully, and

    (15) Prescribes laws, but

    (16) Later he loses favour with the gods and/or his subjects, and

    (17) Is driven from the throne and city, after which

    (18) He meets with a mysterious death,

    (19) Often at the top of a hill.

    (20) His children, if any, do not succeed him.

    (21) His body is not buried, but nevertheless

    (22) He has one or more holy sepulchres.

Let us now apply this pattern to our heroes, and we will start with

Œdipus

His mother, Jocasta, is (1) a princess, and his father is (2) King Laius, who, like her, is (3) of the line of Cadmus. He has sworn to have no connection with her, but (4) does so when drunk, probably (5) in the character of Dionysos. Laius (6) tries to kill Œdipus at birth, but (7) he is spirited away, and (8) reared by the King of Corinth. (9) We hear nothing of his childhood, but (10) on reaching manhood he returns to Thebes, after (11) gaining victories over his father and the Sphinx. He (12) marries Jocasta, and (13) becomes king. For some years he (14) reigns uneventfully, but (16) later comes to be regarded as the cause of a plague, and (17) is deposed and driven into exile. He meets with (18) a mysterious death at (19) a place near Athens called the Steep Pavement. He is succeeded by (20) Creon, through whom he was deposed, and though (21) the place of his burial is uncertain, he has (22) several holy sepulchres.

He does not seem to have been regarded as a legislator; apart from that we may award him full marks.

Theseus

His mother, Æthra, is (1) a royal virgin, and his father is (2) King Ægeus, who is (4) induced to have intercourse with her by a trick. He is also (5) reputed to be the son of Poseidon. At birth he is hidden from the Pallatidæ, who (6) wish to kill him, and (8) reared by his maternal grandfather. We hear (9) nothing of his childhood, but on reaching manhood he (10) proceeds to Athens, (11) killing monsters on the way. He marries (12) several heiress princesses, but (13) succeeds to the kingdom of his father, whose death he (11) causes. For a time (14) he reigns peacefully, and (15) prescribes laws, but later (16) becomes unpopular, is driven (17) from Athens, and (18) is thrown or falls from (19) a high cliff. His supplanter, Menestheus, is (20) no relation. His burial-place is (21) unknown, but bones supposed to be his are placed in (22) a holy sepulchre at Athens.

He scores twenty.

Romulus

His mother, Rhea, is (1) a royal virgin, and his father is (2) King Amuulius, who is (3) her uncle, and (4) visits her in armour. He is also

(5) reputed to be the son of Mars. At birth (6) his father tries to kill him, but (7) he is wafted away, and (8) reared by foster-parents at a distance. On reaching manhood he (10) returns to his birthplace, and having (11) killed his father and gained a magical victory over his brother, he (12) founds Rome and becomes king. His marriage is uncertain, and he is said to have performed some feats after his accession, but he (15) prescribes laws, and (16) later becomes unpopular. Leaving the city (17) after his deposition has been decided upon, he is (18) carried to the sky in a chariot of fire. His successor is (20) a stranger. His body (21) not having been found, he is (22) worshipped in a temple.

We can give him eighteen points.

Heracles

His mother, Alcmene, is (1) a royal virgin, and his father is (2) King Amphitryon, who is (3) her first cousin. He is reputed to be (5) the son of Zeus, who (4) visited Alcmene in the guise of Amphitryon. At his birth (6) Hera tries to kill him. On reaching manhood he (11) performs feats and wins victories, after which he (10) proceeds to Calydon, where he (12) marries the King's daughter, and (13) becomes ruler. He remains there (14) quietly for some years, after which an accidental manslaughter compels him (17) to flee from the country. He disappears (18) from a funeral pyre (19) on the top of Mount Œta. His sons (20) do not succeed him. His body (21) is not found, and (22) he is worshipped in temples.

He scores seventeen points.

Perseus

His mother, Danaë, is (1) a royal virgin, and his father is (2) King Proetus, who is (3) her uncle. He is also reputed to be (5) the son of Zeus, who (4) visited Danaë in a shower of gold. His mother's father (6) tries to kill him at birth, but he is (7) wafted away, and (8) reared by the King of Seriphos. We hear (9) nothing of his childhood, but on reaching manhood he (11) kills a dragon and (12) marries a princess. He then (10) returns to his birthplace, where he (11) kills his father or uncle, and (13) becomes king. We hear (14) nothing of his reign, and his end is (18) variously reported, though in one version he is killed by his successor. His children (20) do not succeed him. His burial-place is (21) unknown, but he is (22) worshipped at shrines.

He scores eighteen points.

Jason

His mother, Alcimede, is (1) a princess, and his father is (2) King Æson. His uncle, Pelias, (6) tries to kill him at birth, but (7) he is spirited away, and (8) brought up at a distance by Cheiron. We hear (9) nothing of his childhood, but on reaching manhood he wins the Golden Fleece, and (12) marries a princess, after which he proceeds (10) to his birthplace, causes (11) the death of Pelias, and (13) becomes king in his stead. He is afterwards (17) driven from throne and city by his uncle's son, and his end is (18) obscure. His children do not (20) succeed him. His burial-place is (21) unknown, but he is (22) worshipped at shrines.

He scores fifteen points.

Bellerophon

His mother, Eurymede, is (1) a princess, and his father is (2) King Glaucus. He is also (5) reputed to be the son of Poseidon. We hear (9) nothing of his childhood, but on reaching manhood he (10) travels to his future kingdom, (11) overcomes a monster, (12) marries the King's daughter, and (13) becomes king. We hear (14) nothing of his reign, but later he (16) becomes hated by the gods, and (17) goes into exile. His fate is (18) obscure, though it includes (19) an attempted ascent to the sky. His children (20) do not succeed him, and his burial-place is (21) unknown, but he was worshipped (22) at Corinth and in Lycia.

He scores sixteen points.

Pelops

His mother, Dione, is (1) a demigoddess, and his father is (2) King Tantalus, but he is also (5) reputed to be the son of Poseidon. His father (6) kills him, but the gods restore him to life. We hear (9) nothing of his childhood, but on reaching manhood he (10) proceeds to his future kingdom, (11) defeats and kills the King, (12) marries his daughter, and (13) becomes king. He (15) regulates the Olympic games, but otherwise we hear (14) nothing of his reign, except that he banishes his sons, who (20) do not succeed him. He has (22) a holy sepulchre at Olympia.

We can give him at least thirteen points.

Asclepios

His mother, Coronis, is (1) a royal virgin, and his father is (5) Apollo, who (6) nearly kills him at birth. He is (7) spirited away, and (8) reared by Cheiron at a distance. On reaching manhood he (11) overcomes death, becomes (13) a man of power, and (16) prescribes the laws of medicine. Later he (17) incurs the enmity of Zeus, who (18) destroys him with a flash of lightning. His burial-place is (21) unknown, but (22) he has a number of holy sepulchres.

He scores at least twelve points.

Dionysos

His mother, Semele, is (1) a royal virgin, and his father is (5) Zeus, who is (3) Semele's uncle by marriage, and who (4) visits her in a thunderstorm. Hera (6) tries to kill him at birth, but (7) he is miraculously saved, and (8) brought up in a remote spot. We hear (9) nothing of his childhood, but on reaching manhood he (10) travels into Asia, (11) gains victories, and (13) becomes a ruler. For a time he (14) rules prosperously, and (15) prescribes laws of agriculture, etc., but later (17) is carried into exile. He (18) goes down to the dead, but afterwards (19) ascends Olympus. He seems (20) to have no children. He has (21) no burial-place, but (22) numerous shrines and temples.

We can give him nineteen points.

Apollo

His mother, Leto, is (1) a royal virgin, and his father is (5) Zeus, who is (3) her first cousin. At birth he is (6) in danger from Hera, but (7) his mother escapes with him, and (8) he is reared at Delos. We hear (9) nothing of his childhood, but on reaching manhood he (10) goes to Delphi, where he (11) kills the Python, becomes (13) king, and (15) prescribes the laws of music, etc.

We can take him no further, but he has scored eleven points.

Zeus

His mother, Rhea, is (1) a goddess, and his father is (5) the god Cronos, who is (3) her brother. His father (6) tries to kill him at birth, but (7) he is spirited away, and (8) reared in Crete. We hear (9) nothing of his childhood, but on reaching manhood he (10) sets forth for Olympus, (11) defeats the Titans, (12) marries his sister, and (13) succeeds his father as king. He (14) reigns supreme, and (15) prescribes laws. Nevertheless he has (22) a holy sepulchre in Crete, and (19) hilltops are particularly sacred to him.

He scores fifteen points.

The lives of the Old Testament heroes have been heavily edited, but the same pattern is nevertheless apparent. Let us take three examples:

Joseph

His mother, Rachel, is (1) the daughter of a patriarch, and his father, Jacob, is (2) a patriarch, and (3) her first cousin. His mother conceives him (4) by eating mandrakes. In his childhood his brothers (6) attempt to kill him, but he is (7) saved by a stratagem, and (8) reared in Egypt. On reaching manhood he is (11) the victor in a contest in dream-interpretation and weather-forecasting, is (12) married to a lady of high rank, and (13) becomes ruler of Egypt. He (14) reigns prosperously, and (15) prescribes laws. We hear nothing of his later years, but the mention of a king who "knew not Joseph" suggests that he fell into disfavour.

Anyhow, we can give him twelve points.

Moses

His parents (1 and 2) were of the principal family of the Levites, and (3) near relatives; he is (5) also reputed to be the son of Pharaoh's daughter. Pharaoh (6) attempts to kill him at birth, but (7) he is wafted away, and (8) reared secretly. We are told (9) nothing of his childhood, but on reaching manhood he (11) kills a man, and (10) goes to Midian, where (12) he marries the ruler's daughter. Returning (10) to Egypt, he (11) gains a series of magical victories over Pharaoh, and (13) becomes a ruler. His rule lasts a long time, and (15) he prescribes laws, but later he (16) loses the favour of Jehovah, is (17) removed from his leadership, and (18) disappears mysteriously from (19) the top of a mountain. His children (20) do not succeed him. His body (21) is not buried, but (22) he has a holy sepulchre near Jerusalem.

He scores twenty points, several of them twice, or, if we include Josephus's account, even three times.

Elijah

After (11) a victory in a rain-making contest, he becomes (13) a sort of dictator. A plot is made against him (16), and he flees (17) to Beersheba, after which he (18) disappears in a chariot of fire. He had previously (19) brought down fire from heaven to a mountain-top. His successor, Elisha, is (20) no relation. His body is (21) not buried, but (22) he has a holy sepulchre.

We know nothing of his parentage and birth, but can give him nine points.

We find the same pattern in the life of a Javanese hero.

Watu Gunung

His mother, Sinta, appears (1) to be a princess, and his father is (2) a holy man. Since his mother sees his father only in a dream, the circumstances of his conception are (4) unusual. When quite young, he incurs his mother's wrath, and she (6) gives him a wound on the head. He (7) flees into the woods and does not return. We are told (9) nothing of his childhood, except that he is brought up by a holy man in (8) a far country. On reaching manhood he (10) journeys to a kingdom where (11) he kills the King, and (13) becomes king in his stead. After this he (12) marries his own mother and sister, who do not recognize him. For a long time he (14) reigns uneventfully, and has a large family, but eventually his mother recognizes the scar she gave him when a child, and is overcome with grief. The gods having (16) refused his request for another wife, he (17) invades heaven, but the gods, having learned by a stratagem the answer to his riddle and the secret of his invulnerability, put him to death (19) there by (18) separating his arms. His sons do not (20) succeed him, and (21) there is no mention of his burial.

His story, as given by Sir Stamford Raffles,[2] is obviously incomplete, yet its resemblance to the Œdipus myth is striking, and we can give the hero eighteen point.

Let us now transport ourselves to the Upper Nile, where we find that Nyikang, the cult-hero of the Shiluk tribe, is represented as following a career that affords a number of resemblances to our pattern.[3]

Nyikang

His mother, Nyikaia, was apparently (1) a crocodile princess, and his father was (2) a king. We hear (9) nothing of his childhood, but when he reaches manhood his brother (6) tries to kill him. He goes (10) to another country, and (12) marries a king's daughter. After (11) a number of victories, actual and magical, he (13) becomes king. For a time he reigns (14) prosperously, and (15) prescribes laws, but at last the people begin (16) to complain against him. Distressed at this, he (18) disappears mysteriously. Though (21) not buried, he (22) has a number of holy sepulchres.

He scores fourteen points.

Let us now come nearer home and consider some of the heroes of northern Europe:

Sigurd or Siegfried

His mother, Siglinde, is (1) a princess, and his father is (2) King Sigmund, who is (3) her brother, and whom she (4) visits in the guise of another woman. On reaching manhood he (10) performs a journey, (11) slays a dragon, (12) marries a princess, and (13) becomes a ruler. For a time he (14) prospers, but later (16) there is a plot against him, and he is killed. He is (19) the only man who can pass through a ring of fire to a hilltop.

He scores eleven points.

The next two examples I shall give are Celtic and are interesting as showing how variations of the same theme can exist in the same culture area. The story of Llew Llawgyffes is given by Professor W. J. Gruffydd.[4]

Llew Llawgyffes

His mother, Arianrhod, is (1) a royal virgin, and his father is apparently Gwydion, who is (2) a prince, and (3) her brother. The circumstances of his conception are (4) unusual, since his mother believes herself to be a virgin at the time of his birth. As soon as he is born he is (7) spirited away by his father, and (8) nursed by a foster-mother. When less than two years old he is (9) a "big lad," and (10) returns to the court. With his father's help he (11) wins magical victories, (12) marries a supernatural being, and (13) becomes a ruler. For a time he rules uneventfully, but later (16) loses favour with his wife, who (17) induces him to leave his court. He is (18) speared, but flies off in the form of an eagle, from (19) a curious elevated position. He has (20) no children and (21) no real death or burial.

He scores seventeen points.

Arthur

He mother, Igraine, is (1) a princess, and his father is (2) the Duke of Cornwall. He is, however, (5) reputed to be the son of Uther Pendragon, who (4) visits Igraine in the Duke's likeness. At birth he is apparently in no danger, yet is (7) spirited away and (8) reared in a distant part of the country. We hear (9) nothing of his childhood but on reaching manhood he (10) travels to London, (11) wins a magical victory, and (13) is chosen king. After other victories he (12) marries Guinevere, heiress of the Round Table. After this he (14) reigns uneventfully, and (15) prescribes the laws of chivalry, but later there is (16) a successful conspiracy against him, while (17) he is abroad. He meets with (18) a mysterious death, and his children do not (20) succeed him. His body is (21) not buried, but nevertheless he has (22) a holy sepulchre at Glastonbury.

He scores nineteen points.

Traces of the pattern are also to be found in the story of

Robin Hood

His father is a Saxon yeoman, but he is also (5) reputed to be the son of a great noble. We (9) hear nothing of his youth, but on reaching manhood he leads a life of debauchery until compelled to fly (10) to Sherwood, where he (11) gains victories over the Sheriff of Nottingham, (12) marries Maid Marian, the Queen of May, and (13) becomes King of May and ruler of the forest. For a long time he reigns, and (15) prescribes the laws of archery, but eventually illness overtakes him, and he (17) has to leave the forest and meets (18) a mysterious death in (19) an upper room. He (20) has no children. The place of his death and burial are (21) variously given, but (22) miracles were performed at his tomb at Kirkley, in Yorkshire.

We can give him thirteen points.

Cuchulainn also scores a good number of points, and it is interesting to compare these heroes of myth with Hengist, who makes a journey, wins a victory, and becomes a king, but otherwise is not alleged to have done anything which brings him within the pattern. But the story of Hengist, as I have tried to show, is not myth but pseudo-history. It may be added that although several of the incidents are such as have happened to many historical heroes, yet I have not found an undoubtedly historical hero to whom more than six points can be awarded, or perhaps seven in the case of Alexander the Great. The differences between the hero of myth and the hero of history will emerge from our discussion of the significance of the pattern, which had better be left to another chapter.

Notes

1. *Vide* my *Jocasta's Crime*.
2. *History of Java*, vol. i, pp. 421–4.
3. *Vide* D. S. Oyler in *Sudan Notes and Records*, vol. i, pp. 107, 283.
4. *Math vab Mathonwy*, pp. 17 ff.

THE HERO
(CONTINUED)

THE fact that the life of a hero of tradition can be divided up into a series of well-marked features and incidents—I have taken twenty-two, but it would be easy to take more—strongly suggests a ritual pattern. I doubt whether even the most fervent euhemerist would maintain that all these resemblances are mere coincidences; and if not, then three possibilities remain. The first is that all, or some, of the heroes were real persons whose stories were altered to make them conform to a ritual pattern; the second is that all, or some, of them were real persons in whose lives ritual played a predominant part; and the third is that they were all purely mythical. A discussion of this question will be attempted in the next chapter; in the present one I shall review the incidents of the hero's career, as they appear in the foregoing stories, and make some suggestions as to their significance.

The first point to be noted is that the incidents fall definitely into three groups: those connected with the hero's birth, those connected with his accession to the throne, and those connected with his death. They thus correspond to the three principal *rites de passage*—that is to say, the rites at birth, at initiation, and at death. I shall have more to say on this when we reach point number nine; let us now start at the beginning.

In connection with the first two points, we note that whenever there are royalties available, the hero is the son of royal parents; that he is nearly always the first child of his mother and, except where his father is a god, of his father, and that with very few exceptions his father does not marry twice. There is, of course, nothing marvellous in all this—some historical heroes have been the eldest child of monogamous royal parents, but I have laid stress upon it because it seems to be typical of the traditional hero, and is definitely not typical of the historical hero.

There is, it is true, a type of folk-tale in which the hero (or heroine), though of obscure origin, obtains a royal spouse and a throne, but this type of tale is probably derived from romances based on the central part of the myth, in which, as we have seen, the hero, though really of royal birth, appears, so to speak, out of the blue. In these tales we are never told of the hero's death, but merely that he "lived happily ever afterwards," which seems to suggest a desire to omit, rather than falsify, the latter part of the myth.

The fact that the hero's parents are often near relatives brings to mind the widespread custom by which kings marry their sisters, with which I have dealt elsewhere.

The circumstances in which our hero is begotten are very puzzling. When, as in the case of Heracles, a god takes the form of the hero's father, we are reminded that the Pharaoh, on particular occasions, approached his queen in the guise of a god.[1] In our stories, however, the circumstances, though almost always unusual, are extremely various, as are the guises in which the god appears. He may take the form of a thunderstorm, a bull, a swan, or a shower of gold. We may suspect, however, that the attribution of divine birth to a hero is not the result of his heroism, but is derived from the ritual union of a princess to her own husband, disguised as a god. It is comparatively easy for a man to disguise himself as a bull or swan, but while the thunderstorm and the shower of gold present greater difficulties and require further investigation, they clearly suggest a ritual rather than a historical origin for the stories.

We now come to the attempt on the hero's life at birth, which happens in almost every case and is one of the most striking features of the pattern. We are all familiar with such rites as that of the Phœnicians, by which the eldest son was burnt as a sacrifice to Moloch; in our stories, it would seem, a pretence is made of sacrificing the child, and sometimes an animal is sacrificed instead. It is often the father who tries to kill the infant hero, and this brings the stories into line with that of Abraham and Isaac. The attempt on the life of Moses, like that of nearly all the other heroes, was made at birth, but the story of Abraham and Isaac suggests that at one period the Hebrews performed this rite at puberty. We may note that while a ram was sacrificed in place of Isaac, Jacob appeared before his father wearing the skin of a kid, and Joseph wore a special garment which was soaked in goat's blood. We

This is not the culture of loss, this
is an orgy of it, a news article blog tagged
all in upper case. This is the culture of culture,
the unwinding way that ravels beneath our heels
as we plummet toward our reasons, feet pressed
to destiny like eyes to television boxes, smashed
with liquor like the poet on a Thursday, wearing
a sock with no sister and gazing through her
empty glass to the frieze of sky, all the numbers
of her grief prismed against her bruise
of a heart, her semblance of a face.

may perhaps suppose that a pretence was made of killing the child, which was wrapped in the skin of a sacrificed goat, and soaked in its blood. Such a rite accounts for some of our stories, such as that of Pelops, and also the widespread story of the Faithful Hound. Sometimes, it would seem, the child itself was wounded in the leg; hence perhaps the name "Œdipus," "swell-foot," and the many heroes who are lame, or who have scars on their legs. Many of the infant heroes, however, are set afloat in baskets or boxes, and these stories are found not merely in Greece and western Asia, but as far east as Japan.[2] I shall discuss them no further, except to say that while the story of the attempt on the infants hero's life can be explained as ritual, it is, though not miraculous, absent or at any rate extremely rare in the case of genuinely historical heroes.

Having escaped death, our heroes are all removed to a distance, and are usually brought up by a foreign king, though Jason and Asclepios are brought up by Cheiron. The latter is easy to understand if we suppose that Cheiron was the title given to a prince's official tutor, but nearly all our heroes are brought up by kings. This suggests several possibilities. The first is that it was actually the practice for kings to send their sons to be brought up by other kings, as we read of in the story of Hakon Adalstein's fostri. The second, which I have put forward elsewhere,[3] but which I am by no means confident about, is that princes succeeded their father-in-law, but became their sons by formal adoption. This might lead to a belief, or a pretence, that they were their real sons who had been removed at birth. The third is the opposite of the second. It is that it was part of the ritual that the prince, though a native, should pretend to be a foreigner. The question needs much more investigation than I have been able to give it.

We next come to point number nine: that we are told nothing of the hero's childhood. This may seen unimportant, since there are, many great men of whose childhood we know nothing. In such cases, however, we equally know nothing of the circumstances of their birth. We may know the place and date, but that is all. With our heroes it is quite different; their birth is the central feature in a series of highly dramatic incidents—incidents that are related in considerable detail, and such as seldom, if ever, occur in the lives of real people. The most exciting things happen to our hero at birth, and the most exciting things happen to him as soon as he reaches manhood, but in the meantime nothing happens to him at all. If, as I suppose, our hero is a figure not of history but of ritual, this is just what one would expect, since as a general rule children take no part in ritual between the rites at birth and those at initiation. The story of the hero of tradition, if I understand it aright, is the story of his ritual progress, and it is therefore appropriate that those parts of his career in which he makes no ritual progress should be left blank. I would compare the blank that occurs during childhood with the blank that occurs after his installation as king has been completed.

The fact that on reaching manhood the hero forthwith sets out on a journey from the land of his upbringing to the land where he will reign is, of course, involved in the problem I have discussed under point number eight—that is, his being reared in a far country. It is a remarkable fact, however, that his victories almost always take place either on the journey or immediately after arrival at his destination. He makes a definite progress from a far country to the throne, and all his feats and victories are connected with that progress. Another remarkable fact is that the hero of tradition never wins a battle. It is very rarely that he is represented as having any companions at all and when he has, he never trains them or leads them. The warrior kings of history, whether civilized or barbarian, have won their renown as leaders. When we think of them we think of serried ranks, of the Argyraspides, of the Tenth Legion, of the Guard which dies but does not surrender, and the impis which think it better to go forward and die than to go back and die. But there is nothing like that in the stories of the heroes of tradition. Our hero's followers, if any, are out of the way or killed off when his crucial fight takes place. All his victories, when they are actual fights and not magical contests, are single combats against other kings, or against giants, dragons, or celebrated animals. He never fights with ordinary men, or even with ordinary animals. And the king whom he fights is the king whom he will succeed, and who is often his own father. It is also possible that the monster with which the hero fights is merely the reigning king in disguise, or, in other words, that the reigning king had to wear an animal costume or mask in which to defend his title and his life. I will return to that later, but will first touch on the magical contest, which seems sometimes to be more important than the actual fight. Œdipus wins his throne by guessing a riddle, Theseus his by finding the way out of a maze. The magical victories of the three Jewish heroes are all connected with rain-making: Joseph successfully prognosticates the weather; Moses is successful in a series of magical contests in which rain-making is included; and Elijah defeats the prophets of Baal in a rain-making contest. Power over the elements is the most unvarying characteristic of the divine king, and it would seem that sometimes at least the candidate for the throne had to pass in a rain-making test.[4]

Our hero, then, has to qualify for the throne in two ways: he must pass a test in some such subject as rain-making or riddle-guessing, and he must win a victory over the reigning king. Whether this was a real fight or a mock contest in which the conclusion was foregone we cannot be certain. There have undoubtedly been many cases in which the king was put to death at the end of a fixed term, or when his powers began to wane. There may have been cases in which there was a fair fight with equal weapons between the king and his challenger, but the evidence for them is rather uncertain. What several of the stories suggest is that the old king was ritually killed, and that his successor had to kill an animal—wolf, boar, or snake—into which his spirit was supposed to have entered. I shall refer to this again when we come to point number eighteen.

After passing his tests and winning his victories, the hero marries the daughter, or widow, of his predecessor, and becomes king. It has often been assumed from this that the throne always went in the female line, and that the reigning queen or heiress could confer the title to it upon her husband simply by marrying him; in other words, that any man who managed to marry the queen became king automatically, whatever his antecedents, and that the only way in which any man could lawfully become king was by marrying the queen. Such an assumption is going a great deal beyond the evidence of the stories, which suggest that the new king established his title to the throne by his birth, his upbringing, and his victories. There were, it would seem, recognized qualifications for the kingship, just as there were recognized qualifications for the queenship. We do not know for certain that the new queen was really the old queen's daughter, any more than we know for certain that the new king was really the old king's son. There may have been a ceremony of adoption in both cases, and in many tales of the Cinderella and Catskin types the future queen has to achieve her journey, her tests, and her victory. There is evidence, too, that at Olympia the winner of the girls' race became Hera, just as the winner of the men's race became Zeus.[5]

Anyhow, the fact that our hero marries a princess and at the same time ascends the throne is far from proving that he ascends the throne by virtue of his marriage. It may merely indicate what we know from other sources to be a fact: namely, that a *hieros gamos* or sacred marriage normally formed an essential and highly important feature of the coronation or installation ceremony. I know of no case, in any age or country, in which a man has become king simply by marrying the queen; he must first, so far I can learn, have qualified for the throne, either by birth or by performing some feat or passing some test, and our heroes seem all to have qualified in all these ways. Even in modern Europe marriage never confers the right to a throne; princes and princesses who marry unqualified persons, who contact, that is to say, what are called morganatic marriages, not merely fail to raise their partners to the throne, but lose their own title to it. It is difficult to believe that the rules were less strict in ages when the ritual functions of a king and queen were far more important than they are today. The chief qualification for the throne has always been the possession of power, the power that is conferred by divine descent and the absorption of divine wisdom, and that is demonstrated by victory over the elements and over man. The conqueror may become king, since by his conquests he proves his possession of power, but that it has ever been believed that such power is conferred by a simple marriage ceremony is unproved and improbable.

Our hero has now become king, and what does he do? It might be supposed that, having shown himself so brave and enterprising before coming to the throne, he would forthwith embark upon a career of conquest; found an empire and a dynasty; build cities, temples, and palaces; patronize the arts; possess a large harem; and behave generally as the conquering heroes of history behaved, or tried to behave. The hero of tradition, however, in this as in most other respects, is totally unlike the hero of history. He does none of these things, and his story, from the time of his accession to the time of his fall, is as a rule a complete blank. The only memorial of his reign, apart from the events that begin and end it, is the traditional code of laws that is often attributed to him. As a fact, however, a code of laws is always the product of hundreds, if not thousands, of years of gradual evolution, and is never in any sense the work of one man. One man, a Justinian or a Napoleon, may cause laws to be codified, or may alter their incidence, but it has never been suggested that all, or even any, of the laws in their codes were devised by these monarchs. It is well known, in fact, that they were not. On the other hand it has been clearly shown by Sir James Frazer[6] that the Ten Commandments, in their familiar form, could have had nothing to do with Moses, since the original Ten Commandments, whoever first composed them, were entirely different. It seems clear, then, that the attribution of laws to a hero of tradition is merely a way of saying that they are very old and very sacred.

Our next point is that the hero of tradition, unlike most heroes of history, normally ends his career by being driven from his kingdom and put to death in mysterious circumstances. Sigurd is the only one of those whom we have considered of whose death we have a clear and non-miraculous account; even of Joseph we are told nothing of what happened between his father's death and his own. We may conclude that deposition and a mysterious death are a part of the pattern, but a puzzling feature is that there is nothing to suggest that the hero suffers a defeat. As he has gained the throne by a victory, one would expect him to lose it by a defeat, but this he never does.

Œdipus kills his father and marries his mother; one might expect that one of his sons, or some other prince, would kill him and marry Jocasta, or, if she were too old, Antigone, and become king. Creon, however, who succeeds him, does so by turning the oracle against him, and several others among our heroes fall out with a god and, of course, get the worst of it. Others become unpopular with their subjects. In either case the hero's fall from favour is not gradual but sudden; at one moment he is apparently in full favour both with gods and men, and the next he has no friends, either human or divine.

The hero's death is mysterious, but one thing clear about it is that it never takes place within the city. Usually he is driven out, but sometimes he has left the city on some sacred mission. Then there is the hilltop, which appears in the stories of Œdipus, Theseus, Heracles, Bellerophon, and Moses, and which is suggested in several of the others. Taken in conjunction with the chariot of fire in which Romulus and Elijah disappear, and the lightning flash that kills Asclepios, it seems justifiable to conclude that in the most usual form of the rite the divine king was burned, either alive or dead, or a pyre erected on a hilltop, and that he was believed to ascend to the sky, in some form or other, in the smoke and flame. It is possible that, before being burnt, he was compelled to fight with and be defeated by his successor, but in the majority of stories there is nothing to suggest this.

The fact that the hero is never succeeded by his son—Nyikang seems to be the sole exception—might suggest that the inheritance went in the female line, but then no hero is succeeded by his son-in-law. If the king reigned for eight years only, and married at his coronation, his children could not succeed him, since they would be to young, but they might succeed his successor, and there is some evidence that this is what happened. The succession at Thebes is not easy to make out, but Creon seems to have preceded and succeeded Œdipus, and also to have succeeded his sons. Perseus is said to have killed and succeeded Proetus, and to have been killed and succeeded by the latter's son. Ægisthus kills and succeeds Agamemnon, and eight years later is killed and succeeded by the latter's son Orestes. There were two royal families at Sparta, and it is possible that originally they reigned alternatively.

The last point to be considered in the hero's career is that although he is usually supposed to have disappeared, yet nevertheless he has a holy sepulchre, if not several. I have attempted to explain his disappearance by suggesting that he was cremated, but if kings were cremated they could hardly have a sepulchre in the usual sense of the term, since we know that in all forms of religion the essential feature of a sepulchre, or shrine, is that it is supposed to contain the bones, or at any rate some of the bones, of the holy person to whom it is dedicated. A great deal has, of course, been written on the customs of the Greeks with regard to the disposal of the dead, and their beliefs about the Otherworld, but I am here concerned merely to consider the rites which are suggested by the hero stories, and what they suggest to me is that, while ordinary people were buried, the bodies of kings were burnt, but not burnt thoroughly, so that the bones were left and could be buried. I understand that this view was put forward by Dörpfeld, though on different grounds, some thirty years ago, but I have not been able to see what he wrote. At any rate, similar customs are found in many parts of the world.

In conclusion, I should like to make it quite clear that I do not claim to have produced final solutions for any of the problems I have discussed in this chapter. What I have tried to show is that they are problems of custom and ritual, and not problems of history.

Notes

1. J. G. Frazer, op. cit., vol. ii, p. 133.
2. B. H. Chamberlain: *The Kojiki*, p. 21. Frazer collects a number of these stories: *Folklore in the Old Testament*, vol. ii, pp. 437 ff.
3. *Jocasta's Crime*, p. 195.

4. Some interesting suggestions on this point are made by Dr. C. B. Lewis: *Classical Mythology and Arthurian Romance*, pp. 41–5.

5. J. G. Frazer: *The Golden Bough*, vol. iv, p. 91.

6. *Folklore in the Old Testament*, vol. iii, p. 115.

THE HERO

(CONTINUED)

IN the last two chapters I have shown, I hope, in the first place that a definite and highly complex pattern is to be traced in the accounts which we have of traditional heroes from many parts of the world, but especially the eastern Mediterranean, and secondly that all the features of this pattern can be identified as features of known rituals. It remains to consider the general meaning and idea at the back of the "hero," and how far traditional heroes were ever real men. Let us consider the latter point first. In so doing we must ask in each case two questions: whether there is any contemporary record of the hero's existence, and whether he is alleged to have done anything that is *not* mythical. As to the former we cannot, of course, be absolutely certain, but it seems pretty safe to say that, although some of them, such as Arthur and Robin Hood, are alleged to have lived at dates when written records were made, yet of none of them, with the very doubtful exception of Elijah, can it be said that we have contemporary evidence for their existence. The exception of Elijah is doubtful not merely because we do not know when the passages relating to him were written, but because he has perhaps less claim than any of the others to be considered historical, since, apart from his running twenty miles across country, nothing is reported of him which is not miraculous.

And this must be our criterion. When we are certain that nothing about our hero was written down till a century or more after his alleged death, we can conclude unhesitatingly that he is mythical, but when we are not certain we must judge as best we can by the reported incidents of his career. They may, of course, have been rationalized, as Elijah's have not been, but even when they have been so rationalized we can often recognize them as mythical, since the rationalizers as a rule cannot get away from the pattern, the pattern I dealt with in Chapter XVI.

The fact, however, that our heroes sometimes go beyond this pattern does not indicate that they are historical, since they may merely get into another pattern. The Twelve Labours of Heracles, for example, are outside my pattern, but they are clearly ritual and not historical; similarly the water that allows Moses to cross safely but drowns his pursuer forms part of a widespread myth with which I have already dealt.[1]

It is possible that some of the heroes were real persons, whose actions were recorded, but whose real careers became for some reason swamped by myth. I shall discuss in the next chapter the attribution of mythical fetures to historical characters, but that is another matter, since in the case of these historical characters it is their historic deeds that are important, and the myths mere excrescence. Alexander's alleged miraculous birth does not affect our view of the Battle of Arbela. But if we subtract the myths from the heroes with whom I have dealt, little or nothing remains. Miracles and mythical incidents are all we are told of them, or at least all that is of any interest. What would the story of Perseus be without the Gorgon's head, or that of Bellerophon without his winged steed? Very little, and even Moses would be much less interesting without his magic rod. It may be suggested that King Alfred is less interesting without the cakes, but though such foolish stories may amuse the unlettered, they are a nuisance to serious students of the life and times of this great ruler. Would anyone, however, venture to say that the story of Medusa is a nuisance to students of the life and times of Perseus? Of course this story, and the dragon-slaying, make up the life of Perseus; apart from these and his mother's brazen tower there is nothing to distinguish him from a score of heroes. The difference between the story of a historical character and that of a hero of tradition is that in the former case we may find myths or fables loosely and as a rule unsuitably tacked on to a record of well-attested fact, while in the latter the story consists of some striking miracles against a background of typical myth.

The old-fashioned view—namely, that all these heroes were real men, whose eminence led to their deification or canonization—was put forward by Sir William Ridgeway, who tells us that "dramatizations of his exploits or sufferings, like dances, eulogies, paintings, and statues, is one of the regular methods of propitiating a man of outstanding personality, at every stage from his actual lifetime, after his death when now canonized as hero or saint, and finally when he may even have been promoted to the foremost rank of the great divinities."[2] Here Sir William, as throughout his works, assumes what he professes to prove; he fails to observe the pattern that runs through these hero stories, and finally he controverts himself, since he shows that those who receive cults are, on the assumption that they were real people, persons of quite insignificant personality. Thus he says that "popular deification often arises out of mere pity for those who have suffered tragic fates, such as the boy-bridegroom, Dhola, who died on his wedding-day,"[3] and that "if it should turn out that in some, at least, of the rites and shrines of Cybele representations of the body of Attis were exhibited ... then the evidence will point still more directly to his having once been a youth, whose tragic fate ... impressed his contemporaries, and led to his worship."[4]

The theory that people are in the habit of making gods out of youths who happen to be killed out hunting or to die on their wedding-day not only is absurd in itself, but is in flagrant contradiction to what he says about outstanding personalities, since if Dhola and Attis had been real persons, they obviously could not have been outstanding personalities.

Sir William Ridgeway and many of those who think like him seem never to have asked themselves why people worship gods. That pity has ever led to worship is both highly improbable in theory and against all the known facts. These show that the idea of deity and the idea of power are and always have been inseparably connected. The power of the god may be for good or for evil, it may be general or particular, but power he always has, and it is this power, and nothing else, that leads to his worship. All the names and attributes of a god are names and attributes of power. The god may die, since death may be a promotion to a higher sphere, but he dies of his own volition. It is in this fact that we must look for an explanation of the phenomenon discussed in the last chapter: namely, that though the hero gains his throne by a victory, he never loses it by a defeat. The end of most of the heroes is, as we have seen, left obscure, but a number of them, such as Dionysos, Heracles, Moses, Elijah, Nyikang, are represented as committing suicide, and thereby securing promotion to divine rank. We have also good reason to believe that Attis was thought of as a hero who attained through suicide his promotion to divine rank. We will return to Attis presently. Here we must note that he was believed by his worshippers to possess power in the highest degree, the power of conferring everlasting life. No attempt, so far as I can learn, has been made to explain why anyone should suppose that a youth of whom nothing was known but that he met with an accidental death should be capable of conferring everlasting life.

A POET TOASTS THE WORLD

Samara Golabuk

This is the culture of loss.
Here is the commitment to grief.
Downtown library, near the bar:
starved frescoes lark along edges
of sky rife with reasons. Silver-pink
newts with their baby skin bodies
throttle up the wall when you
turn the corner to evening.

This is the culture of rise.
Water moves uphill in certain seasons,
lifts off from marshes and bogs
in sparks and eyelets and letters that don't match,
jumbled together after the world's name.
The name, which is here with the letters,
tumbles nonsensically in the poet's mouth
because the world is leftover and sideways.

The world's socks were always prime numbered,
and ma always said it like "How you manage
to do something like that when Tennessee
is under water—" and the rest was implied,
like how there are chemicals that lie in wait
in soil for 50 years to strafe your DNA, or how
all the gulls off Cedar Key are black with oil,
slick with economy clogging their eyes.

Egyptologists fall into a similar error when they suppose Osiris to have been a real man. Dr. Blackman, for example, thinks that he was an early king who "did much to advance agriculture and civilization in general among his subjects, and who met his death at the hands of a rebellious . . . vassal."[5] But in real life no progressive monarch has been deified, or even sanctified; any interest in him that may survive his death is purely historical. Dr. Blackman appears to suppose that the ancient Egyptians, feeling the need for a supreme deity, hunted about for a suitable man upon whom to confer this title, and found him in the shape of a defeated king, or, alternatively, that it was the defeat and death of Osiris that led the Egyptians to believe in the existence of omnipotent deities.

Euhemeros was, of course, a sceptic, and he was concerned rather to explode religious beliefs than to explain the nature of religion, but his theory has had very wide effects, and many people, including those whom I have quoted, have mistaken for science what was really anti-religious propaganda. "The gods, according to this theory," says Professor Bevan,[6] "were kings and great men of old, who had come to be worshipped after their death in gratitude for the beliefs they had conferred. On this view there was nothing monstrous in using the same forms to express gratitude to a living benefactor. In so far as the worship of living men arose from these conditions, it was a product, not of superstition, but of rationalism." In Greece, in the fourth century B.C., there is no doubt that people did say: "X is a very power monarch; let us deify him," and even: "Y *was* a very man; let us deify him," or words to that effect, but such an attitude is, as Professor Bevan says, a product of rationalism. It throws no light on the origin of the belief in gods, nor does it bear any resemblance to the normal attitude of worshippers towards the deities they worship. These are conceived of as superhuman beings of unlimited power, and between these beings and organized bodies of men there exists a continuing relationship of mutual service. With this relationship we are not here concerned further than to try to ascertain what part the hero plays in it. To do so we must study certain heroes from an angle rather different from that adopted in Chapter XVI.

In his *Mexico before Cortez*,[7] Mr. J. E. Thompson tells us that "there is one man who stands out against this background of confusion, although he, too, emerges a shadowy figure in floodlights fogged by contradiction. This was Quetzalcoatl, possibly the last Toltec ruler. Quetzalcoatl, which means quetzal-bird-serpent, was also the name of an important Mexican deity, whose name was borne by the Toltec high priests, who were in turn temporal rulers. Great confusion has naturally ensued, for the acts of god and individual are inextricably confused."

We find that Quetzalcoatl was represented as or by:

1. A sky god.
2. The living representative of a line of priestly rulers.
3. An idol, part man and part bird-serpent.
4. Certain animals; to wit, the quetzal-bird and the serpent.
5. An ancient hero.

Let us now transport ourselves to the Upper Nile and return to Nyikang, whose career we have already examined. We find that he is represented as or by:

1. A sky god.
2. The living representative of a line of priestly rulers, the divine king.
3. An idol, "the effigy called Nyikang."
4. Certain animals, particularly a species of white bird.
5. An ancient hero.[8]

Let us now descend the Nile to ancient Egypt. There we find that Horus was represented as or by:

1. A sky god, whose eye was the sun.
2. The living representative of a line of priestly rulers, the Pharaoh.
3. An idol, showing him as a man with a hawk's head.
4. The hawk.
5. An ancient hero.

Moving on into Asia, we find that Attis, whom, as we saw, Ridgeway supposed to have been a youth, was represented as or by:

1. A sky god, responsible for the weather and the crops.
2. A high priest who regularly bore the name of Attis.
3. An idol made from a pine-tree.
4. A bull.
5. An ancient hero.[9]

The foregoing gods or heroes, whichever one chooses to call them, have all been represented by euhemeristic writers as real men. Now let us consider Dionysos. He was:

1. A sky god, and at his festival at Athens, the great Dionysia, was represented by:
2. His priest,
3. His image, and
4. A bull. He was also
5. An ancient hero.

On this last point we have other evidence than that he scores nineteen points out of twenty-two in my pattern of the traditional hero. He is sometimes actually addressed as a hero in ritual:[10] and at Megara there was a shrine to "Dionysus the Ancestor,"[11] which suggests that the Megarians, at any rate, regarded him as a real man. I cannot find, however, that any scholar regards Dionysos as a real man, though the reasons for so doing seem just as good as those for regarding any other prehistoric hero as a real man.

It seems clear, however, that these and other gods, whether they have been supposed to be promoted men or not, have a definite pattern in their attributes and their cult. In the first place they are sky gods, responsible for the weather and the crops; in the second they are incarnate in kings and priests; in the third they are represented by idols and other objects of cult; in the fourth they have an intimate relation with certain species of animals. Finally they are believed to have been heroes who once lived upon earth, and whose careers corresponded more or less completely to the pattern we have discussed at length in the last two chapters. To assume that these hero stories were earlier than the rest of their attributes is as purely gratuitous as to assume that the non-miraculous is always earlier than the miraculous, or that the gods in the Homeric poems are late interpolations; such assumptions arise from obsession by euhemeristic theories and not from a study of the facts, since the facts, both of myths and of cult, afford no grounds for supposing that any of the attributes is older than the rest. The conclusion that suggests itself is that the god is the hero as he appears in ritual, and the hero is the god as he appears in myth; in other words, the hero and the god are two different aspects of the same superhuman being. The myth describes the victories that the hero won over the forces inimical to his people, the laws and customs which he instituted for their benefit and finally the apotheosis that enables him still to be their guardian and guide. When recited in full it embraces all his attributes, as god, as divine man, as idol, and as animal, and thus explains and justifies the whole of the ritual with which he is worshipped.

With a few distinguished exceptions, such as Professor J.A.K. Thomson, scholars have failed to realize this connection between the god and the hero. The reason for this is that they tend to concentrate on a very limited class of phenomena. Brought up on Homer and the Attic dramatists, they pay less attention to what the heroes are actually alleged to have done than to the words that the poets have put into their mouths. On these they base character studies of the heroes, failing to recognize that the words are not those of the heroes but are those of the poets. The fact is, I am afraid, that scholars as a class are romantically rather than scientifically minded. The reading of the *Iliad* or of the *Seven against Thebes* fills them with emotion, but since they are unwilling to admit that it is emotion of similar type to that experienced by the small boy who reads *Treasure Island*, they attempt to conceal it by throwing over it a veil of pseudo-history. This veil takes the form of a fabled Heroic Age, in which, apparently, the principal features of life were dragons, single combats, and elopements. In my view it is just as reasonable to suppose that there was once a Comic Age, in which life was made up of back-chat, disguises, and practical jokes, and a Tragic Age, in which people were always murdering their nearest relatives, and true love led to untimely death.

This seems to have been the view of Sir William Ridgeway, who believed not only in the Heroic Age, but in a Comic Age as well. He tells us that "it is in the *kyogen* [Japanese comedy] that we get the true pictures of the social and national life of the Oshikaga period (1338–1597). It was a period of high ideals, with a few great men towering above the rest and bearing witness to the priestly holiness and knightly bravery of an age gone by. These are brought before us in the *no* [tragedy]. But it was also a period of mediocre performances; the country swarmed with contemptible and ignoble lords and knights who disgraced their swords, and priests who disregard their religion. Mingled with these were dreamy scholars, who were incapable of managing their money matters, and innocent country people who were the sport of every designing rascal."[12] It is astonishing that he should have taken the stock figures of comedy for real people, but not more so than that he and others should have taken the stock figures of myth for real people. All three conceptions, those of the tragic, the heroic, and the comic, are derived from the poets, and the poets were not interested in historical fact. It may be objected that poets nevertheless do sometimes mention historical facts, and that myths are sometimes attached to real historical heroes. We must next consider how this comes about.

Notes

1. *Supra*, p. 103.
2. W. Ridgeway: *Dramas and Dramatic Dances*, p. 210.
3. Ibid., p. 208.
4. Ibid., p. 92.
5. In *Myth and Ritual*, p. 38.
6. In *Hastings' Encyclopædia*, vol. iv, p. 525.
7. p. 20.
8. C. G. and B. Z. Seligman: *The Pagan Tribes of the Nilotic Sudan*, pp. 37 and 75 ff.
9. Frazer: *Golden Bough*, vol. v, pp. 263 ff.
10. A. C. Pearson in *Hastings' Encyclopædia*, vol. vi, p. 653.
11. L. R. Farnell, op. cit., p. 64.
12. W. Ridgeway: *Dramas and Dramatic Dances*, p. 333.

MYTH AND THE HISTORIC HERO

IF I were to find it stated in one account that X had a black beard, and in another account that X always wore a red coat, I might combine these two statement into one and say: "We are told that X had a black beard and always wore a red coat." By so doing I should be following the example of many historians and of all pseudo-historians, and should be making a statement that is inaccurate, misleading, and quite unjustifiable. For we are not, in the example I have given, told that X had a black beard *and* always wore a red coat. The "and" is supplied by me, and I have no right to supply it unless I give my authorities for the two statements, and show that they are of similar origin and equal value. It is possible that one may be historical, derived, that is to say, from contemporary written records, while the other may be based on dramatic or pictorial representation, or some other form of tradition. To combine into a single narrative statement derived from dissimilar sources is to supply false links, and false links are equivalent to false statements. Yet our pseudo-history, and even our history, are full of such false links; the practice has always been to accept as history any tradition that can be fitted in, and the distinction between history and tradition has thereby become blurred to such an extent that its existence is barely recognized. So far has the process gone that we find eminent writers describing as "historical," characters for whose existence there is no historical evidence at all. If, however, we take any really historical person, and make a clear distinction between what history tells us of him and what tradition tells us, we shall find that tradition, far from being supplementary to history, is totally unconnected with it, and that the hero of history and the hero of tradition are really two quite different persons, though they may bear the same name. I shall illustrate this fact by studying in some detail what is told us by history and by tradition of King Henry V.

King Henry V gained a glorious victory at Agincourt, and afterwards captured Paris. He married the French King's daughter, was recognized as his heir, and became ruler of a great part of France. He died in the midst of his victorious career. This career created a great impres-

sion upon the people, not because England benefited from his victories, which she did not, but because a king's victories have always been
regarded as a proof of divine favour, and a guarantee of national prosperity. The deposition of his son, King Henry VI, was probably due in
the main to a belief that the repeated defeats of his forces in France
were indications of divine disfavour. At any rate the prolonged misfortunes of his reign afforded a striking contrast to the sensational victories of his father. The latter became an ideal hero, and tradition
proceeded, with great promptitude, to provide him with what were
regarded as the requisite antecedents. I shall explain later what I mean
by this.

Into the accounts of Henry V's youth made famous by Shakespeare
it is unnecessary to go in any detail. They tell us that he spent the
years preceding his accession in rioting and debauchery in and about
London, in company with highwaymen, pickpockets, and other disreputable persons; that he was imprisoned by Chief Justice Gascoigne,
whom after his accession he pardoned and continued in office; and
that after his accession his conduct changed suddenly and completely.
The authorities for these stories are Sir Thomas Elyot's *The Governor*
(1531) and Edward Hall's *Union of the Noble and Illustrious Houses of
Lancaster and York* (1542). These two highly respectable authors seem
to have relied largely on matter already in print, some of it traceable
to within fifty years of Henry's death. I know of no argument for the
historicity of any traditional narrative which cannot be applied to
these stories; their credentials are equal to any, and far better than
most—yet there is not a word of truth in any of them.

The facts are these: In 1400, at the age of thirteen, Henry became
his father's deputy in Wales, made his headquarters at Chester, and
spent the next seven years in almost continuous warfare with Owen
Glendower and his allies. In 1407 he led a successful invasion of Scot-
land. In 1408 he was employed as Warden of the Cinque Ports, and at
Calais. In the following year, owing to his father's illness, he became
regent, and continued in this capacity till 1412. During this period his
character as a ruler was marred only by his religious bigotry, and what
seems to be the only authentic anecdote of the time describes the part
he played at the burning of John Badby, the Lollard. In 1412 an attempt was made to induce Henry IV, whose ill-health continued to
unfit him for duties, to abdicate, but his refusal to do so, together with
differences on foreign policy, led to the withdrawal of the future
Henry V from court, probably to Wales, till his father's death a year

later. He did not reappoint Sir William Gascoigne as Chief Justice, and there is no foundation for the story that the latter committed him to prison.

These facts are drawn from the *Dictionary of National Biography*, which sums up the account by saying that "his youth was spent on the battlefield and in the council chamber, and the popular tradition (immortalized by Shakespeare) of his riotous and dissolute conduct is not supported by any contemporary authority." According to Sir Charles Oman, "his life was sober and orderly. . . . He was grave and earnest in speech, courteous in all his dealings, and an enemy of flatterers and favourites. His sincere piety bordered on asceticism. . . . His enemies called him hard-hearted and sanctimonious. . . . The legendary tales which speak of him as a debauched and idel youth, who consorted with disreputable favourites, such as Shakespeare's famous Sir John Falstaff, are entirely worthless."[1]

Even had there been no contemporary records of Henry's youth, there are points in the account adopted by Shakespeare which might lead a sober critic to doubt its veracity. Many of the episodes are in themselves highly improbable; it is difficult to imagine who could have transmitted them with knowledge and safety, and they are quite out of keeping with Henry's activities as king, all of which suggest a long apprenticeship to war and statecraft. An idle and dissolute scapegrace transformed in an instant into the first soldier and statesman of his age would indeed be an astonishing spectacle. Had, however, our critic ventured to express his doubts, with what scorn would he not have been assailed by our rationalizing professors! "Here," they would have said, "is an impudent fellow who pretends to know more about the fifteenth century than those who lived in it. The facts which he dares to dispute were placed on record by educated and responsible persons, the leading historians of their day. Could anything be more absurd than to suppose that they would circulate discreditable stories about a national hero at a time when the facts of his career must have been widely known?"

Yet these stories are, as we have seen, quite untrue. They were written down by men who, if they did not know that they were untrue, could easily have found out, and they have been, and still are, accepted by thousands in preference to the truth.

We cannot, however, suppose that these stories were pure invention. We have seen that imagination is not the faculty of making something out of nothing, but that of using, in a more or less different form, material already present in the mind. We must conclude, then, that those who composed the traditional stories about Prince Henry applied to him, in a more or less modified form, stories which they had heard in a different but not dissimilar connection. We shall fail to explain the origin of these stories unless we can trace the materials from which they were composed.

We have seen that the Falstaff stories, as we may call them, since it is round Falstaff that they revolve, are not a supplement to history, nor even a travesty of history. The Prince Henry of history, who spent his time trying to suppress the Welsh and the Lollards, and the Prince Henry of the stories, who spends his time roistering with Falstaff, may meet on the field of Shrewsbury, but they are really creatures of quite different worlds, and the world of the latter is the world of myth.

In this world of myth the principal characters are two, a hero and a buffoon, who meet with various adventures together, and live on terms of the greatest familiarity. Whence did the imagination of Shakespeare and his predecessors derive their materials for depicting such characters and incidents? The name Falstaff may be a corruption of that of Sir John Fastolf, but their careers and characters bear no resemblance. The figure of Falstaff may have resembled that of some sixteen-century knight, but such knight could obviously not have as-sociated with Prince Henry. What has to be explained is not that there should be supposed to have been a man of that name, figure, and character, but that a man of such characteristics should have been as-sociated, so closely associated, with King Henry V. It is quite clear that Shakespeare and his predecessors regarded Henry as a great hero, and it follows that they regarded association with a man of disreputable character, such as Falstaff was, as being in keeping with the character of a great hero. Elyot and Hall did not need comic relief as an excuse for introducing ribald stories, and the Falstaff incidents in Shakespeare form the principal part of the plays. It seems clear that to Shake-speare's audiences the proper way for a budding hero to behave was to roister with a drunken buffoon.

There is ample evidence that this idea did not arise in the sixteenth century, but is both ancient and widespread. In Greek mythology Di-onysos is, as we have seen, the type or youthful hero, and is in the habit of roistering with Silenos, a fat, drunken buffoon. The great tra-ditional hero of the Arab world, Hârûn ar Rashid, roisters with Abu Nuwâs, his drunken jester, and though Hârûn and Abu Nuwâs are historical, the stories told of them are not.[2] In the Indian drama there is a stock comic character called Vidusaka, who acts as a faithful, though ludicrous, companion to the royal hero, and is represented as a hideous dwarf.[3] Professor Ker gives us some examples from medieval literature. Thus in *Garin of Lorraine* we have Galopin, the reckless humorist. He is ribald and prodigal, yet of gentle birth, and capable of good service when he can be got away from the tavern. In *Huon of Bordeaux*, Charlot, son of Charlemagne, appears as the worthless companion of traitors and disorderly persons. In the saga of *Burnt Njal*, *Kari*, when avenging his father-in-law, is accompanied by one Bjorn, a comic braggart, to whom, as Professor Ker points out, he owes his preservation.[4] Leif the Lucky, the alleged discoverer of America is, as we have seen,[5] accompanied by his father-in-law, who is a figure of fun, gets drunk, and babbles in a foreign tongue. The same idea, that of the noble knight with a comic, drunken squire, appears in Don Quixote.

In the Ampleforth (Yorkshire) folk-play, the clown says:

> "I was always jovial and always will be, always at one time of year,
> "Since Adam created both oxen and plough, we get plenty of store and
>   strong beer."

He makes a series of quips in verse, after which he and the King rattle swords together.[6] In the pantomime the clown is closely associated with the harlequin hero, and at the circus the clown is privileged to joke at the expense of the master of the ring.

There can be no doubt that Falstaff falls within the class of persons who are variously termed fools, clowns, jesters, buffoons, etc., and we shall be able to explain the part he plays only if we can explain the origin of this class. Why did kings and other important people keep a fool or jester, a licentious character whose sallies were often directed at his master? That they did so purely for fun is a cheap rationalization; the official position, the recognized costume, the coxcomb and bladder, emblems of fertility, and the immunity from reprisal or punishment, all mark out the fool as a holy man. We learn that in 1317, when King Edward II was keeping Pentecost at Westminster, a woman disguised as a "histrio" rode into the palace and delivered an insulting letter to the King. The doorkeepers, when blamed, said that it was against the royal custom to deny admission to any "minstrel" upon such a solemn occasion.[7] It would seem that on holy days fools were particularly sacred.

MY GRANDMOTHER'S PLATES

Jennifer L. Freed

—the set I used to stow away
for holidays: fine touch
of gold at the rims, delicate
patterns of green—
I use them

every day,
don't worry that they'll chip
or lose their sheen,
don't leave their offerings

for later. I need
translucent milky teacups
warm against my palms. My softest
sweater. Purple hyacinths
in a pot by the sink, their scent
in February. My brother

has cancer.

I butter my bread
on my grandmother's plates.

The idea of Falstaff as a holy man may seem absurd, and he is, of course, a compound character, but that Shakespeare had at the back of his mind the idea that Falstaff was a holy man is suggested by his death. "Nay, sure, he's not in hell; he's in Arthur's bosom, if ever man went to Arthur's bosom. 'A made a finer end and went away, an it had been any christom child . . . 'a babbled of green fields."[8] It seems clear that Shakespeare intended him to die in the odour of sanctity, and, while it would be dangerous to stress Arthur in this connection, the sanctity seems pagan rather than Christian.

And what did Falstaff do when alive? For the most part he got drunk and then uttered wise saws in a whimsical manner. This suggests that he, or rather his prototype, was a soothsayer or prophet. A soothsayer or prophet is a person who, when in a state of religious ecstasy, usually induced by some intoxicant or narcotic, discloses things that are hidden from the people at large. But that was not his original function, since knowledge of things unseen, even knowledge of the future, was in pre-racing days of little real value. If custom and circumstance mould your life, and you marry, sow, or fight as they dictate, and never otherwise, there is little point in knowing what the result of your actions will be. The original function of the prophet was not to foretell what was going to happen, but to ensure, by the appropriate ceremonies, that what was wanted to happen should happen. The appropriate ceremonies included, as in many parts of the world they still include, the use of intoxicants or narcotics to put the prophet into a proper condition for prophesying.

The story of Balaam contains no mention of intoxicants, but the scene of his meeting with the angel is laid in a vineyard, and his first being unable and then able to see the angel suggests some kind of trance. At any rate we see clearly the function of a prophet: "Come now therefore, I pray thee," says Balak, "curse me this people . . . peradventure I shall prevail."[9] Balaam is to perform the proper ceremonies, which include sacrificing on seven altars, and is then to prophesy the defeat of the Israelites. This will enable Balak to defeat them, for he knows that no king can gain a victory unless that victory has been properly prophesied.

We are told that among the ancient Arabs the menaces which the poet-seer hurled against the foe were believed to be inevitably fatal, and that their pronunciation was attended by peculiar ceremonies, such as anointing the hair on one side of the head, lettle the mantle hang down loosely, and wearing only one sandal. The ancient Irish poet possessed similar powers. "The Irish *glam dichenn*, like the Arabic *hija*, was no mere expression of opinion, but a most potent weapon of war, which might blister an adversary's face or even cost him his life. Like the Arabic *hija*, too, it was at one time accompanied with ritual action; it was uttered 'on one foot, one hand, one eye.' "[10]

It is possible that in very early times every king was his own prophet; that is to say, it was his duty to intoxicate himself and then prophesy whatever was required. Traces of such a custom seem to survive in certain ceremonial drinks that are drunk by chiefs or priests only. We find, however, a general tendency for kings to perform their religious duties by deputy. It would then be necessary for the king's prophet to accompany him to war, and I suggest that this explains the presence of Falstaff, with a bottle of sack in his pocket, on the field of Shrewsbury.

It need not be supposed that Shakespeare had all these ideas present in his mind, but he was soaked in mythology and folklore, and certainly seems to have had some of them. He associates prophecy with drunkenness and drugs: "Plots have I laid, inductions dangerous, by drunken prophecies," says King Richard III,[11] and Banquo, when the witches have prophesied and disappeared, speaks of eating "the insane root that takes the reason prisoner."[12] This root is no doubt the mandrake or mandragora, which Iago includes among the "drowsy syrups."[13]

When Prince Henry sees Falstaff lying apparently dead, he says: "I could have better spared a better man."[14] He has in this scene the character not of a reprobate but a hero, and it is therefore the hero who cannot spare the drunken buffoon. I may perhaps be though to lay too much stress on trifles, but such points are trifles only to those who cherish the illusion that poets derive their ideas from their own inner consciousness.

The discussion has been a long one, but it is intended to serve two purposes. The first is to show that the foundations of tradition are totally different from the foundations of history, and that, if our data are at all adequate, we can easily separate the two. The second is to show that when Sir James Frazer speaks of "the miraculous features which gather round the memory of popular heroes, as naturally as moss and lichens gather about stones,"[15] he is speaking without the book. The traditions that have gathered about the memory of King Henry V are, as I have tried to show, mythical, but there is nothing miraculous about them. Shakespeare, like all his contemporaries, believed in miracles, and used them in his dramas—for example, in the scene in *Macbeth* from which I have just quoted. He did not, however, use them in connection with Henry V, and the reason is simple: the miraculous features associated with victorious heroes in the myths were dragons, magic swords, and helmets of invisibility, and in the sixteenth century people had ceased to believe in these, though they still believed in ghosts, witches, and fairies. The association of myths and miracles with historical characters, far from being a matter of random accumulation, is, like all the phenomena of human culture, the result of processes which can be studied and explained. The subject requires fuller treatment than I can give it here, but that it is governed by rules I have no doubt, and I suggest the following:

First, the person with whom the myths are to be associated must not be too recent, or the true facts of his career will be remembered, nor too remote, or he will have been superseded and forgotten. About fifty years after his death is a probable time for myths to be first associated with a historical character, but this period may be extended if his career has been recorded, and if his fame has not been eclipsed by a later comer of similar character.

Secondly, he must have been famous or notorious in certain definite connections, and his exploits or misfortunes must be such as to afford pegs upon which the myths can be hung.

Thirdly, the miracles that the myths contain will be attributed to the historical character if, when the myths are first attached to him, the possibility of such miracles is still believed in; otherwise they will be omitted.

The first two of these rules follow from the conclusions reached in previous chapters, and indeed should be fairly obvious. It should, however, be noted that this association of myths with historical characters is literary and not popular. There is no evidence that illiterates ever attach myths to real persons. The mythical stories told of English kings and queens—Alfred and the cakes, Richard I and Blondel, Queen Eleanor and Fair Rosamund, Queen Margaret and the robber, and so on—seem to have been deliberately composed; a well-known character and an old story were considered more interesting when combined. "Even from very early times," says Professor Nicoll,[16] "there had been a tendency in the morality to substitute for a pure abstraction some typical and well-known royal figure. Bale's *King Johan* is a good example of this."

As regards the third rule, I cannot find that anyone has studied the attribution of miracles to real people. Miracles fall into two classes: those which people believe to be possible in their own times, and those which they believe to have taken place only at certain periods in the past. There is nothing natural in the belief in miracles; people have to be taught to believe in them just as they have to be taught everything that is not patent to the senses. The idea that a stupid and ignorant person will necessarily believe in werewolves or magic swords is quite baseless. A miracle is a phenomenon that can be produced, on the appropriate occasions, by gods and sacred personages, but never by ordinary people. Early man, however, knew nothing of gods or sacred personages. No doubt he was often surprised at occurrences of which he had no experience, but mere surprise does not lead to a belief in miracles; it has first to be combined with certain definite religious beliefs. A miracle, as we have seen, is not any wonder, but a particular type of wonder—that is, a ritual wonder—and it must have needed a long and intensive subjection to ritual influence before people learned to believe that the ritual transformation of a man into a wolf was a real transformation.

The history of the Devil affords an interesting example of this process. Originally, it would seem, he was a ritual character who wore the horns of a bull or goat, probably the divine king in his capacity as the promoter of fertility. Later, apparently, the horns came to stand for the old king, their actual wearer, as opposed to the new king, their future wearer, and so the Horned Man became the antagonist of the Hero. Eventually he stepped out of the ritual into real life, and became, what to millions he still is, a figure far more real than any historical character has ever been to anyone.

The date at which the life of a saint was written can be judged by the part played in it by the Devil. Many of the early saints are purely mythical; their lives are nothing but hero myths with the sacred marriage left out. Later we get lives of saints who were real persons, into which encounters with the Devil and other mythical features have been introduced, but it is quite untrue to say that such incidents gather naturally abou them. They have been introduced deliberately in order to make the stories conform to what at the time was regarded as the correct type. But whereas the utmost that can be allowed to a modern saint are limited powers of supernatural healing, encounters with supernatural beings are still tolerated in the lives of ancient saints.

The same tendency is to be seen in Shakespeare. In plays such as *Macbeth* or *The Tempest*, staged in remote regions or long-past ages, the hero's familiar, Hecate, or Ariel, may appear and disappear miraculously, since the audience was prepared to accept miracles under such conditions. But Prince Henry could not convincingly have been given an attendant sprite; Falstaff, though as mythical as Hecate or Ariel, is very much more solid.

I have dealt at length with Prince Henry and Falstaff because the myths are familiar and the facts readily accessible, but a study of any hero to whose name myths have become attached would show the clear-cut line that separates the historical hero from his mythical namesake. "From the researchers of J. Bédier upon the epic personages of William of Orange, Girard de Rousillon, Ogier the Dane, Raoul de Cambrai, Roland, and many other worthies, it emerges that they do not correspond in any way with what historical documents teach us of their alleged real prototypes."[17]

"All history," said Dr. Johnson, "so far as it is not supported by contemporary evidence, is romance."[18] This is perfectly true, since romance is often myth in disguise, and if historians, instead of telling us what, in their opinion, is "not improbable," were to bear it in mind and consider carefully the channels by which any alleged fact has been or could be transmitted, we should less often find myth masquerading as history.

Note.—Professor Hocart, though in general agreement with my views, disagreed with my explanation of the clown. "The clown," he said, "is the earth-cousin of the sky-king, and so does everything topsy-turvy."

Notes

1. C. W. Oman: *A History of England*, pp. 219–220.
2. W. H. Ingrams: *Abu Nuwâs, passim.*
3. E. Welsford: *The Fool*, p. 62.
4. W. P. Ker, op. cit., pp. 281, 310, 314.
5. Raglan, op. cit., p. 69.

6. E. K. Chambers: *The English Folk-play*, p. 140.

7. E. K. Chambers: *The Mediæval Stage*, vol. i, p. 44.

8. *King Henry V*, Act II, Scene iii.

9. Numbers xxii, 6.

10. E. Welsford, op. cit., pp. 80, 89.

11. Act I, Scene i.

12. *Macbeth*, Act I, Sc. iii.

13. *Othello*, Act III.

14. *King Henry IV*, Pt. I, Act V, Scene iv.

15. *Folklore in the Old Testament*, vol. iii, p. 97.

16. *The Theory of Drama*, p. 164.

17. A. van Gennep, op. cit., p. 173.

18. J. Boswell: *A Tour to the Hebrides*, p. 335.

PART III

THE HERO PATTERN AND THE LIFE OF JESUS

by Alan Dundes

THE HERO PATTERN AND THE
LIFE OF JESUS

THE New Testament in general and the life of Jesus in particular have not received much critical attention from folklorists. This is in marked contrast to the considerable body of folklore scholarship devoted to the Old Testament. Frazer could pen a three-volume work entitled *Folklore in the Old Testament*, but he said relatively little about folklore in the New Testament. Similarly, Fraser devoted a considerable portion of his monumental *Golden Bough* to "Dying and Reviving Gods," most of them Near Eastern, but he said next to nothing about their possible relationship to the life of Jesus. Lord Raglan in his fascinating delineation of the hero pattern was perfectly willing to take three examples from the Old Testament—Joseph, Moses, and Elijah—but he does not so much as mention Jesus, despite the fact that the life of Jesus is demonstrably as similar to Raglan's twenty-two incident hero pattern as the lives of the three Old Testament heroes he does cite.

Perhaps one reason for the neglect of the New Testament by folklorists is a combination of prejudice and self-interest. Folklorists as well as folk feel ambivalence towards folklore. On the one hand, there is pride in folklore insofar as it represents a traditional expression of one's heritage. On the other hand, to the extent that folklore is considered to be synonymous with error and fallacy (and to the extent that the folk are considered to be the *vulgus in populo*), one tends to be ashamed of one's folklore and may even repudiate it. Raglan, for example, was anxious to show that the lives of traditional heroes were "folklore" rather than history. Thus it was perfectly all right to argue that Old Testament or Jewish heroes were folkloristic rather than historical. But heaven forbid that a proper member of the British House of Lords should apply this line of reasoning to the life of Jesus! Moses might be folklore but Jesus was history or, to put it another way, Moses was "false" while Jesus was "true." Raglan even went so far as to remark that "the compilers of the 'historical' books of the Old Testa-

HARLEM GENTRIFICATION

Adrienne Christian

The old Kenyan
makes a living now
slaughtering goats.

Not for Curry Goat.
For whites'
dogs.

ment were not historians writing for students, but theologians writing for the faithful" (Raglan 1956:112), an observation, which, of course, could be equally well applied to the New Testament!

This may be a somewhat exaggerated statement of Lord Raglan's position; but since he does not discuss Jesus, it would appear reasonable to assume that he felt Christ was fact while Moses was fiction. (In 1958 Lord Raglan told Professor Albert B. Friedman that of course he had thought of Jesus in connection with the hero pattern, but that he had no wish to risk upsetting anyone and therefore he elected to avoid even so much as mentioning the issue—personal communication from Professor Friedman, April, 1977.) To be sure, Raglan does not categorically deny the historicity of any of the heroes he considers. It is rather their common biographies which he labels as nonhistorical. Moses and the others may have lived, but inevitably the folk reportings of their lives tend to conform to the hero pattern. The common biographical pattern, Raglan claimed, derived from a common ritual pattern, namely, ritual regicide. In this articulation of myth-ritual theory, Raglan offers no suggestion of why ritual regicide should have arisen. Actually, myth-ritual theory rarely, if ever, accounts for ultimate origins. To say myth comes from ritual is not to say where the alleged ritual came from.

Inasmuch as Raglan and others insist upon referring to the accounts of heroes as myths, it might be appropriate to indicate that if one defines myth in the folkloristic sense of a sacred narrative explaining how the world and man came to be in their present form, then it is abundantly clear that Raglan's hero narratives are *not* myths. The narrative which originally inspired Raglan to undertake his hero pattern study was Oedipus, which folklorists recognize as a folktale, namely Aarne-Thompson tale type 931 (Thompson 1961). The story of Oedipus is not a myth. Similarly, the story of Perseus, also analyzed by Raglan, is generally considered by folklorists to be a version of Aarne-Thompson tale type 300, The Dragon-Slayer. Many of the narratives treated by Raglan, e.g., Arthur, Robin Hood, are legends rather than myths. What this means is that the hero pattern articulated by Raglan (and a number of other scholars) is part of folktale and legend, not myth. I would argue that the lives of Joseph, Moses, Elijah, and Jesus would, from the folklorists' point of view, be considered legends (cf. Bascom 1965).

If folklorists have neglected the life of Jesus, it cannot be said that theologians concerned with reconstructing the biography of Christ have not been concerned with folklore (though they usually insist upon referring to folklore under the misleading rubric of "myth"). The various "quests for the historical Jesus" invariably set as their goal the disentangling of fact from fiction, history from folklore. It would be a gross understatement to say that there exists a proliferation of books and monographs devoted to the life of Jesus. It would take more than one lifetime to read them all, assuming one had the requisite polyglot linguistic competence to do so. However, it is possible to note the consistent concern with attempting to separate out the folkloristic elements from the New Testament so as to come as close as humanly possible to unalloyed "gospel" truth.

The utilization of comparative folklore materials to illuminate the historicity of portions of the New Testament is by no means anything new. Celsus (circa 178), writing an anti-Christian tract in the second century, compared the virgin birth of Jesus with Greek myths about Danae, Melanippe, Auge, and Antiope. Furthermore, in speaking of the resurrection, he asked why, if other stories are myths, should the Christian account be regarded as "noble and convincing" (Grant 1961:73, 75)? There is other evidence attesting to the early recognition of possible analogues or parallels to the story of Jesus. For example, Justin Martyr, also writing in the second century, used a form of the comparative method in two distinct ways. On the one hand, he implies that the existence of analogues weakens the credibility of the Jesus narrative. Into the mouth of Trypho the Jew in his "Dialogue with Trypho," Justin put the following argument: "Besides, in Greek mythology there is a story of how Perseus was born of Danae, while she was a virgin, when the one whom they call Zeus descended upon her in the form of a golden shower. You Christians should be ashamed of yourselves, therefore, to repeat the same kind of stories as these men, and you should, on the contrary, acknowledge this Jesus to be a man of mere human origin" (Justin Martyr 1948:254). On the other hand, Justin in "The First Apology" actually used the existence of comparable stories as an argument for believing in the story of Jesus. "When, indeed, we assert that the Word, our Teacher Jesus Christ, who is the first-begotten of God the Father, was not born as the result of sexual relations, and that He was crucified, died, arose from the dead, and ascended into Heaven, we propose nothing new or different from that which you say about the so-called sons of Jupiter. You know exactly the number of sons ascribed to Jupiter by your respected writers: Mercury, who was the interpretative word and teacher of all; Aesculapius, who, though himself a healer of diseases, was struck by a thunderbolt and ascended into heaven; Bacchus, who was torn to pieces; Hercules, who rushed into the flames of the funeral pyre to escape his sufferings; the Dioscuri, the sons of Leda; Perseus, the son of Danae; and Bellerophon, who, though of human origin, rose to heaven on his horse Pegasus" (Justin Martyr 1948:56–57). Justin goes on to claim that such Greek myths had been invented by demons to counterfeit and thereby demean the true and miraculous events in the life of Jesus. "And, Trypho (I said), when I hear it asserted that Perseus was born of a virgin, I know that this is another forgery of that treacherous serpent" (Justin Martyr 1948:262, 57, 92, 259).

The problem of how to treat apparent or actual parallels to biblical materials has yet to be solved. If the same narrative exists in a variety of cultures, why is one version of the story singled out as being true or valid while all others are dismissed as being false or untrue? This fundamental question, which invariably arises from any honest application of the comparative method, continues to bedevil conscientious students of theology. Gunkel put the matter thus: ". . . it should not be forgotten that many of the legends of the Old Testament are not only similar to those of other nations, but are actually related to them by origin and nature. Now we cannot regard the story of the Deluge in Genesis as history and that of the Babylonians as legend" (Gunkel 1964:10). A number of alternatives exist. One can stubbornly cling to the notion that one's own version of the narrative is God's truth and simply not worry about the probable or possible cognate versions of the narrative in other cultures. A second possibility is to accept all versions of the narrative as God's truth. A third possibility is to accept the comparative data as bona fide evidence for the multiple existence of a narrative (thereby confirming the narrative as folklore) and to remove it from the sacred canon. This is, generally speaking, the course which has been followed by scholarly theologians. The folklore elements are to be identified and then culled out of the Bible. Through this process of "demythologizing," unadulterated sacred truth will remain.

I do not propose to survey all of the various attempts to demythologize the Old and New Testaments, for truly there is a massive amount of scholarship devoted to the subject (cf. Doane, Saintyves, Henderson, Childs, and Ohler). However, it might be useful to cite several of the earlier illustrations of the trend. One of the most influential treatises was the *Leben Jesu* of David Friedrich Strauss, first published in 1835. Using a modified form of the comparative method, Strauss viewed the four gospels as variants and he tried to isolate contradictory elements. One of his principles was: "An account which shall be regarded as historically valid, must neither be inconsistent with itself, nor in contradiction with other accounts" (Strauss 1892:88). His honest detailing of the contradictory elements as part of his elaborate effort to apply "the notion of the mythus to the entire history of the life of Jesus" (1892:65) led to a veritable ground swell of vituperative criticism from both his peers and the general public. The book cost Strauss his teaching position and his academic career (Schweitzer 1968:71; McCown 1940:6). Twentieth-century folklorists can nevertheless appreciate his accurate awareness of the difference between the narrative genres of myth and legend (Strauss 1892:62) even though he stubbornly chose to use the term *mythus* to refer to the folkloristic patterns underlying Christ's biography. Folklorists can certainly empathize with such statements as "The knowledge of the fact, that the Jews were fond of representing their great men as the children of parents who had long been childless, cannot but make us doubtful of the historical truth of the statement that this was the case with John the Baptist; knowing also that the Jews saw predictions everywhere in their writings of their prophets and poets, and discovered types of the Messiah in all the lives of holy men recorded in their Scriptures; when we find details in the life of Jesus evidently sketched after the pattern of these prophecies and prototypes, we cannot but suspect that they are rather mythical than historical" (Strauss 1892:89). The field of comparative folklore was scarcely sufficiently developed at the time Strauss wrote for him to have been able to cite parallels from non-Judeo-Christian traditions.

By the end of the nineteenth century, various advocates of a 'myth' approach to the life of Jesus were much more sophisticated in terms of knowledge of other narrative traditions, but at the same time they were much less convincing in their arguments because of rigid adherence to one or another particular theory of interpretation: e.g., solar mythology. So another German critic, Arthur Drews, in his book *The Christ Myth*, which appeared initially in 1909, sought to "prove that more or less all the features of the picture of the historical Jesus, at any rate all those of any important religious significance, bear a purely mythical character, and no opening exists for seeking an historical figure behind the Christ myth" (Drews 1911:19). Drews, called by one scholar "perhaps the outstanding representative of the denial of the historicity of Jesus in the twentieth century" (McCown 1940:71), attempted through tortuous reasoning to show that the sun god who dies in winter to rise again in the spring is related to a fire god, specifically the Indic Agni. A brief example of Drews' specious use of comparative folklore should suffice: "At dawn, as soon as the brightening morning star in the east announced that the sun was rising, the priest called his assistants together and kindled the fire upon a mound of earth by rubbing together two sticks in which the God was supposed to be hidden. As soon as the spark shone in the 'maternal bosom,' the soft underpart of the wood, it was treated as an 'infant child.' " He concludes, "There is no doubt that we have before us in the Vedic Agni cult the original source of all the stories of the birth of the Fire-Gods and Sun-Gods" (Drews 1911:99–100), adding later "Accordingly we have before us in the story of the transfiguration in the Gospels only another view of the story of the Light-God or Fire-God, such as lies at the root of the story of the baptism of the Christian Saviour" (1911:127). One must keep in mind that the reigning folklore theories of the day included both Indic origins and solar mythology. In any case, the flawed reasoning and faulty scholarship of Drews and other would-be folklore Bible critics of the period were fairly easy to attack. (Conybeare's *The Historical Christ* published in 1914, for example, did so with a good deal of acerbic glee!)

The excesses of solar mythologists may be partly responsible for the failure of later students of the history of religion and folklorists to have made any concerted effort to systematically consider the life of Jesus Christ as a variant of a standard European (or perhaps Indo-European) hero pattern. (The hero pattern in question actually includes Semitic as well as Indo-European exemplars.) Biblical scholars have shown a willingness to draw upon developments in folklore and mythology research. Bultmann, for example applies Olrik's celebrated "epic laws of folk narrative" to biblical materials (1963:188–189). But neither

Bultmann, Dibelius, nor Boman makes mention of the extensive research devoted to the hero pattern. Even with the recent tendency to consider and even to embrace structural folklore studies, e.g., Propp (Ricoeur 1975:39–51) or Lévi-Strauss (Patte 1976, cf. Leach 1975), I am not aware of any application of Raglan's hero pattern, published in the mid-1930s, to the life of Jesus.

The hero pattern has been the subject of frequent discussion for over a century, but few of the discussions have even so much as mentioned the possible relevance of the pattern to Christ. E. B. Tylor in an essay written in 1863 noted the widespread stories of children being brought up by animals and he referred specifically to Romulus and Remus, Moses, and Cyrus. But it was not until the posthumous publication of J. G. von Hahn's "Arische Aussetzungs-und-Rückkehr-Formel" (The Aryan Expulsion and Return Formula) in 1876 that modern hero pattern research may be said to have been properly launched. Von Hahn used the biographies of fourteen heroes to arrive at a sixteen-incident biographical paradigm. Von Hahn's pioneering effort passed virtually unnoticed by folklorists with perhaps the single exception of Alfred Nutt, who applied the pattern to Celtic materials in 1881. The heroes analyzed by von Hahn included Perseus, Hercules, Oedipus, Romulus and Remus, Siegfried, Cyrus, Karna, and Krishna.

Some of the subsequent hero studies centered on Cyrus. In 1882, Adolf Bauer published a comprehensive monograph. In the first part of "Die Kyros-Sage und Verwandtes," Bauer concentrated upon different versions of the Cyrus story, but in the second part he discussed such possible cognates as Romulus and Remus, Siegfried, Karna, and Sargon. Bauer also noted that the expulsion of children, miraculous rescue from water, the nursing by an animal, and the foster parenthood undertaken by a shepherd, fisherman, or some other poor individual were widely found in *märchen* as well (Bauer 1882:566–570). Other studies of Cyrus appeared including Heinrich Lessmann's *Die Kyros-sage in Europa* in 1906. Lessmann gave a summary of the hero pattern (1906:49–50), but it was far less detailed than von Hahn's of 1876.

In 1908 French folklorist Emmanuel Cosquin published a fascinating essay entitled "Le Lait de la Méré et Le Coffre Flottant." Taking a Javanese Moslem legend as a point of departure, Cosquin proceeded to show the parallelism of the biographies of Sargon, Romulus and Remus, Perseus, Karna, Cyrus, Judas, and Moses. He also documented the existence of the same or similar pattern in folktales. Cosquin's essay stimulated further discussion (Hertel), including a study of the pattern in Jewish tradition apart from the Old Testament (Lévi). In 1909 Otto Rank published his brilliant monograph *The Myth of the Birth of the Hero* in which he used fifteen biographies as the basis of his formulation of the hero pattern. (The heroes analyzed by Rank were: Sargon, Moses, Karna, Oedipus, Paris, Telephus, Perseus, Gilgamesh, Cyrus, Tristan, Romulus, Hercules, Jesus, Siegfried, and Lohengrin.) Rank is unique among early students of the hero pattern in that he included the life of Jesus as one of his representative biographies. Rank chose to give a composite narrative synopsis of the hero pattern rather than giving a detailed listing of individual incidents.

Additional studies of the hero appeared. In 1911 came Karl Schmeing's dissertation, *Flucht- und Werbungssagen in Legende*, which was largely concerned with Christian saint's legends. In 1916, Paull Franklin Baum published a lengthy discussion of the medieval legend of Judas, remarking that "practically the whole of Judas' story can be related by means of the 'formulas' to which Hahn has reduced a large mass of myth and Heldensage" (1916:594, n. 39). Baum was attempting to determine whether the Judas story was a direct derivative of the Oedipus plot or whether it could have developed independently. Baum argued that the existence of a standard, distinct hero pattern involving a mother's dream of a son predestined to a wicked career, the exposure of the newborn child on the sea, his rescue and murder of his father, and the unconscious incest with his mother tended to suggest that the Judas story was not necessarily a conscious borrowing from Oedipus (Baum 1916:590, 603). In 1925, Eugene S. McCartney surveyed some forty classical versions of animal-nurtured children including Romulus and Remus, Cyrus, Paris, Aesculapius, Gilgamesh, and a host of lesser-known figures. In 1928 Vladimir Propp's *Morphology of the Folktale* was published. This important study might be said to outline the typical biography of a hero or heroine as it is found in fairy tales (Aarne-Thompson tale types 300–749). Since the story of Perseus is similar to tale type 300, The Dragon-Slayer and since Oedipus is tale type 931 (though strictly speaking this tale type doesn't fall in the Aarne-Thompson tales of magic category analyzed by Propp [1968:19]), one might well expect Propp's analysis to apply to the hero pattern. However, Propp is concerned solely with the fairy tale genre. His pattern ends with the marriage of the hero. In other words, Propp's scheme does not provide the full life of a hero ending with the hero's death. This is not a criticism of Propp but rather an acknowledgment that the fairy tale genre ends with marriage, not death. Most hero narratives are, or were told as, true stories; they are legends rather than fairy tales. For this reason, Propp's pioneering morphology of the fairy tale has only limited applicability to the totality of the legendary hero pattern.

In 1933 Alexander Haggerty Krappe wrote a brief essay in which he pointed out the similarity of the stories of Moses, Cyrus, Zeus, and Perseus. In 1934 Lord Raglan published his paper "The Hero of Tradition," which shortly thereafter (1936) formed the basis of his book *The Hero*. Raglan's hero pattern is one of the most ambitious inasmuch as he used the biographies of twenty-one heroes to illustrate a proposed scheme consisting of twenty-two incidents. Raglan wrote in complete ignorance of earlier scholarship devoted to the hero, and he was therefore unaware of the previous studies of von Hahn and Rank, for example. Raglan was parochial in other ways too. For one thing, the vast majority of his heroes came exclusively from classical (mostly Greek) sources. The first twelve heroes he treats are: Oedipus, Theseus, Romulus, Heracles, Perseus, Jason, Bellerophon, Pelops, Asclepios, Dionysos, Apollo, and Zeus. Raglan could have strengthened his case had he used some of the same heroes used by von Hahn and Rank and other scholars, e.g., such heroes as Sargon and Cyrus. On the other hand, one overall advantage of the fact that von Hahn, Rank, and Raglan made independent investigations of essentially the same textual material is the support it provides for the reliability of their hypothesized accounts of the hero pattern. In other words, since all three were able to inductively extrapolate hero biographical incident sequences from a more or less common body of data, sequences which reveal a fairly high degree of uniformity, it is more reasonable to defend the proposition that an empirically demonstrable hero biography pattern for (Indo-)European (and Semitic) heroes exists.

Before considering the pattern as described by von Hahn, Rank, and Raglan, it should be mentioned that the steady stream of hero pattern studies has continued. Joseph Campbell in his 1956 work *The Hero with a Thousand Faces* tries to delineate a "monomyth" which might apply to heroes from all cultures. However, Campbell's pattern is a synthetic, artificial composite which he fails to apply in toto to any one single hero. Campbell's hero pattern, unlike the ones formulated by von Hahn, Rank, and Raglan, is not empirically verifiable, e.g., by means of inductively extrapolating incidents from any one given hero's biography. In 1964 Gerhard Binder considered stories of exposed children citing no less than one hundred twenty-one examples from a variety of European and Asian cultures. For the present purposes, however, it is doubtful whether an overly ambitious attempt to define a universal hero pattern allegedly applicable to all human societies or an intensive study of one specific incident, e.g., the exposure of infant heroes, is as useful as an empirical study of the entire life stories of individual heroes. Let us therefore briefly consider the patterns of von Hahn, Rank, and Raglan.

von Hahn (1876)	*Rank (1909)*	*Raglan (1934)*
1. hero of illegitimate birth	child of distinguished parents	mother is royal virgin
2. mother is a princess	father is a king	father is a king
3. father is a god	difficulty in conception	father related to mother
4. prophecy of ascendance	prophecy warning against birth (e.g., parricide)	unusual conception
5. hero abandoned	hero surrendered to the water in a box	hero reputed to be son of god
6. suckled by animals	saved by animals or lowly people	attempt (usually by father) to kill hero
7. hero raised by childless shepherd couple	suckled by female animal or humble woman	hero spirited away
8. hero is high-spirited	—	reared by foster parents in a far country
9. he seeks service abroad	hero grows up	no details of childhood
10. triumphant homecoming	hero finds distinguished parents	goes to future kingdom
11. slays original persecutors and sets mother free	hero takes revenge on his father	is victor over king, giant dragon or wild beast
12. founds cities	acknowledged by people	marries a princess (often daughter of predecessor)

13. extraordinary death	achieves rank and honors	becomes king
14. reviled because of incest and dies young	—	for a time he reigns uneventfully
15. hero dies as an act of revenge by an insulted servant	—	he prescribes laws
16. he murders his younger brother	—	later, he loses favor with gods or his subjects
17. —	—	driven from throne and city
18. —	—	meets with mysterious death
19. —	—	often at the top of a hill
20. —	—	his children, if any, do not succeed him
21. —	—	his body is not buried, but nevertheless
22. —	—	he has one or more holy sepulchers

It is difficult to compare the three patterns. Von Hahn had sixteen incidents, Rank did not divide his pattern into incidents as such, and Raglan had twenty-two incidents. Raglan himself admitted that his choice of twenty-two incidents (as opposed to some other number of incidents) was arbitrary (Raglan 1956:186). So one could hardly expect complete agreement among the three pattern studies in terms of the number of incidents. Rank, because of his particular psychoanalytic bias, tended to emphasize the birth of the hero and for this reason he seems to have slighted the death of the hero. It is not my purpose in any case to try to reconcile the differences between von Hahn, Rank and Raglan. Nor am I interested in comparing the relative importance of individual incidents or traits in any of the schemes. Cook's statistical analysis of Raglan's pattern revealed two things. One was that the pattern was *not* truly cross-cultural. It did not apply, generally speaking, to selected American Indian, African, or Oceanic heroes. Moreover, even among the European heroes selected by Raglan, not all the traits occurred with the same frequency. Only one of the months later, my mind goes blank—I forget the moves, my body is totally numb. I am smiling but it is pasted on, like the pink cardboard things on my nipples. I block out the four-and-a-half minutes on stage, but the warmth from the well-seasoned women afterwards makes me feel connected. They welcome us to their ranks, as one naked organism.

Day Rest of My Life

I spend much of the first year after her death trying to negotiate something with my body. I wonder when these breasts will fail. I begin checking them for lumps. I try to admire them, just in case I will lose them soon. I decide to start treating myself the way I wanted my dying mother to be treated. *Dignity, without shame.* I decide to stand taller, grounded in the earth, shoulders back, glitter-covered breasts held high. I try to claim my body. I get my nipple pierced. I get my first tattoo. A year later I start seeing a somatic therapist. I tell her that my body is still mostly a human meat carriage that I drive around. I learn the word that people use for this: *disassociation.* Isn't that what everybody does? *No. You learned this to survive.*

Much of my softening happens in the bathtub. Looking down the length of my naked body, I can't help but see my mother, her white abdomen and tan legs jutting out. I imagine her farmer's tan on my feet. I try to take care of myself. My right nipple hurt this morning, throbbed when the metal ring was pushed through. I soak it in salt water, allowing the solution to enter and exit the piercing like water at a cave entrance. I am usually a bit rougher, but this time I am gentle as I swish the ceramic cup suctioned over my breast.

twenty-two traits occurred in the biographies of all twenty-one heroes: trait 11, the victory over the king *et al.* Five of the traits (3, 4, 15, 16, 19) occurred in only eleven or twelve biographies (Cook 1965:149). The point is that there is some arbitrariness in Raglan's selection of traits. Raglan remarks that he used the story of Oedipus as his starting point although he gives no particular justification for doing so. But this may be why Oedipus earns an almost perfect score of twenty-one points (out of twenty-two), the highest score of any hero Raglan considered. (Theseus and Moses both score twenty.)

There have been relatively few follow-up studies utilizing the Raglan scheme. Just as Nutt had applied von Hahn's pattern to Celtic material, so Rees (1936) applied Raglan's pattern successfully to a number of Celtic saints—including Saint Patrick. Raglan's methodology has also inspired attempts to delineate commonalities in the biographies of traditional heroines (Jezewski 1984). Utley applied the pattern somewhat tongue-in-cheek to the biography of Abraham Lincoln and found that Lincoln scores no less than the full twenty-two points (Utley 1965:4, 28). The significance of Utley's essay is that it underscores the distinction between the individual and his biography with respect to historicity. The fact that a hero's biography conforms to the Indo-European hero pattern does not necessarily mean that the hero never existed. It suggests rather that the folk repeatedly insist upon making their versions of the lives of heroes follow the lines of a specific series of incidents. Accordingly, if the life of Jesus conforms in any way with the standard hero pattern, this proves nothing one way or the other with respect to the historicity of Jesus.

To determine to what extent, if any, the life of Jesus might be related to the standard Indo-European hero pattern, one might ask which version of the life of Jesus is the one to choose. Biblical scholars are wont to distinguish sharply between the different versions told in each of the four gospels. A distinction is also made between the synoptic gospels (Matthew, Mark, and Luke) and the gospel of John. Moreover, the materials in the four gospels are often considered separately, as being more authoritative, from details contained in the so-called apocryphal gospels. As a folklorist, I find it difficult to give a priori preference or precedence to one or more versions of a legend as opposed to other versions. As a genre, legend rarely exists in any one single version in any community in the world. Rather, a cluster of legends surrounds an important political or religious figure. It may be that no one individual in a community can relate the entire legendary life history of a particular figure. For this reason, a folklorist normally collects as many versions of a legend as possible before trying to reconstruct a composite notion of a legendary figure's life story. In the present instance, I have chosen to regard all four gospels as primary sources for the life of Jesus although I will on occasion cite what I consider to be relevant data from the apocrypha. I do not intend to treat Jesus as miracle worker or healer or religious teacher. Rather, my purpose is to examine his life in the light of the hero pattern as this pattern has been described by folklorists.

If one wished to apply Raglan's twenty-two incident pattern to the life of Jesus, one might include (1) virgin mother, (4) unusual conception, (5) hero reputed to be son of god, (6) attempt to kill hero, (7) hero spirited away [flight into Egypt], (8) reared by foster parents [Joseph], (9) no details of childhood, (10) goes to future kingdom, (13) becomes "king" [cf. the mock title of king of the Jews: INRI], (14) "reigns" uneventfully for a time, (15) prescribes laws, (16) loses favor with some of his "subjects" (e.g., Judas), (17) driven from throne and city, (18) meets with mysterious death, (19) at the top of a hill, (21) body is not buried, and (22) he has a holy sepulcher. While one may well quibble about the applicability of one or two of Raglan's twenty-two points, it would appear that Jesus would rate a score of seventeen (which would rank him closer to Raglan's ideal hero paradigm than Jason, Bellerophon, Pelops, Asclepios, Apollo, Zeus, Joseph, Elijah, and Siegfried). If one accepts the validity of the general outlines of the European hero pattern as delineated by Raglan (and others), then it would appear reasonable to consider that the biography of Jesus does in fact conform fairly well to this pattern.

Raglan's pattern provides a new vantage point for those who seek to understand the life of Jesus as it is reported in the gospels. For example, Bible scholars have bemoaned the lack of information about the youth and growing up of Jesus. Luke and John tell us almost nothing of the period between birth and adulthood. The point is that this is precisely the case with nearly all heroes of tradition. That is why Raglan included his trait 9 "We are told nothing of his childhood" (1956:174).

The versions of the pattern delineated by von Hahn and Rank are also helpful. For example, both include the animal nurse detail. It is tempting to see an echo of this incident in Jesus being born in a manger (Luke 2:12). The word "manger" (cognate with French *manger*, to eat) does refer to a box or trough from which animals feed. The image of the manger is thus consonant with the animal nurse incident in the hero pattern. It is true that no animal participates in the actual nursing of Jesus, but the later iconographic tradition of having an ox and ass watching over the infant Jesus (cf. Ziegler) might possibly be related to this part of the hero pattern (cf. Rank 1956:52, n. 7). There is no scriptural authority for the iconographic tradition though there is a passage in Isaiah (1:3) "The ox knoweth his owner, and the ass his master's crib." A striking piece of evidence confirming the present analysis of the manger detail as part of the hero pattern comes from one of the New Testament apocrypha, namely, the Protevangelion of James the Lesser. In this account, the manger as a box or trough clearly functions as the floating chest in which the imperiled infant male is ensconced. Moreover, the placement of Jesus in the manger immediately follows Herod's massacre of the innocents, a sequence following the hero pattern to the letter: "Then Herod perceiving that he was mocked by the wise men, and being very angry, commanded certain men to go and to kill all the children that were in Bethlehem being two years old and under. But Mary hearing that the children were to be killed, being under much fear, took the child, and wrapped him up in swaddling clothes, and laid him in an ox-manger" (Protevangelion 16:1–2). Then follows a sudden shift to John the Baptist and his mother Elizabeth who take flight from Herod's decree. In other words, the hero pattern continues to be followed but with different personages filling the traditional slots.

Another detail possibly illuminated by the hero pattern consists of presence of the shepherds at the nativity scene. Dibelius (1932:75) discusses at some length the traditionality of having a shepherd present at the birth of a hero or god. While only two of the thirty-two versions of "the literary motif of the exposed child" surveyed by Redford have shepherd rescuers, there are commonly comparable figures such as three herdsmen, a fisherman, a farmer, etc. (Redford 1967:225). Von Hahn did have as his seventh incident "Hero raised by childless shepherd couple." The inference to be drawn is that in Luke's account, the shepherds' role is diminished—they come to observe rather than to save the newborn infant (Luke 2:8–20). Nevertheless, it could be argued that the shepherds do constitute another reflection of the influence of the overall hero pattern.

There is a methodological issue which it might be well to mention and that is that the above observations were facilitated by the perspective provided by a knowledge of the general Indo-European hero pattern. Previous scholarship, in my opinion, has been greatly handicapped by its self-imposed parochial nature. The comparative approach may have been employed, but the comparisons were typically restricted or partial. A comparison of the birth of Jesus with just the birth of Moses (e.g., Bourke, Winter) or with just a possible Egyptian (Brunner-Traut) or Indic (Kennedy) precursor failed to yield the same insights. The comparative method requires more than a limited comparison with only one or two presumed parallels. I submit that biblical scholars have failed to utilize the relevant comparative tools available from folkloristics. The error of making too limited a comparison, e.g., Jesus with Moses, has another dimension. By comparing only a single element of the hero pattern, e.g., just the virgin birth, scholars deprive themselves and their readers of perceiving the entire pattern. Thus Dibelius treats the virgin birth and the manger-child as two separate legends (1932:80) whereas I am arguing that both elements are part of single legendary hero sequence. Bultmann (1963:3) makes clear that his aim is to reconstruct the history of the "individual units of the tradition", a praiseworthy and useful goal to be sure, but the atomistic study of small units can unfortunately result in seeing trees instead of the forest.

Having established, albeit tentatively, that the life of Jesus is a variant of the standard biography of the hero of tradition, we have tried to note similarities in the life of Jesus and in the hero pattern. But of equal importance are the differences between the life of Jesus and the typical hero. From our folkloristic vantage point, we can observe just how Jesus departs from the pattern. Recalling Raglan's trait sequence, we can easily see that what is "missing" from the life of Jesus are traits 11 and 12: a victory over a king, giant, dragon or wild beast; and a marriage with a princess. (One might go so far as to argue that to the extent that Jesus resisted the temptations of Satan [Matthew 4:1–11; Luke 4:1–13] he could be said to have vanquished a villainous antagonist. And in this same connection, it is of interest that in one of the apocryphal accounts of Christ's infancy, namely, the Gospel of Pseudo-Matthew [chapter 23], Jesus descends from his mother's lap to tame threatening dragons. But there can be no question that Jesus does not marry a princess.) In theory, that is, according to the folkloristic hero pattern, Jesus should have taken revenge upon Herod (or some other authority figure) and married his daughter.

The absence of marriage with a princess provides a significant clue to the particular worldview which produced the various versions of the life of Jesus. It was a male-oriented worldview which denied power to females—the one female power acknowledged was that of procreation. Women from Eve to Delilah to Salome were not to be trusted. If one wished to consider the life of John the Baptist in the light of the hero pattern, one can see that instead of the hero marrying the king's daughter, he is beheaded at her request (Mark 6:17–41). Propp's thirty-one function analysis of Russian fairy tale structure ends with the hero's or heroine's wedding which further supports the notion that traditional narratives included a marriage. It is thus the denial of women generally and the failure of Jesus to marry which sets him apart from other Indo-European heroes.

The significance of the lack of marriage in some versions of the Christian ideal (cf. the continuing argument over the necessity of celibacy for the truly devout) is even more crucial when one considers the possible psychological implications of the European hero pattern. Up to this point, we have considered only formal features of comparison with respect to the life of Jesus and the hero pattern. But pattern description is not an end in itself. Describing a pattern is but one step towards the end of studying meaning. What, if anything, does the European hero pattern mean? and how does its meaning bear on our understanding of the life of Jesus? To attempt to answer such questions, we must venture into the treacherous areas of interpretation and speculation. It is one thing to point out empirically verifiable parallels between one narrative and another; it is quite another to offer an interpretation of the possible meaning(s) of such narratives.

For an understanding of the psychological significance of the hero pattern, we must turn first to the insightful analysis offered by Otto Rank, in 1909. Rank made a number of extremely astute observations about the hero pattern. First, he suggested there were three actors: the hero and his parents. Second, he explained that the pattern exemplified the psychological principle of projection inasmuch as the son who would like to get rid of his father is transformed into a father who tries to get rid of his son. Through this projection, the son is freed from any guilt caused by hating his father since the father is depicted as a wicked villainous figure. Third, the son's Oedipal wish to repudiate his father (so as to have his mother all to himself) finds its ultimate expression in the virgin birth (Rank 1959:81). There have been numerous folkloristic studies of the virgin birth (Charencey, Hartland, Van Gennep, Saintyves) though not nearly so many as theological studies of the same phenomenon (cf. the bibliography in Boslooper), but none have offered a more fascinating (and persuasive) interpretation of this puzzling detail. A son who is born of a virgin can deny that his father ever had sexual access to his mother.

Despite his brilliant insights, Rank went astray on one point and unfortunately it was a major point in his analysis. Rank interpreted the placing of the infant hero in a box floating in water as the "symbolic expression of birth." Rank's extended emphasis upon the importance of the alleged "birth" symbolism (as opposed to his application of Freud's Oedipal rationale to the lives of heroes) perhaps anticipated his later book *The Trauma of Birth* in which he argued that it was the act of being born which was primarily responsible for adult neuroses. Rank, in fact, attempted to offer his birth trauma theory as a rival theory to Freud's Oedipus complex. In any event, there are some serious theoretical difficulties in this aspect of Rank's analysis of the hero pattern which one must remember Rank called "the myth of the *birth* of the hero."

For one thing, the hero is *not* surrendered to the water in a box in all versions of the hero biography. Von Hahn is more accurate when he refers to the abandonment of the hero. The child is just as often abandoned on land as at sea. Redford's study of thirty-two versions of the "literary motif of the exposed child" shows that only twelve have a watery place of abandonment. Thus Moses is abandoned in water but Oedipus is abandoned in the wilds. Slightly more than half of the specific heroes selected by Rank himself for his analysis have the water abandonment. What this means is that the hero pattern is *not* dependent upon the particular motif of S 331, Exposure of child in boat (floating chest). The critical motif is rather M 371, Exposure of infant to avoid fulfillment of prophecy. Since the hero's biography can conform to the overall pattern without reference to exposure to water, Rank's analysis of the hero pattern in terms of birth trauma would seem to be in error.

There are other problems with Rank's birth analysis. Consider the fact that the hero is already born when he is abandoned. Why would he need to be born again? Consider also that in several versions of the hero story involving water, the protagonist is abandoned *with* his mother, as Rank himself observed, and they are *both* placed in the box or floating chest, e.g., the case of Perseus. Since the mother is placed in the chest, is she also being born or reborn? Holley in his study of "the floating chest" suggests, not very convincingly, that "the pres-

ence of the mother in the chest, a mythological doubling of the function of the chest itself" is related to a supposed ritual involving a
mother-goddess and a young child-god who must be reborn to ensure
the earth's annual vegetative fertility (1949:45).

I should stress that the weakness of Rank's interpretation of the
birth symbolism of the hero pattern in no way affects the aptness of his
more or less Oedipal reading of the pattern. After the father has gotten
rid of his son (which in terms of inverse projection means "after the
son has gotten rid of his father"), he is invariably nursed by a kindly
animal or peasant woman. It was Cosquin in 1908 who specifically
pointed out the repeated connection between the act of exposing the
hero and his being suckled. In some of the legends discussed by
Cosquin, the act of nursing is initiated to prevent sexual relations. For
example, in the Javanese Moslem legend which inspired Cosquin's research, an ascetic cures a king's daughter after the king had promised
to embrace Islam. The king has the ascetic sheik marry the princess
but the ascetic returns to his home without her. The princess gave
birth to a handsome son but at the same time an epidemic breaks out.
The king's astrologers claim the baby is the cause of the calamity. The
king builds a watertight chest and placing the infant in it, he throws
the chest into the sea. A passing ship notices a strange light and picks
up the chest. The infant is turned over to the ship's owner, a woman.
The woman raises the child and after some time conceives a grand
passion for him. The boy then says to her that if she will uncover her
breasts, he will remedy the situation. She does so and the boy nurses.
By this means, the woman becomes the proper mother of the boy. (For
references to additional mythological parallels to symbolic nursing as
a means of ritual adoption, see Deonna's excellent essay "La légende
de Pero et de Micon et l'allaitement symbolique" [1955:5–50] and Renard 1964:616 n. 1.) Presumably the act of nursing cures the woman
of her passion for the boy. (In terms of projection, the boy's passion for
the mother [surrogate] is transformed into her passion for him and so
the alleged curative act for *her* problem provides an opportunity for
him to fulfill *his* desire.) In some versions of the story, it is stated that
the miracle consists of the fact that the woman was able to produce
milk even though she had never given birth to a child. In still other
Indic and Javanese legends, the abandoned boys return to their original homeland to attack the king. The king's wife, their mother, squirts
milk into their mouths, thereby proving to the boys her relationship to

them. Cosquin suggests that these legends may be cognate with the stories of Sargon, Romulus and Remus, Moses, Judas, etc.

I submit that the act of nursing is a confirmation of the mother-child constellation vis-à-vis the father. In many societies, a father must abstain from sexual intercourse so long as his wife is nursing a baby. Thus the longer an infant nurses, the more he succeeds in keeping his father away. In terms of the hero pattern, one finds a variety of means for the hero to keep his father away from his mother. The unusual means of conception, the virgin birth, and the emphasis upon abandonment plus nursing are all techniques for denying the father. (For numerous creation myths from East Indonesia which tell of the mother-son bond to the exclusion of a visible father image, see Muensterberger 1939.) Since breast-feeding in biblical times might have lasted as long as three or four years, according to Patai (1959:194-197), this would have solidified the mother-child relationship. It is worth noting also that Jesus was the firstborn—assuming that he did have brothers and sisters. His frequent depiction in iconography and art in the act of nursing from his mother suggests that he succeeds as no other firstborn ever has insofar as he is never displaced by younger sibling rivals. Von Hahn's delineation of the hero pattern ends with the hero murdering his younger brother. It is not certain just how common this is (though it does occur), but it would seem to reflect a sibling rivalry component of the hero pattern. (For the notion that Jesus and Judas might represent "brothers," see Tarachow 1960:546.)

The importance of the mother-infant nursing configuration in the hero pattern is suggested by one of the numerous ancient etymologies for the names "Romulus" and "Remus," which derives them from "ruma" or "rumis," allegedly old Latin words for "breast" (McCarthy 1935:32, citing Plutarch and Pliny). Regardless of the linguistic validity of what might be a folk etymology, the fact that it was proposed at all supports the notion that the heroes are closely associated with the act of suckling. If the etymology were accurate, it would seemingly apply to the current name Rome and thus support Rank's general notion of the city as a mother symbol (cf. the modern word 'metropolis' derived from the Greek for mother and city) and his particular observation that "the seven hills of Rome correspond to the teats of the she-wolf" (1952:18, n. 2).

Other philological data is less suspect. For example, in Latin and in derivative languages, the words for mother and breast are similar if not identical. Even in English, "mamma" can refer affectionately to one's mother or to the breast. The semantic connection between mother and breastfeeding makes both logical and psychological sense (and may have been a factor in the decision of Linnaeus to coin the term "mammalia" to refer to the class of animals whose young are brought forth alive and then nourished with milk from the mother's breasts). Also relevant is the likelihood that the Latin word for son, *filius*, appears to have meant originally "suckling" from the Latin root *felare*, "suck"—cf. fellatio—(Buck 1949:105). The English word daughter is also of interest in this connection. Buck (1949:106) claims the root connection is obscure. It agrees in form with Sanskrit *duh* "milk" and with a Greek root meaning fashion or make, but Buck remarks that "in neither case is there a convincing semantic explanation." One wonders if a daughter isn't perceived as a milk-maker (as opposed to a son who sucks). Females give; males take (cf. Thass-Thienemann 1957:30).

It is tempting to argue from linguistic data that being thrown into or onto a body of water does not so much symbolize birth, as Rank contended, as it symbolizes being thrown onto a mother. The word for sea in Latin is *mare* which could conceivably be related to *mater*. (In French, the words *mer* and *mère* are homophonic.) I am not arguing that the words for sea and mother are related in all languages or even in all Indo-European languages. But the phonetic if not etymological similarity of the words for sea and mother in even one language is surely of interest. One wonders if the name "Mary" isn't derived from either sea or mother. The origins of the name are obscure but Mary may be related to the name Miriam which could be construed as containing the Hebrew *yam* meaning sea. (Ernest Jones in his extended discussion of the "MR" root (1951b:326–339) suggests that "milk" is related to it.) It is certainly curious that in Latin the word for lake is *lacus* and the word for milk is *lac*. The floating "chest" might be literally just that, a floating female bosom (cf. in French *boite* and *poitrine*). This would explain Cosquin's observation that there was a close connection between the floating chest and the giving of maternal milk. Please note that the association exists *regardless* of the validity of the above admittedly highly speculative philological musings.

The importance and antiquity of the mother-child nursing configuration is well attested in mythology and art. Besides such traditions as Juno suckling Hercules (Deonna 1955:31–38; Renard 1964), there is considerable evidence from the ancient Near East. Statues show Ishtar nursing a child or the cow-headed Egyptian goddess Hathor suckling Osiris (Jeremias 1911, I:118). Sometimes the image takes the form of a cow nursing a calf with the characteristic motif of the maternal cow twisting its head around so as to see or lick the young calf (Matthiae 1962). The configuration was found in Egypt, Syria, and Mesopotamia. This bovine imagery is present in both the Old and New Testament. Samson refers to his bride as a heifer in his suggestive metaphor rebuking her kinsmen who with her help were able to answer his neck riddle: "If ye had not plowed with my heifer, ye had not found out my riddle" (Judges 14:18). The ashes of a ritually slain heifer were used to purify the unclean. The requirements were: a red heifer without spot, wherein is no blemish, and upon which never came yoke. In any case, a heifer is, so to speak, a virgin cow. In terms of such an imagery pattern, one is reminded of the centrality in Mithraism of killing the bull (a father figure?) coupled with the worship of the golden calf (a son figure?) (Exodus 32:1–8). The mythological association of a heifer or cow with a mother figure is also attested in the Greek story of Zeus' affair with Io (plus the formulaic epithet "cow-eyed," used to describe Hera). One could cite numerous examples of gods mating with cows in Sumerian and Canaanite myths (Astor 1965:80–92). There is even Neolithic evidence of this metaphorical pattern which includes the head of a bull on a wall, right next to which are two protruding human breasts (Mellaart 1963:72).

Although the cow' was perhaps one of the most logical forms of the animal nurse motif, other animals apparently served equally well. Wolves, goats, and dogs on occasion provided the necessary source of milk. One of the most curious nurturant agents consisted of bees, e.g., in the case of Zeus. It might be worth mentioning that the combination of milk and honey associated with the idyllic "paradise" of earliest infancy could well account for the presence of the same nutrient combination in the promised land or afterlife paradise. One thinks of "and the hills shall flow with milk" (Joel 3:18) and the image of the ideal of "honey and milk" under the tongue (Song of Solomon 4:11). The idiom of "a land flowing with milk and honey" as a metaphor for abundance occurs no fewer than twenty-one times in the Bible (Beck and Smedley 1971:167). One might logically assume that infants were in fact fed milk and honey (Usener 1902, Roheim 1940:182). Guidi (1903:241) argued that the biblical phrase should be translated as milk accustomed to love and a gentle touch, now surrounded by coffee grounds and cat shit.

Day 28

She spends her second to last night on Earth throwing up strawberries. I alternate between comforting her and sleeping. Her breathing becomes loud, like an animal. She is suffering, and I am tired. In the morning I feel ashamed when I see that the oxygen tubes have slid partway off her nose, and the tip of her nose has turned blue. Around 10am, our hospice nurse, John, arrives. He gives me a look and we leave the room. John tells me that she probably isn't going to communicate with us again. I nod. We re-enter the room and give her a full body massage with Frankincense and grapeseed oil. John tucks her shirt down from where it has bunched up around her ribs. He lifts up her torso and gently massages her back.

"Do you like that, Elise?" he asks turning his face towards hers. Her eyes are closed.

"Yeah," she says with a smile. "I like that." These are her last words. I take this as her blessing that I have done a good enough job.

After a long night holding her and chanting songs to her with my best friend, she stops breathing. I climb into bed with her, still holding her hand, and go to sleep. When I wake, the sun has come up and her body is much cooler. Her jaw has relaxed and her eyes are open. She looks dreamy and at ease. I take off her clothes and wash her whole body with a washcloth. I decide to dress her in blue silk pajamas. I put on her makeup, which seems silly, but it also seems silly not to do it right one last time. I arrange her hands over her abdomen and straighten the legs of her pajama pants. When everything feels done, I close the door and wait for the men to come and take her.

Day 36

I sign up for a burlesque class. It feels obscene to take a class on striptease so close to my mother's death, but I do it anyway. I feel like I have nothing left to lose. I join half a dozen other women in a cold warehouse in rainy autumnal San Francisco and learn the correct way to apply carpet tape to pasties. When our class performs a couple of with honey rather than milk and honey. In any event, the parallelism of earliest infancy with the concept of afterlife suggests an infantile origin for the equation of *Urzeit* and *Endzeit*, as Gunkel and others refer to the beginning and end of human time on earth. Some scholars have suggested an infantile origin for paradise, but they tend to think that the model is the prenatal state (Rank 1952:116, 162, n. 1, Rubenstein 1972:147, 165). I think it is more reasonable to argue that postnatal breast-feeding is a more likely infantile model, especially in view of such phrases as "the hills shall flow with milk." In this regard, a passage from the Coptic Gospel of Thomas (Plate 85, lines 20–22) is germane: "Jesus saw children being suckled. He said to his disciples, 'These children who are being suckled are like those who enter the Kingdom' " (cf. Isaiah 66:10–13).

The semantic connection between honey and milk is also suggested by the curious coincidence that the initial portion of the English word *milk* is phonetically similar to the Latin root for honey *mel*. Thus combining the Latin words for honey and milk would be *mel lac*, which is close to Gothic *miluks* (cf. Danish *melk*, Old English *meolc*, Polish *mleko*, Russian *moloko*, etc. Buck 1949:385). Another association between honey and milk comes from an equation of bees and breasts (Bradley 1973) supported by such mythological data as the many-breasted Artemis of Ephesus, a mother goddess of western Anatolia, having her cult administered by a group of sixty priestesses called bees "melissai" (Mellaart 1963:80). The notion of Zeus, father of the gods, as an infant being nurtured by bees is also suggestive in philological terms. *Abba* is Aramaic for father (Mark 14:36) (cf. *babbo* in Italian). Bee in Latin is *apis*. French *abbé*, the head of an abbey, is at least homonymically similar to French *abeille*, bee. If one were speculatively inclined, one might be tempted to see a parallel between the social organization (and nurturant qualities) of bees and abbeys. With respect to man-made objects, Bradley (1973:304) remarks that until relatively recently, men tended to build beehives in the shape of the human breast. Even if one rejects some of the questionable etymological speculation crossing unrelated languages (Aramaic and French), there remain to be explained such facts as Zeus' being nursed by bees or the many-breasted Artemis' having helpers called "*melissai*" (bees).

What is at issue here is not the symbolism of bees and honey, or the difficulties of a dubious etymological equation so much as trying to understand one of the principal elements in the Indo-European (and

Semitic) hero pattern. The abandonment and exposure of the infant and his being rescued by an animal that suckles him could very well represent the deep-seated anxiety produced by weaning. But whether he is displaced by a younger sibling or engaged in a struggle with the father for exclusive possession of the mother, the hero of the hero pattern finds an ideal solution. He succeeds in separating his parents and in being lavishly and lovingly nursed. It should be noted that the basic plot of a son who desires to separate his father from his mother is also to be found in myth.

The hero pattern, as I have noted, is rather a matter of the genres of legend and folktale. But in the widespread creation myth of the world parents (motif A 625, World parents: sky-father and earth-mother as parents of the universe), we find that the sky-father has descended upon the earth-mother to beget the world. Often the culture hero pushes the sky away (motif A 625.2, Raising of the sky), leaving him alone with his earth-mother. (In Egypt, it is the sky which is female and the earth which is male, but the crucial point is that they are torn asunder.) It has been suggested that in those myths in which father sky leaves mother earth in the morning, we find a parallel to the custom of visit marriage. "When morning comes, the man, like Uranos, must leave the woman. Therefore the myths have merely transferred what happens every morning to the first morning of the beginning of the universe" (Numazawa 1953:34). I might add that the withdrawal of the father either for a day or for a longer period of time (e.g., if there were multiple households as is not uncommon in societies with polygamous marriage) might through a projection of the infantile experience account for the idea of *deus otiosus*, in which a creator departs after having completed the initial act of (pro) creation.

Once armed with the hypothetical possibility that the stories of gods are child's projections of parents, one can more easily understand what previous generations have considered trivial or absurd narratives. For example, Hooke in *Middle Eastern Mythology* (1963:131) describes the Babylonian flood myth as follows: "In the Babylonian myth of the Flood the gods decided to destroy mankind for the rather absurd reason that they had become so noisy that they prevented the gods from sleeping at nights." If one reads "parents" for "gods" and "infants" for "mankind," one can see that the absurdity is not absurd at all. Rather, we have another version of the child's wish to disturb or separate the parents in bed.

In the separation of parents in folk narrative, the son ideally seeks to possess the mother while the daughter seeks to have the father for herself. The projection of Oedipal or Electral complexes in the Bible is a subject which deserves separate study. For the Electra complex, for example, one might profitably examine the story of Lot. His wife is turned to salt—the elimination of the mother is a common bit of wishful thinking in girl-centered fairy tales. This removes the principal rival for the father's affections. In the case of Lot, his daughters succeed in seducing him (Genesis 19:30–36).

This world parent creation myth is extremely widespread (Fischer, Numazawa, Staudacher) and it was common in classical Greek tradition (Maròt). It is of interest that in perhaps the best-known Greek version, Kronos castrates Uranos as he approaches his consort Gaia. The castration of the father by the son would, like the virgin birth, be an ultimate expression of the son's repudiation or rejection of his father.

The relationship of castration to the hero pattern, however, is not always attached to the son's success. Castration is sometimes applied to the son. For example, the story of Attis, though not treated by von Hahn, Rank, or Raglan, appears to be related to the hero pattern. (Attis is mentioned by Redford as an example of the literary motif of the exposed child and by McCartney as an example of an animal-nursed infant [Redford 1967:212, McCartney 1925:22].) Attis, the son of Nana, was conceived by contact with a pomegranate (from a tree growing from the severed phallus of a previous son of a mother-goddess). Disgraced by this miraculous conception, Nana's father Sangarius exposes the baby, who is rescued and suckled by a goat. Attis grows up to become the beloved of the mother-goddess Cybele. Eventually, Attis castrates himself. In one version, Zeus responds to the plea to bring Attis back to life by granting only that his body should not decay, that his hair should continue to grow, and that his little finger should remain alive and move (Weigert-Vowinkel 1938:356).

In the story of Attis and comparable heroes, we find that the mother-goddess figure becomes absolutely infatuated with a son figure. It is the mother who passionately pursues the son. This seems to be another instance of projection in the hero pattern (Weigert-Vowinkel 1938:371). Just as the father's attempt to eliminate the son is a projection of the son's wish to eliminate the father, so the son's wish to love his own mother, love in a sexual sense, that is, is projected onto the mother figure. (Cf. the Javanese Moslem legend cited by Cosquin in which it is the mother-rescuer who suddenly conceives a grand passion for the grown youth.) In the case of Jesus, he is pursued by women; he does not pursue them. It is women who seek him out and who come to the sepulcher. Even Frazer after his exhaustive consideration of the various major mother-son constellations in the ancient Near East does "surmise that the Easter celebration of the dead and risen Christ was grafted upon a similar celebration of the dead and arisen Adonis" and, further, that "the type, created by Greek artists, of the sorrowful goddess with the dying lover in her arms, resembles and may have been the model of the *Pietà* of Christian art, the Virgin with the dead body of her divine Son in her lap" (Fraser 1964:356). Fraser, to be sure, draws no inferences whatsoever of the possible further implications of seeing a parallel between the relationship of various sets of mother-son lovers and the relationship of Mary and Jesus. (For a truly remarkable examination of the erotic symbolism of the *Pietà* tradition, see Steinberg 1970.)

The possible parallelism between Mary and Jesus and the widespread mother-son mythological pattern has frequently been noted. Ishida, in several ambitious studies of mother-son relationships in folk narrative, documents the antiquity and distribution of the pattern. In east Asian tradition, he finds a three-element pattern consisting of (1) a divine boy from the water world, (2) the boy's miraculous birth, or no mention of his father, and (3) his mother or a motherlike female is worshipped with him (Ishida 1956:411). Sometimes the male is very small in size (1964:31). In some tales, a small snake is put in a cup but it "grew so quickly during the course of each night that soon no container was big enough to hold it" (1964:33). Ishida concludes that the east Asian tradition is part of a larger pattern and that the pattern of a mother-goddess coupled with a small male deity was widespread in "the entire pre-Aryan and probably pre-Semitic cultural zone of the ancient Orient from Southwest Asia to the Eastern Mediterranean" (1964:49). In this pattern, "the Mother, a goddess of fertility, was often accompanied by a young male deity who was both her son and her consort: Isis with Horus, Astaroth with Tammuz, Kybele with Attis, Rhea with the young Zeus. Everywhere she bore her son by parthenogenesis; then, in union with him, she bore all living things" (1964:49–50). Ishida continues, "Even after the Christian conquest of paganism, the Mother maintained her prominence as an object of pious worship, holding in her arms the baby Jesus, the divine child" (1964:51). He also comments upon the frequency of an incestuous marriage between mother and son (1964:45–48). Earlier, both Freud and Jones had commented upon the similarity of the relationship between Mary and Jesus to the mother-son pattern common in the Near East (Freud 1913:152–53; Jones 1951a:370–71.) Jones argued that the maternal component of the sacred nuclear family of father, mother, and son was replaced in early Christianity by the Holy Ghost, thereby making an all-masculine Trinity (Jones 1951a:210; cf. Rank 1952: 121–29). He felt that the suppression of a mother goddess followed the example of the highly patriarchal Hebrew tradition. Accordingly, he insisted that Mary represented a weakened version of the mother-goddess figure. The psychoanalytic position has been summarized as follows: "It has been recognized, for example, that Mary represents a sort of younger sister of the great goddesses of love of antiquity; and that her relationship with Jesus was an incestuous one, in the tradition of such mother-goddesses and their son-husbands, for instance, Ishtar and Tammuz, Astarte and Adonis, Isis and Osiris, Cybele and Attis. Within this tradition, then, Jesus' crime was an incestuous one, part of which was an attempt to equal or to displace his father, and for this reason he has to die" (Reider 1964:523).

The delineation of the mother-son pattern reveals both that the life of Jesus belongs to it *and* that it departs from it in several respects. Jesus does not have an incestuous relationship with Mary nor in fact does he have a sexual relationship with any woman. It is true, however, that there is far more mention of Mary in the Gospels than of Joseph. The extremely low profile of Joseph, a father figure, would tend to support the idea that the life story of Jesus does concern a mother-son relationship. Occasional father-son rivalry does occur in some of the apocryphal gospels. The Infancy Gospel of Thomas contains several examples. In one instance (chapter 5), an angry Joseph violently pulls the ear of the boy Jesus. In another (chapter 13), Jesus helps Joseph solve a carpentry problem. Joseph, in the process of constructing a couch, ineptly makes one piece of wood shorter than another and he doesn't know what to do. Jesus instructs him to lay the two pieces down alongside each other. Jesus then grasps the shorter beam and stretches it, making it equal with the longer piece. The possible phallic significance of this deed is obvious enough. Yet the overall lack of sexuality in Jesus and his failure, as noted earlier in this discussion, to marry a princess, as dictated by the norms of the hero pattern, suggest a departure from the mother-son bond.

One way of appreciating the departure of Jesus from the Near Eastern mother-son pattern is to consider how the relationship of Jesus to Mary changed over the centuries. A most compelling piece of data bearing on the relationship of Mary and Jesus to the general mother-son pattern is the rise of Mariolatry. The folk, in effect, have over the course of centuries succeeded in redressing the imbalance caused by the particular male-centered worldview which created the Gospel accounts of the life of Jesus. It is as though the paradigm of the mother-son pattern re-asserted itself. Over the years, the worship of Mary restored the mother goddess to the place she would have held if the Jesus biography had conformed more closely to the original hero pattern. I shall not attempt here to recapitulate the complex history of hyperdulia, but suffice it to say that in the centuries since the first articulations of the life of Jesus, there have been as many or more sightings of the Virgin Mary on the surface of the earth than sightings of Jesus. It is the Virgin Mary who has continued to intervene in the affairs of men and whose appearances have inspired the construction of numerous sacred shrines, e.g., Lourdes, Fatima, etc. By the end of medieval times, the Virgin Mary had assumed many of the attributes of the mother figure in the hero pattern. An eminent art historian remarked on what to him seemed the curious depiction of the Virgin Mary as the bride of Christ. "However anomalous such a union may appear to us, the conception of Mary as the bride of Christ (in addition to being his mother and daughter) was current in the Late Middle Ages" (Meiss 1951:109, cf. Steinberg 1970:237–238). From the perspective afforded by a knowledge of the hero pattern, we can see that the notion of Mary as mother and bride is but a reaffirmation of the very same details noted by Ishida: "the Mother, a goddess of fertility, was often accompanied by a young male deity who was both her son and her consort."

If Jesus is a cognate of the son figure in the mother-son pattern then we may wish to consider the manner of his death in this light. It is curious to see how St. Augustine (though in a passage which may not have been written by him) viewed the crucifixion: "Like a bridegroom Christ went forth from his chamber; he went out with a presage of his nuptials into the field of the world. . . . He came to the marriage-bed of the cross, and there, in mounting it, he consummated his marriage. And when he perceived the sighs of the creature, he lovingly gave himself up to the torment in place of his bride, and he joined himself to the woman for ever" (Jung 1967:269). Numerous symbolic interpretations of the crucifixion exist, e.g., it has been analyzed as a scapegoat ritual (Runeberg), but it is not clear how many scholars would concur with St. Augustine's sexual reading of the event. Yet the sexual component of the crucifixion is also signalled by its being subsumed under the term *Passion*, which connotes both suffering and also strong amorous feeling. Later folk narratives can be adduced to support a sexual interpretation of the cross. In the legend of St. Elizabeth of Hungary, a suspicious husband rushes into the saint's bedroom and whisks off the blankets to discover the crucified Jesus in his wife's bed (Thurston and Attwater 1956:387). There is also a folktale (Aarne-Thompson tale type 1359c, Husband prepares to castrate the crucifix) in which a discovered paramour assumes the pose of the crucified Jesus until the husband prepares to take action against him.

St. Augustine, or the author of the passage attributed to St. Augustine, may have been intuitively correct in stating that the crucifixion contained a metaphorical meaning of marriage or sexual intercourse, but it is also true that the crucifixion implies punishment and a denial of intercourse. Again from the perspective of the hero pattern, we can observe that it is not uncommon for the hero's masculinity to be threatened. Samson, betrayed by Delilah, is shaved by his enemies. The loss of hair, perhaps a form of symbolic castration, results in a loss of strength. Samson is also blinded, and blindness often serves as an expression of symbolic castration. Oedipus, after killing his father and marrying his mother, self-inflicts blindness—just as Attis self-inflicts literal castration. The symbolism of the cross is surely multifaceted, but it is conceivable that it has, as a symbol of life, a phallic dimension. For those who doubt the possibility of a phallic component in the Bible, it might be well to recall that if one swears by all that is holy, it may be significant that one swears by the phallus. "And the servant put his hand under the thigh of Abraham his master, and sware to him concerning that matter" (Genesis 24:2, 9 cf. Genesis 47:29, Jeremias 1911, II:77, n. 1). From this custom, we get our idiom of giving *testi*mony and for that matter ultimately the names of Old and New Testament. (The phallic nature of the cross might also illuminate the practice of nuns wearing one around the neck—to protect their maiden heads? and especially the custom of monks wearing one exposed and hanging down from the waist.)

If the cross has a phallic component, then it is of interest that according to John (19:17), Jesus carried his own cross. (Matthew 27:32 and Mark 15:21 say that one Simon bore the cross while Luke 23:26 implies that Simon merely helped Jesus carry it.) In any event, Jesus, having denied the father (by being born of a virgin), yields to the father by being nailed to a symbolic phallus. (Earlier nineteenth-century interpretations of the cross as phallic failed to see it in the context of the entire hero pattern.) If the number three is a masculine or phallic symbol (Dundes 1968), then the image of Christ being one of three crucified might be relevant. As the figure in the middle, he would be the phallus—with the two thieves being testicles. (Cf. Allegro's controversial assertion (1970:35) that the name Jesus stems from a Sumerian word which means "semen.")

The idea of castration being an extreme form of the denial of sexuality is found in the New Testament. According to Matthew (19:12), Jesus himself refers specifically to men making themselves into eunuchs for the kingdom of heaven's sake. "For there are some eunuchs, which were so born from their mother's womb; and there are some eunuchs, which were made eunuchs of men: and there be eunuchs, which have made themselves eunuchs for the kingdom of heaven's sake" (cf. Nock 1925, and Phipps 1973:144).

The humiliation of the son in terms of masculinity is exacerbated in the crucifixion insofar as Jesus is physically penetrated—both by the nails and by the spear which is later thrust into his side. In circum-Mediterranean male verbal dueling, there is honor for the active penetrator, for the male who puts his opponent down just as for the matador who sinks his sword into the bull; there is only shame for the passive victim who is penetrated. The distinction also applies to active and passive homosexuals—as is clear from accounts of pederasty in classical Greece and modern Turkey (cf. Vanggaard 1972; Dundes, Leach, and Özkök 1970). In this case, Jesus is curiously hoist on his own petard by being nailed to a symbolic phallus which entails his being penetrated by male representatives of an authority figure.

The paradoxical irony of being put to *death* on a symbol of *life*, the cross, is reminiscent of the Garden of Eden story. The crucifixion is the continuation of the Eden story (with Eve and Mary, Adam and Jesus explicitly equated). In Eden, discovery of the tree of *life* resulted in *death* thereafter for mankind. (Several references in the New Testament specifically refer to the cross as a tree, e.g., Acts 5:30; 1 Peter

2:24.) More importantly we find a continuity of theme. Twentieth-century ethnography confirms that in Mediterranean cultures, "Sex, sin and death [are] related; similarly virginity, continence, and life" (Campbell 1964:280). The original sin was sexual in nature (Levy, Róheim) and the result was the origin of death (Cohon, Morgenstern, Krappe 1928). Similarly, the crucifixion involves sexuality, sin, and death. In Eden, disobedience led to forfeiting the tree of life; in the case of Jesus, obedience led to being nailed to it.

Yet if the crucifixion is a form of symbolic castration, analogous to a similar incident in the lives of other heroes, it is not the end. A hero can evidently overcome even an obstacle of this magnitude. Recall that the hair of Samson's head began to grow again after he was shaven, and he regained enough strength to pull down the pillars and the temple of his enemies (Judges 16:22–30). Similarly, in the previously cited version of Attis, Zeus granted that his hair should continue to grow and that his little finger should remain alive and move, indications that the castration is rescinded or transcended (Weigert-Vowinkel 1938:372). So in the life story of Jesus, the hero is able to rise from the dead, a phallic triumph of the highest order. D. H. Lawrence in his fictionalized life of Jesus, originally entitled "The Escaped Cock," depicts Jesus as being rescued by a young virgin devotee of Isis: " . . . He crouched to her, and he felt the blaze of his manhood and his power rise up in his loins, magnificent. 'I am risen!' . . . " (Lawrence 1952:444, 386–393, cf. Garth 1950:40, n. 52). At least the irrepressible Lawrence refrained in his literary 'exejesus' from punning on Jesus having a "cross" to "bare"! (In English, a punster might well have been tempted by the potential double entendre of a "second coming" meaning both a second advent and a second orgasm.) The association of the "erection" of a phallus with the notion of resurrection has been suggested by scholars not at all influenced by psychoanalytic thought. For example, Jeremias in his respected treatise, *The Old Testament in the Light of the Ancient East*, remarks that "the phallus planted by Bacchus at the gate of Hades is a symbol of the Resurrection" (1911 I:122, n. 2). Metaphorically, it certainly makes sense for an erect phallus to represent the overcoming of death; and this is surely involved in the shape and form of memorial monuments (consider the appropriateness of the Washington Monument erected by grateful Americans for the *father* of their country).

In the light of the present interpretation of the 'crucifiction,' it may not be amiss to remember the individual to whom the risen Christ first appeared. If the resurrection is a form of re-erection, then it would be reasonable for the observer of this marvel to be a woman. Matthew (28:1) indicates that Mary Magdalene and the other Mary came to the sepulcher where an angel told them Jesus wasn't there and asked them to tell the disciples. Mark (16:9) says that Jesus appeared first to Mary Magdalene, while John (20:14–18) reports that Jesus revealed himself first to Mary Magdalene in the famous scene where Jesus orders her not to touch him.

Phipps has astutely pointed out (1973:67) that the word *touch* might possibly carry a nuance of sexual intercourse, especially since it does so elsewhere in the Bible. In 1 Corinthians 7:1–2, we find "It is good for a man not to touch a woman. Nevertheless to avoid fornication, let every man have his own wife. . . ." In Genesis 20:6, Abraham told Abimelech that Sarah was his sister, not his wife, which led Abimelech to believe that Sarah was available to him as a partner. God prevented Abimelech from taking advantage of the misunderstanding by appearing to him in a dream to explain the situation: "for I also withheld thee from sinning against me: therefore suffered I thee not to touch her." Similarly in Proverbs 6:29, "So he that goes in to his neighbour's wife; whosoever toucheth her shall not be innocent." Whether touching refers simply to a physical caress or serves as a euphemism for intercourse, there would seem to be a definite sexual connotation. So when Jesus tells Mary Magdalene, the very first person to see him "arisen" not to "touch" him, it is at least within the realm of logical possibility that Jesus is fending off a sexual advance.

Mary Magdalene had been healed of evil spirits—seven devils had been cast out of her life (Luke 8:2, Mark 16:9). She is generally identified as the repentant sinner whom Jesus forgave (Luke 7:37–50). The implication is that she was a prostitute (cf. Phipps 1970:64–67, 1973:69, Garth 1950:21) and she is so regarded in popular Christian iconography. The critical question is why should Jesus appear first to a reformed prostitute whose name just coincidentally happens to be the same as that of his own mother? From the point of view of the mother-son pattern, Jesus should be a son-consort. This would require a Mary mother and a Mary bride (cf. Leach 1975). There is some evidence of a tradition which declared that Mary Magdalene was the wife

clothes. Help her move downstairs. Adjust oxygen. More conversation on the staircase. Find a movie for her to watch. Make lunch. Adjust oxygen. Get something for her from upstairs. Continue making lunch. Get something else from upstairs. Deliver lunch. She requests Chipotle instead. Dignity, without shame. Adjust oxygen. Get something else from upstairs. Text your friend, forget to hit send. Help your mother to the bathroom. Conversation on the stairwell, she can't go any further. Deliver leftover Chipotle to her on the stairs. Bring her a paper towel. Bring her a pillow. Read her Pema Chodron. Get yourself dressed. Breathe. She is resting in the stairwell, staring up at the ceiling. Go to the kitchen and wash dishes. Notice there is a world outside. The sight of the sky is shocking. Feel ashamed that your mother is convalescing in the stairwell. Maybe people with money don't die like this. You notice the farmer's tan on her pale feet, her heels weathered from a summer of gardening. Toes still painted salmon pink. She likes to make the extra effort to keep her nails painted just in case she meets someone. She's still hoping someone will fall in love with her. Eat some food; it has no flavor. She wants some fruit and asks for three strawberries. Bring her three strawberries. She is a grateful and gracious patient and she makes you feel like you've won the World Series when she sees the plump red fruit. Wonder how long you can do to this. Never allow that thought to land.

I see my arms outstretched, and I feel like the ends of myself are far away.
They're touching stars.
Only they don't warm me.
They burn me.
I imagine I am made of paper.
And when I hug myself, I ignite.

Day 24
My mother no longer needs her favorite underwear. I don't know what to do with them. They make me emotional. I photograph them and put them in the garbage can—the one by the curb, so I won't fish them back out. I hear them whimpering in there that night. Once

of Jesus (Phipps 1970:64, 137–38), a tradition recorded in the Gospel of Philip (Wilson 1962:35). For example, a passage from this source reads "And the consort of [Christ is] Mary Magdalene. [The lord loved Mary] more than [all] the disciples, and kissed her on her [mouth] often" (Wilson 1962:39). This tradition of Mary Magdalene being the wife of Jesus is perhaps as old as the second century and it continued for centuries, e.g., at least up until the sixteenth century (Garth 1950:73).

The double tradition of a Virgin Mary and a harlot Mary is a long-standing one. The initial situation of an unmarried virgin's becoming pregnant has always suggested adultery and whoring. In Redford's survey of thirty-two examples of "the literary motif of the exposed child," he found three motivations for the exposure. The first was exposure because of shame at the circumstances of the child's birth. The second was the prophecy of parricide or some similar misfortune for those in power. The third was a general massacre, i.e., motif M375, Slaughter of innocents to avoid fulfillment of prophecy. (The third motivation appears to be a special adaptation of the second.) Shame, then, is the crucial factor in fourteen instances (of thirty-two examples) and the shame commonly involves illegitimate birth or perhaps using the birth as prima facie evidence of the prior occurrence of sexual promiscuity. So in Matthew (1:18–19), it is told "Now the birth of Jesus Christ was on this wise: When as his mother Mary was espoused to Joseph, before they came together, she was found with child of the Holy Ghost. Then Joseph her husband, being a just man, and not willing to make her a public example, was minded to put her away privily." An angel convinces him to do otherwise and Joseph knew (sexually) his wife "not till she had brought forth her firstborn son" (Matthew 1:25) But even if Mary is not a reformed harlot (cf. Phipps 1973:106), Mary Magdalene certainly seems to be one.

Freud has explained the psychological origin of the 'harlot' component of the mother figure in terms of the shock of a young boy's discovery that his very own mother must have indulged in sexual activities with his father. In Freud's words, "he says to himself with cynical logic that the difference between his mother and a whore is not after all so very great since basically they both do the same thing" (Freud 1910:171). Thus Jesus born of a virgin Mary reveals his resurrection first to a harlot Mary. It is tempting to see a parallel to Jesus' possible relationship with a harlot in the story of Samson. There can be no question about Samson's consorting with a harlot (Judges 16:1). Interestingly enough, after Samson meets the harlot, he takes the doors of the gate of the city and carries them away. Jesus rolled the stone away from the door of his sepulcher right before he revealed himself to Mary Magdalene. However, Jesus, in contrast with Samson, rejects the woman's overtures.

What is the significance, if any, of the fact that the life of Jesus seems to be related to the European or Indo-European hero pattern? What sense can we make of his attitudes towards women? We have seen that one important omission in terms of the standard hero pattern is the failure of Jesus to marry a princess. How can one explain the resurgence of the Virgin Mary in so many circum-Mediterranean cultures? Ernest Jones suggested that the Protestant Reformation was in part a reactionary attempt to oppose Mariolatry and to restore the original Christian version of the hero pattern (Jones 1951a:372). I would add that in the circum-Mediterranean area where the original mother-son pattern was so strongly entrenched, such Protestantism reform has not had much impact. The cult of the Virgin in Greece, Italy, France, Spain, and Ireland continues. The question is why should the mother-son paradigm be so strong in this geographical-cultural area. It is one thing to describe a pattern; it is quite another to explain its origin or psychological significance. Surely there are critical factors which might account for the phenomenal success and continued appeal of this religious pattern.

To the extent that religious or sacred family structure mirrors ordinary human family structure, one might reasonably look at Mediterranean family organization. The isomorphism between family structure among the gods and among men is signalled in Roman mythology by the very name of the head of the gods, Jupiter, the latter portion of which is cognate with Sanskrit *pitar-* (cf. Latin *pater*) which means father. The equation of divine and human family is explicit in Christianity inasmuch as God is termed the father, Jesus is the son, and Mary the mother of God. (Even the name 'pope' etymologically comes from father. Priests continue to be addressed as father while various religious orders insist upon using family kinship terms such as brothers and sisters.)

Circum-Mediterranean social organization traits include rigid sexual segregation. Men associate with one another, leaving women largely to themselves. Men tended to marry late and often in serial succession according to birth order (cf. Genesis 29:26). In modern Greece, for example, sons, or sometimes just the youngest son, are supposed to wait to marry until all the daughters of the house are married (Westermarck 1922 I:373, Campbell 1964:178, Slater 1968:24). A man might marry a woman much younger than himself. According to Joachim Jeremias, the usual age for a Jewish girl to be betrothed at the time of Jesus was between twelve and twelve-and-a-half (1969: 365). Slater reminds us of a tradition that Helen was abducted when she was only twelve (1968:392). If a man took a second wife, the chances were that the second wife would be much younger than the man. In the contemporary Near East, one of the rationales given for selecting a young wife is that a young bride will be strong enough to take care of the man when he has grown old (Granqvist 1931:42–43). In ancient Greece, the age at which males married was estimated to be around thirty (Slater 1968:26). Certainly the traditional view is that Joseph was much, much older than Mary—just as Laius was much older than Jocasta, and for that matter, just as Freud's father was twenty years older than his mother! (Wellisch 1955:32, 38).

The age differential coupled with the enforced sexual segregation meant that affection-starved wives often poured their unrequited love upon their sons. The sons thereby became husband-substitutes for their own mothers. I believe this may be why there are so many son consorts for so many mother goddesses in the Near East. However, the husband-hating and resenting females tended to smother (the verb choice is intentional) their sons, making it difficult for the boys to break away from the world of women to join the sexually segregated domain of men. Sons in their later struggles with distant or strict fathers would often ask their mothers to intervene on their behalf. The communication chain would involve a son asking his mother to ask his father for some boon rather than the son's asking the father directly. (So adult males found it comfortable to ask favors from the Virgin Mary or to request her to act as intermediary to God the father.)

Sons raised in such an atmosphere might well develop excessive feelings of attachment towards their mothers to the point where they wished to possess the mothers and to do away with their fathers completely. The Oedipal situation was reinforced by the social realities and it is understandable how a warm, proximate, succoring mother could be worshipped in favor of a distant, sometimes uncaring father.

Women in Mediterranean societies were invariably divided into two categories: good and bad. The good, the virgins, were mothers and wives and they were not to be thought of in sexual terms; sisters and daughters were to be guarded against sexual attacks by outsiders. The evil women were harlots and they were perceived in sexual terms. Since all women, according to this worldview, had inherent predispositions to become evil, the good women had to be protected from such temptations or rather from tempting other men by being guarded behind walls, veils, and the general overall protection of male members of the immediate family. Good women were expected to be virgins and to produce a son. Thus a virgin mother-wife who produces a son is truly an ideal model of Mediterranean male chauvinistic values. Since "good" women were not supposed to enjoy sexuality, men often sought mistresses in addition to wives. This attitude also encouraged neglected mothers to lavish undue affection upon their sons, the affection they might have offered their husbands. According to Slater, who has brilliantly analyzed this pattern, Greek boys learned to fear mature women, a factor which also led them to prefer much younger wives (who would not smother or dominate them). Again, these younger wives, not being able to manage their older husbands, would give their affection to their sons and so the cycle would continue ad infinitum (Slater 1968:45, 52, 132, 307). With a distant or absent father, a son raised in a mother-dominated household (often sleeping with the mother until replaced by a younger sibling) might take on cross-sex identificational characteristics which could be construed as effeminacy (Slater 1968:224, 227).

I do not pretend to have given an exhaustive description of Mediterranean family dynamics, but if the holy family represents a projection of human family roles, then perhaps what Nelson has described for Mexico (1971:74) may apply to Mediterranean cultures generally. She suggests that the Virgin Mary provides a female ideal (mother, wife) but there is no clear counterpart for the male. Joseph is regarded as a cuckold, God is too remote to be perceived as a role model, and Jesus for all his compassion—or because of it—is effeminate. (On the other hand, the cultural relativity of the projective aspects of Christ must also be taken into account. It has been suggested [Richardson, Pardo, and Bode 1971:247], for example, that in Catholic Latin America Christ provides a model of how to suffer [e.g., on the cross] whereas in Protestant North America, the emphasis is on the resurrection or the conquering of death, a distinction which, if valid, might well be correlated with critical differences in general worldview.)

In Mediterranean family structure, one of the crucial problems for boys remains breaking the strong bond existing between them and their mothers so as to join the world of mature men. I suggest that the hero pattern in general and the life of Jesus in particular are an expression of this problem. In this sense, the hero pattern is analogous to male puberty rites. In male initiation rites, young boys are separated from their mothers to join a males-only group. The male initiates are born again, but this time from exclusively male progenitors. The rebirth ceremony often involves a ritual mutilation of the phallus, e.g. circumcision or subincision. These mutilations explicitly entail a feminization of the initiates. (The incised urethra may be referred to as a vulva and the bleeding is likened to menstrual bleeding, etc.) The young boys are deemed inferior to the older males and they must play the parts of women (sometimes in homosexual activities) to demonstrate this (Dundes, 1976). Yet the ceremony permits the boys to join the world of adult men, to become one with their fathers.

Jesus must leave the world of women to join a males-only group (his disciples). Then he undergoes symbolic castration to join (be at one with his) father. As the symbolic castration is no more devastating than ritual circumcision/subincision, Jesus, like male initiates everywhere, is reborn, resurrected. Evidence supporting the notion that the life of Jesus involves a rejection of the mother in favor of the father includes Jesus' response to the woman who praised Mary: "Blessed is the womb that bare thee, and the paps which thou has sucked". Jesus replied, "Yea, rather, blessed are they that hear the word of God and keep it" (Luke 11:27–28). In other words, father's word is more important than mother's womb and breasts. There is also Jesus' direct rebuff of Mary, "Woman, what have I to do with thee?" (John 2:4). In initiation ritual, a boy is required to reject his mother so as to be accepted by his father. While Jesus refuses to allow Mary Magdalene to touch him (John 2:17), he specifically invited doubting Thomas to do so (John 20:27). Jesus rejects women and accepts men.

From the perspective of an individual male trying to choose between remaining on earth with his mother or joining his father in heaven, we see the crucifixion as a critical state in which the child is suspended between his parents (cf. Endelheit 1974:195). After resurrection, Jesus shakes off Mary Magdalene's attempt to "touch" him and he leaves the world of women to join his heavenly father. Joining one's father in afterlife is a continuation of a conventional metaphor in the Old Testament. Heidel thoroughly documents (1963:144–146) the use of the idiom "to lie down with one's fathers" or "to sleep with one's fathers" as a formula signifying death. In a partriarchally determined worldview, just as one would ideally deny the role of woman in childbirth—Eve is created from Adam's body (rather than vice versa), so similarly in death, one would not be laid to rest in mother earth. Rather one would be said to lie or sleep with one's father or to be "carried by the angels into Abraham's bosom" (Luke 12:22). So it is a father's bosom rather than a mother's which serves a euphemism for the land of the dead. And so it is that Jesus is described as the "only begotten Son, which is in the bosom of the Father" (John 1:18).

I have tried to show that the life of Jesus must be understood as a version, a very special version, of the standard Indo-European hero pattern. The life of Jesus is related to the lives of Cyrus, Romulus and Remus, Oedipus, Moses, and many, many other heroes. But his life must also be understood in relation to the norms of Near Eastern and circum-Mediterranean family structure. Freud was essentially correct in observing that whereas Judaism is a religion of the father, Christianity was a religion of the son (Freud 1939:88, 136; 1913:154. Cf. Tarachow 1960:550, who argues that the Judaic pattern renounced the Oedipal object, that is, the mother figure; whereas the Christian pattern retained the Oedipal object.) But Freud did not spell out the full implications of the Holy Family being in some sense a projection of ideal or typical earthly families. If we add a psychoanalytic perspective to both the hero pattern and Mediterranean family structure, we might summarize the life of Jesus as follows: A young virgin is impregnated by her heavenly father, a plot element which contains the appeal of the Electra complex for females. The pregnant virgin is then married to a man much older than she, perhaps old enough to be her father. The infant Jesus is imperiled by a threat on his life by Herod. In one version (Protevangelion), Mary wraps him in swaddling clothes and places him in a manger for protection. In psychoanalytic terms, the son's wish to get rid of the father is translated into the father's attempt to eliminate the son. (We know that Mediterranean fathers specifically wanted sons—as proof of masculinity and to continue the patronymic line.) The son succeeds in keeping his mother to himself (eventually represented in Christian art in the form of the Madonna del Latte). However, unlike the majority of heroes in the hero pattern who kill their father figures and who marry their mothers or a mother surrogate, Jesus yields to (paternal) authority and is crucified. He renounces the world of women to join the world of men and to become one with his father. A mother watching her son agonize in a suspended state over leaving the protective world of women to join the men's world (leaving the mother for the father, leaving the earth for heaven) is common enough in Mediterranean family dynamics. The resurrection suggests a triumph over symbolic castration. He reveals himself to Mary Magdalene, a harlot counterpart of his mother Mary, but he refuses to allow her to "touch" him. By becoming one with his father, Jesus achieves the Oedipal ideal of being his own begetter (thus assuming his father's sexual role with his mother). So Jesus has it both ways: he is the dutiful son obeying a distant, powerful father, but he becomes one with that father—just as boys growing up in circum-Mediterranean households have to learn to progress from a close and prolonged association with protective mothers to a world of men dominated by elders to a time finally when they themselves become distant fathers to their own children as they seek virgin wives and attempt not to become cuckolded (like Joseph).

The life of Jesus cannot be understood in isolation from the cultural context from which it arose. Nor can it be understood apart from comparable hero patterns in cognate cultures. Nor finally can it be understood without reference to the social and psychological factors inherent in the circum-Mediterranean and Near Eastern form of the family.

References

Allegro, John M. 1970. *The Sacred Mushroom and the Cross*. New York: Bantam.

Astour, Michael C. 1965. *Hellenosemitica: An Ethnic and Cultural Study in West Semitic Impact on Mycenaean Greece*. Leiden: E.J. Brill.

Bascom, William 1965. The Forms of Folklore: Prose Narratives. *Journal of American Folklore* 78:3–20.

Bauer, Adolf 1882. Die Kyros-Sage und Verwandtes. *Sitzungsberichte der Philosophisch-Historischen Klasse der Kaiserlichen Akademie der Wissenschaften* 100:495–578.

Baum, Paull Franklin 1916. The Mediaeval Legend of Judas Iscariot. *Publications of the Modern Language Association* 31:431–632.

Beck, Bodog F., and Smedley, Dorée 1971. *Honey and Your Health*: A Nutrimental, Medicinal and Historical Commentary. New York: Bantam.

Binder, Gerhard 1964. *Die Aussetzung des Konigskindes Kyros und Romulus*. Beiträge zur Klassischen Philologie 10. Meisenheim am Glan: Verlag Anton Hain.

Boman, Thorleif 1967. *Die Jesus-Uberlieferung im Lichte der neueren Volkskunde*. Göttingen: Vandenhoeck and Ruprecht.

Boslooper, Thomas 1962. *The Virgin Birth*. Philadelphia: The Westminster Press.

Bourke, Myles M. 1960. The Literary Genius of Matthew 1–2. *Catholic Biblical Quarterly* 22:160–75.

Bradley, Noel 1973. Notes on Theory-Making, on Scotoma of the Nipples and on the Bee as Nipple. *International Journal of Psycho-Analysis* 54: 301–14.

Brunner-Traut, Emma 1960. Die Geburtsgeschichte der Evangelien im Lichte ägyptologischer Forschungen. *Zeitschrift für Religions-und Geistesgeschichte* 12:97–111.

Buck, Carl Darling 1949. *A Dictionary of Selected Synonyms in the Principal Indo-European Languages*. Chicago: University of Chicago Press.

Bultmann, Rudolf 1958. *Jesus Christ and Mythology*. New York: Charles Scribner's Sons.

———. 1963. *The History of the Synoptic Tradition*. Oxford: Basil Blackwell.

Campbell, J.K. 1964. *Honour, Family, and Patronage*. New York: Oxford University Press.

Campbell, Joseph 1956. *The Hero with a Thousand Faces*. New York: Meridian.

Charencey, Hyacinthe de 1879. *Le Fils de la Vierge*. Havre: Imprimerie Lepelletier.

Childs, Brevard S. 1960. *Myth and Reality in the Old Testament*. Studies in Biblical Theology no. 27 London: SCM Press.

Cohon, Samuel S. 1919. The Origin of Death. *Journal of Jewish Lore and Philosophy* 1:371–96.

Conybeare, Fred. C. 1914. *The Historical Christ*. London: Watts & Co.

Cook, Victor 1965. Lord Raglan's Hero—A Cross Cultural Critique. *Florida Anthropologist* 18:147–54.

Cosquin, Emmanuel 1908. Le Lait de la Mère et le Coffre Flottant. *Revue des Questions Historiques* 83:353–425.

Deonna, W. 1955. *Deux études de symbolisme religieux.* Collection Latomus 18. Berchem-Bruxelles: Latomus.

Dibelius, Martin 1932. *Jungfrauensohn und Krippenkind.* Sitzungsberichte der Heidelberger Akademie der Wissenschaften, Philosophisch-historische Klasse 22, 4. Abhandlung.

Dibelius, Martin 1935. *From Tradition to Gospel.* New York: Charles Scribner's Sons.

Doane, T.W. 1882. *Bible Myths and Their Parallels in Other Religions.* New York: The Commonwealth Company.

Drews, Arthur 1911. *The Christ Myth.* Chicago: Open Court Publishing Company.

Dundes, Alan 1968. The Number Three in American Culture. In *Every Man His Way.* Englewood Cliffs, N.J.: Prentice-Hall. Pp. 401–24.

———. 1976. A Psychoanalytic Study of the Bullroarer. *Man* 11:220–38.

Dundes, Alan, and Jerry W. Leach and Bora Özkök 1970. The Strategy of Turkish Boys' Verbal Dueling Rhymes. *Journal of American Folklore* 83: 325–49.

Edelheit, Henry 1974. Crucifixion Fantasies and Their Relation to the Primal Scene. *International Journal of Psycho-Analysis* 55:193–99.

Fischer, Henri Théodore 1929. *Het Heilig Huwelik van Hemel en Aarde.* Utrecht: Drukkerij J. van Boekhoven.

Frazer, James 1918. *Folklore in the Old Testament.* 3 vols. London: Macmillan.

———. 1964. *The New Golden Bough.* New York: Mentor.

Freud, Sigmund 1910. A Special Type of Choice of Object Made by Men. *Standard Edition* 1957, 11:162–75. London: The Hogarth Press.

———. 1913. *Totem and Taboo. Standard Edition* 1955, 13:1–161. London: The Hogarth Press.

———. 1939. *Moses and Monotheism. Standard Edition* 1964, 23:7–137. London: The Hogarth Press.

Garth, Helen Meredith 1950. *Saint Mary Magdalene in Mediaeval Literature.* The Johns Hopkins University Studies in Historical and Political Science 67 (3). Baltimore: Johns Hopkins University Press.

Gennep, Arnold van 1904. Lucina sine concubitu (III), notes ethnographiques. *La Revue des Idees* 1:554–58.

Granqvist, Hilma 1931. *Marriage Conditions in a Palestinian Village,* Vol. I. Helsinki: Societas Scientiarum Fennica.

Grant, R.M. 1961. *The Earliest Lives of Jesus.* London: S.P.C.K.

Guidi, I. 1903. Une Terre Coulant du Lait avec du Miel. *Revue Biblique* 12:241–44.

Gunkel, Hermann 1964. *The Legends of Genesis.* New York: Schocken.

Hartland, Edwin Sidney 1894–96. *The Legend of Perseus.* 3 vols. London: David Nutt.

Hahn, Johann Georg von 1876. *Sagwissenschaftliche Studien.* Jena: F. Mauke.

Heidel, Alexander 1963. *The Gilgamesh Epic and Old Testament Parallels.* Chicago: University of Chicago Press.

Henderson, Ian 1952. *Myth in the New Testament.* Studies in Biblical Theology no. 7. London: SCM Press.

Hertel, Johannes 1909. Zu den Erzählungen von der Muttermilch und der schwimmenden Lade. *Zeitschrift für Volkskunde* 19:83–91.

Holley, N.M. 1949. The Floating Chest. *Journal of Hellenistic Studies* 69: 39–47.

Hooke, S.H. 1963. *Middle Eastern Mythology.* Baltimore: Penguin.

Ishida, Eiichirô 1956. The Mother-Son Complex in East Asiatic Religion and Folklore. In *Die Wiener Schule der Volkerkunde.* Vienna. pp. 411–19.

Ishida, Eiichirô 1964. Mother-Son Deities. *History of Religions* 4:30–52.

Jeremias, Alfred 1911. *The Old Testament in the Light of the Ancient East.* 2 vols. New York: G.P. Putnam's Sons.

Jeremias, Joachim 1969. *Jerusalem in the Time of Jesus.* London: SCM Press.

Jezewski, Mary Ann 1984. "Traits of the Female Hero: The Application of Raglan's Concept of Hero Trait Patterning." *New York Folklore:* 55–73.

Jones, Ernest 1951a. *Essays in Applied Psychoanalysis,* Vol. II, Essays in Folklore, Anthropology and Religion. London: The Hogarth Press.

Jones, Ernest 1951b. *On the Nightmare.* New York: Liveright.

Jung, C.G. 1967. *Symbols of Transformation.* 2nd ed. Princeton: Princeton University Press.

Justin Martyr, Saint 1948. *Writings of Saint Justin Martyr* New York: Christian Heritage.

Kennedy, J. 1917. The Gospels of the Infancy, The Lalita Vistara, and the Vishnu Purana: Or the Transmission of Religious Legends Between India and the West. *Journals of the Royal Asiatic Society of Great Britain and Ireland* 209–43; 469–540.

Krappe, Alexander Haggerty 1928. The Story of the Fall of Man. *Nieuw Theologisch Tijdschrift* 17:242–49.

Krappe, Alexander Haggerty 1933. La naissance de Moise. *Revue de l'Histoire des Religions* 107:126–133.

spend time with my kids, the kids that don't exist yet, the ones she is hoping to live long enough to meet. She dictates the features she wants in her new car: colorful, no brown or black anything. I begin spending hours on Craigslist trying to find the perfect everything.

One day, without much warning, she buys a plane ticket and I have to tell my housemates that my mother and her oxygen machine are coming to live in our queerdo house—like, tomorrow. *I'm sorry. She says her body told her not to wait.* We're in the emergency room on her first day in California, because it's unhealthy to breathe in jet fumes when you have fifteen percent lung capacity and you ignore your doctor's orders not to fly without oxygen. That's when the Emergency Room doctor finally shows us her x-rays. Her cancer is stage four. This is our first time with that news.

I have a magnet on my refrigerator of a little girl looking out at the ocean. The world is hopeful, composed. It is dark outside but the stars are shining. Nobody can see her face. She is far away out among the seemingly endless horizon.

Four days later in our new dream house, two small rooms rented from an old friend, I enter her bedroom. My mom rolls onto her belly and pulls her shirt up for me to rub Frankincense on her back. The window is open; the cool air and the chirping of crickets join us. I warm my hands with my mouth before making contact with her skin, rubbing sweeping circles over her lungs and the enlarged lymph nodes under her armpits. I am afraid of touching her more intimately but I know the day is coming when it will be necessary. I am afraid that my touch will make her uncomfortable because thinking about it makes me uncomfortable.

When her breathing and mobility get worse, I sit down and write the kind of experience I want my mom to have. I am determined to give her a good death. I need something short and simple to guide me; a mantra for my frayed heart. *Dignity, without shame.*

Day 13
Rise. Check on her. Short conversation about which seeds to plant in California. Prepare incredibly detailed Budwig Diet breakfast. Deliver. More conversation. Meds. Breakfast for me. Help her change

Lawrence, D.H. 1952. *The Later D.H. Lawrence*. New York: Alfred A. Knopf.

Leach, Edmund 1976. Jesus, John and Mary Magdalene. *New Society* 34: 686–88.

Lederer, Wolfgang 1967. Historical Consequences of Father-Son Hostility. *Psychoanalytic Review* 54:248–76.

Lessmann, Heinrich 1906. *Die Kyrossage in Europa*. Wissenschaftliche Beilage zum Jahresbericht Uber die Städtische Realschule zu Charlottenburg. Ostern.

Lévi, Israel 1910. Le Lait de la Mére & Le Coffre Flottant. *Revue des Etudes Juives* 59:1–13.

Levin, A.J. 1957. Oedipus and Samson: The Rejected Hero-child. *International Journal of Psycho-Analysis* 38:105–16.

Levy, Ludwig 1917. Sexualsymbolik in der biblischen Paradiesgeschichte. *Imago* 5:16–30.

McCartney, Eugene S. 1925. Greek and Roman Lore of Animal-Nursed Infants. *Papers of the Michigan Academy of Science, Arts and Letters* 4:15–42.

McCown, Chester Charlton 1940. *The Search for the Real Jesus*: A Century of Historical Study. New York: Charles Scribner's Sons.

Maròt, Károly 1951. Die Trennung von Himmel und Erde. *Acta Antiqua* 1: 35–66.

Matthiae, Paolo 1962. Il motivo della vacca che allatta nell'iconografia del vicino oriente antico. *Revista degli Studi Orientali* 37:1–31.

Meiss, Millard 1951. *Painting in Florence and Siena After the Black Death*. Princeton: Princeton University Press.

Mellaart, James 1963. Excavations at Catal Hüyük, 1962. *Anatolian Studies* 13:43–100.

Morganstern, Julian 1919. The Sources of the Paradise Story. *Journal of Jewish Lore and Philosophy* 1:105–23; 225–40.

Münsterberger, Warner 1939. *Ethnologische Studien an Indonesischen Schopfungsmythen* Ein Beitrag zur Kultur-Analyse Südostasiens. The Hague: Martinus Nijhoff.

Nelson, Cynthia 1971. *The Waiting Village*. Social Change in Rural Mexico. Boston: Little, Brown.

Nock, Arthur Darby 1925. Eunuchs in Ancient Religion. *Archiv für Religionswissenschaft* 23:25–33.

Numazawa, Frank Kiichi 1946. *Die Weltanfange in der Japanischen Mythologie*. Paris: Librairie du Recueil Sirey.

Numazawa, Frank Kiichi 1953. Background of Myths on the Separation of

Sky and Earth from the Point of View of Cultural History. *Scientia* 88: 28–35.

Nutt, Alfred 1881. The Aryan Expulsion-and-Return Formula in the Folk and Hero Tales of the Celts. *The Folklore Record* 4:1–44.

Ohler, Annemarie 1969. *Mythologische Elemente im Alten Testament.* Düsseldorf: Patmos-Verlag.

Patai, Raphael 1959. *Sex and Family in the Bible and the Middle East.* Garden City: Doubleday.

Patte, Daniel 1976. *What is Structural Exegesis?* Philadelphia: Fortress Press.

Phipps, William E. 1970. *Was Jesus Married?* New York: Harper & Row.

Phipps, William E. 1973. *The Sexuality of Jesus.* New York: Harper & Row.

Propp, Vladimir 1968. *The Morphology of the Folktale.* Austin: University of Texas Press.

Raglan, Lord 1934. The Hero of Tradition. *Folklore* 45:212–31.

Raglan, Lord 1956. *The Hero. A Study in Tradition, Myth, and Drama.* New York: Vintage.

Rank, Otto 1952. *The Trauma of Birth.* New York: Robert Brunner.

Rank, Otto 1959. *The Myth of the Birth of the Hero.* New York: Vintage.

Redford, Donald B. 1967. The Literary Motif of the Exposed Child. *Numen* 14:209-28.

Rees, Alwyn D. 1936. The Divine Hero in Celtic Hagiology. *Folklore* 47: 30–41.

Reider, Norman 1960. Medieval Oedipal Legends about Judas. *Psychoanalytic Quarterly* 29:515–27.

Renard, Marcel 1964. Hercule allaité par Junon. In Marcel Renard and Robert Schilling, eds., *Hommages a Jean Bayet.* Collection Latomus 70. Bruxelles-Berchem: Latomus. Pp. 611–18.

Richardson, Miles, and Marta Eugenia Pardo and Barbara Bode 1971. The Image of Christ in Spanish America as a Model for Suffering. *Journal of Inter-American Studies and World Affairs* 13:246–57.

Ricoeur, Paul 1975. Biblical Hermeneutics. *Semeia* 4:29–148.

Róheim, Géza 1940. The Garden of Eden. *Psychoanalytic Review* 27:1–26; 177–99.

Rubenstein, Richard L. 1972. *My Brother Paul.* New York: Harper and Row.

Runeberg, Arne 1952. *Jesu Korsfästelse.* Stockholm: Natur och Kultur.

Saintyves, Pierre [Nourry, Emile Dominique] 1906. *Les Vierges Méres et les naissances miraculeuses.* Paris: E. Nourry.

———. 1923. *Essais de Folklore Biblique.* Paris: E. Nourry.

Saliba, John A. 1975. The Virgin-Birth Debate in Anthropological Literature: A Critical Assessment. *Theological Studies* 36:428-54.

Schmeing, Karl 1911. *Flucht- und Werbungssagen in der Legende*. Münster: Aschendorffsche Buchdruckerei.

Schweitzer, Albert 1968. *The Quest of the Historical Jesus*. New York: Macmillan.

Slater, Philip E. 1968. *The Glory of Hera*: Greek Mythology and the Greek Family. Boston: Beacon Press.

Staudacher, Willibald 1968. *Die Trennung von Himmel und Erde*. 2d ed. Darmstadt: Wissenschaftliche Buchgesellschaft.

Steinberg, Leo 1970. The Metaphors of Love and Birth in Michelangelo's *Pietàs*. In Theodore Bowie and Cornelia V. Christenson, eds., *Studies in Erotic Art*. New York: Basic Books, Pp. 231–335.

Strauss, David Friedrich 1892. *The Life of Jesus*. 2nd ed. London: Swan Sonnenschein.

Tarachow, Sidney 1960. Judas the Beloved Executioner. *Psychoanalytic Quarterly* 23:528-54.

Taylor, Archer 1964. The Biographical Pattern in Traditional Narrative. *Journal of the Folklore Institute* 1:114–129.

Thass-Thienemann, Theodore 1957. Oedipus and Sphinx: The Linguistic Approach to Unconscious Fantasies. *Psychoanalytic Review* 44:10–33.

Thompson, Stith 1955–58. *Motif-Index of Folk-Literature*. 6 vols. Bloomington: Indiana University Press.

Thompson, Stith 1961. *The Types of the Folktale*. Helsinki: Academia Scientiarum Fennica.

Thurston, Herbert, and Donald Attwater, eds. 1956. *Butler's Lives of the Saints*. Vol. IV. New York: P.J. Kennedy & Sons.

Tylor, E. Burnet 1863. Wild Men and Beast-Children. *Anthropological Review* 1:21–32.

Usener, Hermann 1902. Milch and Honig. *Rheinisches Museum für Philologie* 57:177–95.

Utley. Francis Lee 1965. *Lincoln Wasn't There or Lord Raglan's Hero*. CEA Chap Book. Supplement to CEA Critic 22, no. 9. Washington, D.C.: College English Association.

Vanggaard, Thorkil 1972. *Phallos*: A Symbol and Its History in the Male World. New York: International Universities Press.

Weigert-Vowinkel, Edith 1938. The Cult and Mythology of the Magna Mater from the Standpoint of Psychoanalysis. *Psychiatry* 1:347–78.

Wellisch, E. 1955. *Isaac and Oedipus*. New York: Humanities Press.

Westermarck, Edward 1922. *The History of Human Marriage*. 3 vols. New York: Allerton Book Company.

Wilson, R. McL. 1962. *The Gospel of Philip*. New York: Harper & Row.

Winter, Paul 1954–55. Jewish Folklore in the Matthaean Birth Story. *Hibbert Journal* 55:34–42.

Ziegler, Joseph 1952. Ochs und Esel an der Krippe. *Münchener Theologische Zeitschrift* 3:385–402.

LIBRARY OF CONGRESS CATALOGING-IN-PUBLICATION DATA

IN QUEST OF THE HERO.

P.   CM. — (MYTHOS)

CONTENTS: THE MYTH OF THE BIRTH OF THE HERO—

THE HERO: A STUDY IN TRADITION, MYTH, AND DRAMA,

PART II—THE HERO PATTERN AND THE LIFE OF JESUS.

ISBN 0-691-02062-0 (PBK.: ALK. PAPER)

1. HEROES—MYTHOLOGY.   2. HEROES—RELIGIOUS ASPECTS.   3. JESUS

CHRIST—HISTORY OF DOCTRINES.   4. BIBLE. N.T. GOSPELS—CRITICISM,

INTERPRETATION, ETC.   I. RANK, OTTO, 1884–1939. MYTHUS VON DER GEBURT

DES HELDEN. ENGLISH. 1990.   II. RAGLAN, FITZROY RICHARD SOMERSET, BARON,

1885–1964 HERO. PART 2. 1990.   III. DUNDES, ALAN. HERO PATTERN AND THE

LIFE OF JESUS. 1990.   IV. SERIES: MYTHOS (PRINCETON, N.J.)

BL 325.H46I5   1990

291.2'13—DC20   90-38204

MYTHOS

The Princeton/Bollingen Series in World Mythology